Central Asian Music

CENTRAL ASIAN MUSIC

Essays in the History of the Music of the Peoples

of the U. S. S. R.

BY VIKTOR M. BELIAEV

Edited and Annotated by Mark Slobin

Translated from the Russian by Mark and Greta Slobin

WESLEYAN UNIVERSITY PRESS

Middletown, Connecticut

This abridged English translation from the Russian was made from the first volume of Viktor M. Beliaev's *Očerki po istorii muzyki narodov SSSR*, which was published by Gosudarstvennoe Muzykal'noe Izdatel'stvo in Moscow in 1962.

Library of Congress Catalog Card Number: 74-5913

ISBN 0-8195-4083-8

Manufactured in the United States of America

First edition

Contents

Editor's Introduction

VIKTOR MIKHAILOVICH BELIAEV (1888-1968) was one of the leaders of Soviet ethnomusicology. Up to the end of his long and distinguished career he wrote widely on the music cultures of Asian and Eastern European peoples (for a bio-bibliography, see B. Krader, 1968).* Thus it was fitting that in his later years he undertook a practical summary of the music cultures he knew so well, and it is equally appropriate to introduce that summary to Western scholars as the first comprehensive survey of Central Asian music cultures.

My method of editing Beliaev's work has been to include everything but the long sections on ethnohistory at the opening of each chapter, since such data are readily available in English (*e. g.*, L. Krader, 1966), and ideological passages that interrupt the general narrative. I have tried to maintain the tone of the original while restricting the content mainly to musical matters. All deletions are indicated.

Some Western readers may still feel that the Soviet Marxist tone of the writing weighs too heavily. Since intellectual bias permeates the classic works of Euro-American ethnomusicology, it is only the shock of unfamiliar prejudices that may strike the reader of this volume. It is my hope that through the present book ethnomusicologists and other scholars may become better acquainted with the thinking of their Soviet colleagues, who have produced so extensive and so valuable a reference library on folk musics of the Soviet Union and neighboring lands.

---

*Since Krader's bibliography was published, a posthumous volume of previously published and unpublished works of Beliaev has appeared (Beliaev, 1971), with a promise of more such volumes to come. Krader's bibliography includes a number of items that Beliaev published in English and a list of foreign periodicals to which he contributed, none of which is included in the 1971 bibliography of Beliaev. It does include reviews and books edited by Beliaev, omitted in the latter, as well as a useful section entitled 'References on Beliaev.'

Preparation of this book was made possible by a grant from the Wenner-Gren Foundation for Anthropological Research and the Lloyd Postdoctoral Fellowship of the University of Michigan. I should like to thank Barbara Krader for her very helpful suggestions and Alice Pomper for her editorial work on the manuscript.

Mark Slobin

Middletown, Connecticut
August, 1975

Note on Transliteration and Translation

TRANSLITERATION of Russian words follows the Library of Congress system, with the substitution of *j* for *dzh*. Transliteration of Kirghiz, Kazakh, Turkmen, Tajik, and Uzbek words follows the system presented in Allworth (1971), with the substitution of š, č, ǧ, and ž for *sh, ch, gh,* and *zh*. Local terms and proper names with long-established English spellings (*e. g.*, Kazakh, Bukhara, Khan) are kept in that form. Names of non-Russians that have been given Russian endings (*e. g.*, Iskhak Valiev) are transliterated as if they were Russian.

Translations of song texts were in all cases from the Russian version given by Beliaev rather than from the original language. I regret the ensuing discrepancies in meaning, but without the aid of a panel of specialists it was not possible to translate from the original in most cases.

Preface

THE present *Essays on the History of the Music of the Peoples of the USSR* constitutes a textbook for conservatories. The content is defined by "Working materials for the program of the course in the history of the music of the peoples of the USSR up to the Great October Socialist Revolution for conservatories" approved by the Department of Educational Institutions of the Ministry of Culture of the USSR.

Essays consists of three separate publications: 1) the music cultures of Kirghizia, Kazakhstan, Turkmenia, Tajikstan, and Uzbekistan; 2) the music cultures of Azerbaijan, Armenia, and Georgia; and 3) the music cultures of the Ukraine and Belorussia. [1]

The course in music history of the peoples of the USSR up to the Great October Socialist Revolution, as reflected in the present *Essays*, includes the following questions: a) the history of folk music [2] and professional music of the oral tradition of all aforementioned peoples of the USSR; and b) the history of professional composition of the peoples of the Ukraine (from the last quarter of the eighteenth century), Georgia, Armenia (from the last quarter of the nineteenth century), and Azerbaijan (from the beginning of the twentieth century), *i. e.*, of those peoples of the Soviet Union who were able to establish the bases for national music cultures while still under the yoke of autocracy.

The scope of the individual essays of the present textbook depends more or less on the extent of current knowledge of the various national music cultures.

Since this textbook is designed for the conservatories of the Soviet Union, the examples of folk and composed vocal compositions are provided with texts in the language of the given nationality and prose line-by-line translations into Russian. This affords an acquaintance with both the textual and the structural content of the vocal compositions of various peoples. In some cases an isometric line-by-line translation of a national text is also given. At the same time, it should be noted that a line-by-line translation of song texts into a different language conveys their meaning more precisely than does a verse translation. Thus it is more suitable for works of a scientific or pedagogical nature, whereas a verse translation is indispensible for purposes of performance. [3]

In the bibliographical sections at the end of each chapter of *Essays* only basic materials are given. For the most part these consist of anthologies of folk music and those works which can be found in the libraries of local conservatories and in more available editions. Less available editions and unpublished materials are mentioned in remarks within the text or in prefaces to the separate volumes of *Essays*.

As a first attempt at a textbook for the history of the music of the peoples of the USSR, *Essays* is only a beginning step on the road to creation of a course of history of the music of the peoples of the USSR with wider scope, including the music cultures of the fraternal peoples of the multinational Soviet Union.[4] Work on the *Essays in the History of the Music of the Peoples of the USSR* was undertaken in the Department of Russian and Soviet Music of the Moscow Conservatory. Sections of *Essays* were also inspected in the national republics at the departments of the history of music of the Tashkent and Alma-Ata conservatories, in the institutes of the Academy of Sciences of Tajikistan, Turkmenia, and Kazakhstan and in the Composers' Unions of the Tajik and Turkmen Republics. . . .

The following key is used for the structure of sample musical compositions:

1) A, B, C, D *etc.* indicate separate melodic structures corresponding to lines of text and constituting parts of the strophe;

2) a, b, c, d *etc.* correspond to parts of refrains;[5]

3) aa, bb *etc.* correspond to opening calls;[6]

4) *var*, indicates variation of a basic musical phrase at its repetition;

5) In some cases roman numerals are introduced to indicate entire individual strophes of a song;

6) Underlining marks off the text of refrains, as well as of exclamatory syllables or words interpolated into the basic text; . . .

This key holds as well for the structure of instrumental works with allowance for their specific structure.

Notes

1. The present edition includes only volume I of *Essays*. Volume II was published in the Soviet Union in 1963, but Volume III, though apparently completed, has not yet been published.

2. *Narodnoe tvorchestvo* can be translated as "folk music" in the context of the present work, but can also generally denote all of folk tradition in the arts and handicrafts, with stress on elements learned through oral transmission.

3. This reference to performance is indicative of the practical nature of Soviet ethnomusicological study. In translating song texts I have not attempted to reproduce in English the Russian isometric translations sometimes given by Beliaev.

4. This would perhaps includes peoples of Siberia, the Volga, smaller groups of Central Asia and the Caucasus and others, not included in the three volumes of *Essays*.

5. The Russian word *pripev* may or may not correspond to the English "refrain" in the sense of an invariable melodic-textual segment regularly repeated after each stanza. As used by Beliaev, the term has the flexibility of the refrain structures of medieval French verse.

6. The Russian word *zapev* usually refers to the leader's call in the call-response style of Russian folk songs, but is used in the present work mostly to mean an opening call in a solo song.

Introduction

THE first volume of *Essays in the History of the Music of the Peoples of the USSR* consists of five chapters containing short characterizations of the music cultures of the Kirghiz, Kazakhs, Turkmen, Tajiks, and Uzbeks. Since ancient times these peoples have been territorially contiguous and have found themselves in tightly knit historical relationships. One of the important bases for these ties was their common struggle against both local oppressors and foreign conquerors. Though not in equal measure, these peoples carried on continuous warfare with the Achaemenids of Iran in the sixth to fourth centuries B.C., the Greco-Macedonians in the fourth to second centuries B.C., the Sassanians in the fourth to sixth centuries A.D., the Arab conquest in the seventh to ninth centuries, and the invasion of the Mongol hordes of Chingis Khan in the thirteenth century. Popular uprisings, under the leadership of Spitamen, Mazdak, Mukanna, and Tarabi gained wide fame.

The ancestors of these peoples founded their own ancient cultures, distinguished by outstanding achievements. Among these the most noteworthy were: remarkable irrigation systems, a high level of textiles, carpet weaving, woodcarving and metalworking, the creation of objects in sculpture and the fine arts, the erection of outstanding architectural monuments, the invention of writing systems, among others. The distinctive cultures of the Kirghiz, Kazakh, Turkmen, Tajik, and Uzbek peoples, each with individual traits, developed on this basis.

The Kirghiz, Kazakhs, and Turkmen preserved their pastoral nomadic way of life over a long period of time, while the Tajiks and Uzbeks developed sedentary agriculture and urbanization quite early. The Uzbeks Turkmen, Kirghiz, and Kazakhs belong to the Turkic peoples and speak languages of the Turkic family, while the Tajiks are an eastern Iranian people, speaking one of the languages of the Iranian family. Close similarities must be noted between the general culture and music cultures of the Kirghiz and Kazakhs on the one hand, and the Tajiks and Uzbeks on the other. The basis of this similarity is due primarily to ethnic affinity and secondarily to long term territorial contiguity. The Turkmen occupy a somewhat special position, in that they are not in close contact with either their northern or eastern neighbors, which sets a special stamp on their culture. [1]

Notes

1.   Beliaev's division of Central Asian music cultures does not correspond to the assessment of Viktor Sergeevich Vinogradov, a specialist in Kirghiz music. Vinogradov has made a much broader classification which includes peoples not mentioned by Beliaev (Vinogradov, 1958, as summarized in Slobin, 1969a:3):

> The first group consists only of the Azerbaijanis, who are closely tied to Caucasian traditions. Next comes a broad band of northern peoples, including the Tartars, Bashkirs, some Altai Turks, the Oirots and the Tuvins, all of whom show strong affinity to the musical practice of the Mongols, Buriats and Chuvash. The Uzbeks, with their Tajik ties, constitute another group. The fourth heading takes in the Kazakhs and Turkmens and the final category includes the Kirgiz, Khakas and a number of Altai tribes. The fourth and fifth groups have much in common due to their recent nomadic background.

Vingradov's splitting of the basic Kazakh-Kirghiz group established by Beliaev and the resulting connection of the Kazakhs and Turkmen is curious, but it is noteworthy that he follows Beliaev in emphasizing the close ties between Uzbeks and Tajiks.

Perhaps the best summary of the current state of such typologies has been given by E. Gippius (1964, as quoted by Slobin, 1969a:xiii):

> The working-out of this set of problems on the basis of comparative historical study of the national musical art of the Tuvins and related Turkic peoples of the Altai, Ural, Volga regions and Central Asia, as well as of the Mongols and Buriats, awaits its researcher. The ground for such research is as yet inadequately prepared by existing Soviet and outside literature in scientific publications and studies.

Central Asian Music

The Music Culture of Kirghizia

IN the pre-Soviet period Kirghiz music developed as an unwritten art, arising and existing in the conditions of pastoral nomadism. Being closely tied to the life and history of the people, Kirghiz music was well developed in the areas of song, instrumental creation, epic and professional music in the oral tradition, and was characterized by a striking national style and profound originality. Thus, a firm basis was created for the development of Kirghiz music in the Soviet epoch . . .

THE BASES FOR THE DEVELOPMENT OF KIRGHIZ MUSIC CULTURE

Kirghiz Folk Song

. . . Many varieties of Kirghiz folk song developed, reflecting various sides of the nomadic life, social relations, psychological make-up, and ideology of the working people. This content received artistic embodiment in national forms worked out over the centuries.

Genres of Kirghiz Folk Song. In Kirghiz, "song" is *ïr* or *obon*. Work songs are the main genre of Kirghiz folk song, and form the basis of all the other genres and types. Bearing a close connection to nomadic life, these songs are largely pastoral. They can be divided into two types: *bekbekei*, a song of girls and women who guard flocks of sheep against wolves near the settlement at night, and *širïldang*, songs of cowboys leading herds of horses to pasture. The content of both types of song is inseparably connected to the work activities they accompany. However, their thematic material is often broadened by lyric digressions and by reflections on the condition of forced service by the poor, in which the motive of social protest is introduced.

1

The first type of song received its name from the watchman's cry "bekbekei!" ("Guard closely!"). Individual verses of these songs usually end with the exclamation "Oy, du uyt!" often chanted outside the scale of the song. Sïrïldangs are songs of brave riders and fearless tamers of unbroken steppe horses. Here are typical examples of the bekbekei and šïrïldang (Exs. 1, 2):

Ex. 1. "Bekbekei" (A. Maldibayev, *Sbornik pesen*, No. 32). Freely.

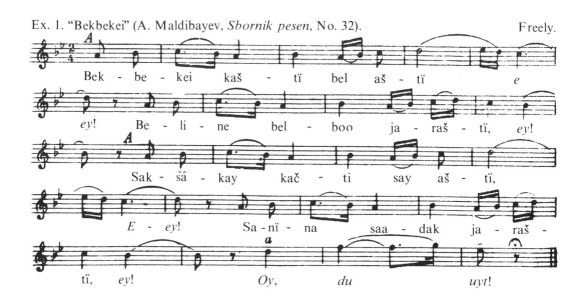

Bekbekei kašti bel ašti	Bekbekei ran across the pass,
Beline belboo jarašti	The sash belted the waist.
Saksakay kačti say ašti	Saksakai flew across the river-bed;
Sanïna saadak jarašti.	The quiver hanging at his hip. Oi du-uyt!
Oy, du uyt!	

Iynemding učun maytardïm	I bent the end of the needle
Bügün da koroo kaytardïm	Guarding the sheep tonight.
Ukuruk uču dolobo,	The end of my lasso is made of hawthorn;
Oy, du uyt!	Wolf-thief, don't let me catch you!
	(Refrain)

Tündü tündey jügürgen,	The fox, running at night,
Tülkününg kolu sögülsün.	May he twist his legs.
Tün uykumdu tört belgön,	Let the blood be spilled
Börününg kanï tögülsün.	Of the wolf who interrupts my sleep.
Oy, du uyt!	(Refrain)

Kïrdï kïrday jügürgen,	The fox who runs along the crest of the mountain,
Karsakting kolu sögülsün.	May he twist his legs.
Karanggï tündö angdïgan	The bandit who lies in wait for a victim in the dark,
Karakchï kanï tögülsün.	Let his blood flow.
Oy, du uyt!	(Refrain).

Ex. 2. "Shirildang" (A. Maldibayev, *Sbornik pesen*, No. 31).   Quickly.

Šïp - šï - rïl - dang šïr ë - ken, *ey*,   Jïl - kï - či - nïng ir ë - ken, *ey*.

Ka - rï - lar - dïng nark ë - ken,   *ey*,   Ji - git - ter - ding ayt ë - ken, *ey*.

Ay - ïl uu - lap   tün dör - de,   *ey*,   Ay - ta jür - čü   salt ë - ken, *ey*.

Šïrïldang is a smart song.
It is sung by the cowboy.
Old men sing it in the old way.
The *jigits** sing it in a holiday spirit.
It has long been sung
In the settlements at night.

**Jigit*, adopted from Turkic to Russian,
is roughly comparable to American "brave"
adopted from pseudo-Indian parlance.

In addition to pastoral songs, the Kirghiz have agricultural work songs. "Op maida!," a song in recitative style,[2] is an example of Kirghiz threshing songs. While performing the song, a man drives animals that thresh sheaves of wheat by treading on them with their hooves while circling the threshing ground. The text of this song consists of the cries of the driver, directed to the animals (Ex. 3).

Hunting songs must be added to the list of Kirghiz work songs, as well as songs connected with various types of women's domestic work: spinning, weaving, preparing animal by-products, manufacturing felt and carpets, and working hand-mills among other activities.

Wedding songs and funeral laments belong to the category of ceremonial songs, one of the earliest types of Kirghiz folk art.[3] Kirghiz weddings are preceded by gatherings of youth for prewedding games called *kiz oyunu*. The wedding ceremony itself is not marked by the great elaboration observed among other peoples. The *kiz uzatuu*, or lament of women for the bride, sung while sending her to her husband's settlement, occupies a central place in the ceremony. The kiz uzatuu stems from funeral laments called *košok*. The same type of wail accompanies laments for the dead. The lament is generally cast in an improvisatory verse form with varied repetition of a single sorrowful tune. Falling glissando turns of a fourth below the tonic are often used as cadences (Ex. 4).

Ex. 3. "Op mayda" (V. Vinogradov). In the character of a recitative.   Fairly quickly (♩=96).

Ex. 4. "Košhok" (V. Vinogradov).   Freely (♩ = 120).

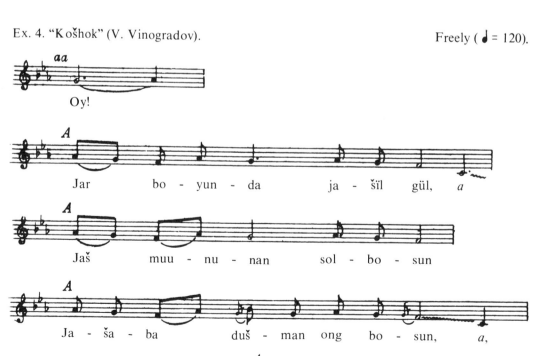

> The flower growing at the precipice's edge
> May it not wither at the root.
> May the enemy be defeated,
> And youths, having lost their fathers,
> Not undergo my fate.

A large group of Kirghiz daily-life songs[4] includes a whole series of independent genres, unusually varied and rich both in content and means of expression.[5] These are lullabies, children's, youths' and maidens' songs, lyric songs, game songs, joking and satirical songs. The richest of these genres is that of lyric songs, which in turn has many types: songs of love, family, nature, and domestic or wild animals. As is the case with other genres, the themes of daily-life songs are greatly enriched by connection with songs of social protest, work, and the like. Being later in origin, with a few exceptions (lullabies, children's songs), daily-life songs, and among these especially lyric songs, are also the most highly developed type of Kirghiz music.[6] Here is an example of a Kirghiz lullaby, "Bešik ïrï" (Ex. 5):

Ex. 5. "Bešik Ïrï" (V. Vinogradov).   Smoothly (♩= 54).

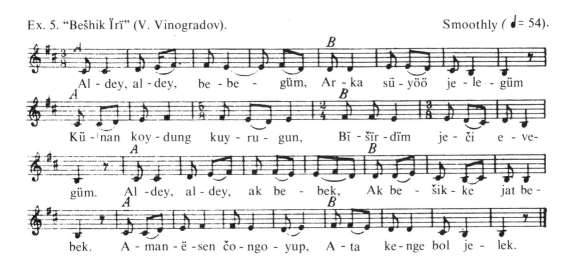

Rock-a-bye my little one
You are my support
I cooked a lamb's tail
Fat, my darling.

Rock-a-bye, little one
Lie down in the white cradle
Grow up in good health
And be the support of your father.

Ex. 6. "Jal-jal" (A. Zataevich, *250 pesen*, No. 208, transl. Beliaev). Drawn-out (♩ = 72).

Ë - ki be - ting al - bï - rïp

A - nang al - ma - nïng kï - zïl gü - lün - dey

Sa - may ča - čing selk ë - tip

O, jal jal to - tu kuš -tung jü - nüng - dey.

The blush of your cheeks is bright red
Brighter red than the spring blossoms of
    the pomegranate.
The play of colors on your plaits shines
Brighter than the feathers of a peacock playing.

Ex. 7. "Kïzïl gül" (A. Zataevich, *250 pesen*, No. 209, Drawn-out and thoughtful (♩ = 96).
transl. Beliaev).

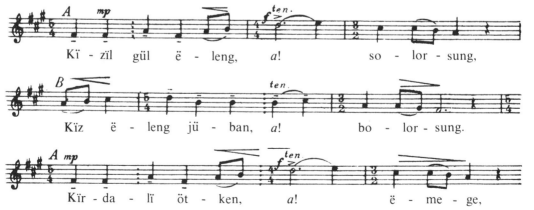

Kï - zïl gül ë - leng, a! so - lor - sung,

Kïz ë - leng jü - ban, a! bo - lor - sung.

Kïr - da - lï öt - ken, a! ë - me - ge,

Kant - ken   de teng tüš,   a!   bo - lor - sung.

We are young, ah!
Like flowers, when time passes, ah! you start to fade.
You are to all jigits, ah! like sweet honey.
Whose wife, whose, ah! will you become?

The structure of this melody is typical of Kirghiz folk song in its gradual rise and subsequent fall and also in its two part structure.[7]

Melody is highly developed in lyric (especially love) songs, which use images of nature as background. The following are basic and unique genres of Kirghiz lyric songs: *seketbai* (bright songs), *küigön* (songs of passionate love and of love's burning) and *arman* (songs of unrequited love, complaints, and sadness).

"Jal-jal" ("The Beauty") and "Kizil gul" ("The Red Flower") are striking examples of the seketbai genre with wide-ranging melodies. The melody of the latter was composed by A. Maldybayev in folk style with all its typical traits (Exs. 6, 7).

The *küigön* genre can be represented by a song of the same name (Ex. 8).

Ex. 8. "Küigön" (M. Rauchberger, *Deviat' pesen*).   Tunefully (♩ = 92).

Ma - ši - na, *ga - na - le*, tik - tim,   *e*,   Zin - ger - den,

Mü - cheng - dü, *ga - na*, ay - tam,   *o*,   i - yil - gen.

A - dam - dïng, *ga - na*, köö - nün oo - rüt - pas,

A - kïl - man, *ga - na*, ö - züng,   *o*,   til bil - gön.

I sew on a Singer machine   You don't let anyone get the better of you
And sing of your delicate figure.   Clever and sharp-tongued.

One of the characteristic types of Kirghiz lyric songs, both in terms of text and musical structure and unique national content, connected with Kirghiz nomadic life, is the song "Küngötay" (Ex. 9).

Ex. 9. "Küngötay" (A. Maldybaev, *Pesni*).   Lively.

Ak boz attïng takasï	The horseshoe of the skewbald horse,
Ak irim köldüng jakasï.	The shore of the white lake.
Aytmayïnča jazïlbayt,	Until you tell them, they won't separate.
O kurgur!	Damn them!
Küngötay kïzdïng kapasï.	The sadness of the girl Küngötay,
O-oy, bay-bay-bay-bay!	Oy, bay-bay-bay-bay,
Küngötay kïzdïng kapasï.	The sadness of the girl Küngötay.
Kök boz atting takasï,	The horseshoe of the greyish horse,
Kök irim köldung jakasï.	The bank of the blue lake.
Körmöyünče jazïlbayt,	Until you tell them, they won't separate
O, kurgur!	Damn them!
Küngötay kïzdïng kapasï.	The sadness of the girl Küngötay, etc.
O-oy, bay-bay-bay-bay!	
Küngötay kïzdïng kapasï.	
Teskeydegi kuu kazïk,	In the shadow an old stake is driven.
Tekenin ëti jol azïk.	Mutton—food for the road.
Tengtušun taap algan song.	If she found herself a friend of the same age
O kurgur!	Damn them!
Küngötay kïzda ne jazïk.	How is the girl Küngötay to blame?
	O-oy, etc.
	How is the girl Küngötay to blame?

8

Toptoy učkan taranči	The sparrows fly in a bunch,
Tobun buzbayt karači.	Not departing from the flock.
Top biykečtin ïčinde,	Look: among many girls
O kurgur!	Damn them!
Küngötay barbï karači	Isn't that the girl Küngötay?
O-oy, bay-bay-bay-bay	O-oy, etc.
Küngötay barbï karači.	Isn't that the girl Küngötay?

Songs of a didactic-moralistic and educational character, representing a generalization of folk wisdom and morals, played a great role in the old Kirghiz way of life, although they were marked by historical limitation of viewpoint at times. They are close to lyric songs in musical structure . . . .

Melodies of Kirghiz Folk Song. Melody with a clearly defined structure lies at the basis of Kirghiz song, in which a gradual rise is followed by a counterbalancing gradual descent. This type of melodic motion will henceforth be termed rising-falling. It is characteristic of both the general structure of Kirghiz songs and of their individual parts, *i. e.*, it typifies both simple and complex forms.

The ceremonial spring play song "Selkinček" ("Swings") can serve as a typical example of this structure (Ex. 10).[8]

Ex. 10. "Selkinček" (V. Vlasov & V. Fere, *Altïn kïz*).   Quickly.

Kïl ar - kan - dïn sel - kin - ček, Kïz - dar oy - nor ěr - kin - dep.

Swings made of a lasso
Girls are swinging.

Even in a well developed lyric song of Atay Ogonbaev [of whom more below—M. S.], "Ësimde" ("I Remember"), one can see how the turning back of the melodic motion can occur either in the structure of a whole work or in individual sections (Ex. 11).

Every line of text of this excellent Kirghiz song receives its expression in rising and falling melodic formations, in which the highest peak of the melody occurs in the second and third lines of the verse, *i. e.*, in the middle of the strophe, as can be seen in Example 12.

Ex. 11. "Esimde" (Transc. A. Maldybaev). Drawn out, with feeling.

Jay - dïng bir *ga - na,* to - luk, *ey!* ke - zin - de
a! A - dïr - luu, *ga - na,* too - nung, *a,* be - tin
de, Sang gül - dön tan - dap bird üz - gön, *oy,*
Jay - da - rï *ga - na,* sel - ki ey! ë - sim - de!

Jaydïng bir toluk kezinde
Adïrluu toonung betinde,
Sang güldön tandap birdi üzgön,
Jaydarï selki ësimde!

Agarïp toodon tang atkan,
Suyulup jïldïz baratkan,
Kaldïgo beken ësingde,
Kïyïšbay külö karaškan.

Özümdü saga beröm dep,
Ömürdüng gülün teröm dep,
Jaš bašïm oygo čömülgen,
Turmuštung sïrïn terengdep.

At the height of summer
On a mountain slope
I remember how you plucked
The most beautiful flower for me.

When dawn gilded the mountain tops,
And you put out the stars,
Do you remember those pure, frank smiles
Which you exchanged with me?

I wanted to give you my whole self.
I wanted to gather the flowers of life.
But my darling was busy with thoughts,
Trying to discover the secrets of life.

I remember your vow, given at twilight.
My thoughts are always with you.
O, if only every one of us
Could find a companion equal to himself.

The range of Kirghiz melodies is usually no wider than an octave, but in a majority of cases it is narrower, and even in well developed tunes it might not exceed a sixth.

Ex. 12.

Internal cadences in Kirghiz melodic structures are most often made on the tonic, second, or fourth degrees of the scale. As for final cadences, outside of the tonic another typical cadence ends on a switch from the tonic to the fourth below in both simple and more complex forms (Ex. 13).[9]

Ex. 13.

This can also be observed in Russian, Ukrainian, and Belorussian songs. However, there is no basis at all for discussing mutual influence here.

Kirghiz melody arises as free declamation of the text. In songs held to a quick tempo, the melody is almost "undeveloped," *i. e.*, each syllable of text corresponds to one note. All of these notes have equal duration except for the last, which is twice as long. The same type of declamation in a slow tempo is found in drawn-out[10] Kirghiz songs for projecting the text. More florid passages correspond to interjections inserted in the lines of text or to junctures of the refrain with the basic strophe. Melismatic vocalise episodes are closely connected to all the other elements of melodic development, making an organic artistic whole.

Certain episodes outlining accented passages and climaxes are often formed from a cambiata-like phrase in drawn-out Kirghiz songs. These phrases consist of a rising major second and a consequent fall of a third from the seventh, sixth, fifth, or fourth scale degree, depending on previous melodic motion (Ex. 14).

Ex. 14.

11

Broader melodic formations arise on the basis of such sequences (Ex. 15).

Ex. 15.

Refrains are created in similar fashion as, for example, the refrain of the song "Küydüm čok" (Ex. 16).[11]

Ex. 16

Rhythmic Basis of Kirghiz Folk Song. The rhythmic basis of Kirghiz folk song consists of measured declamation of seven-syllable trochaic verse lines with a pause on the last syllable (Ex. 17).

Ex. 17.

A free breeze in the silence
Skims over the wave.

Typical of this Kirghiz verse line is the frequent addition of a one-syllable exclamation after the fourth syllable (Ex. 18).

12

Ex. 18.

The systematic introduction of such exclamations into the seven-syllable verse line leads to the formation of a second type of line of song text: the eight-syllable line, made up of two groupings of 5+3 syllables (Ex. 19).

Ex. 19.

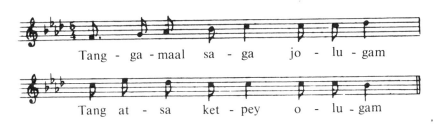

I meet the dawn with you
And do not look at the color of the dawn.

This type of complex verse line can in turn be broadened by inserting exclamatory vowels after the fifth syllable, which can be seen in Example 6. Occasionally in Kirghiz song an eleven-syllable trochaic verse line of 4+4+3 syllables is used, which is the third type of Kirghiz verse line (Ex. 20).

It is important to note that duple rhythms are almost exclusively used in Kirghiz folk songs; triple rhythms are extremely rare.

In Kirghiz folk verse one finds elision of the last vowel of a word if the following word also begins with a vowel; for example, instead of "takasy ai" one sings "takas ai."

Ex. 20.

13

Forms of Kirghiz Folk Song. The Kirghiz, like the majority of other peoples, use the quatrain as the basic strophe of song texts. The lines of a Kirghiz song do not always rhyme regularly, but are often united by beginning assonance, a device characteristic of the song-text structure of Turco-Mongol peoples. In Kirghiz the *aaba* formula predominates. This rhyme scheme is widespread among the Central Asian and Caucasian[12] peoples and also among some of the Volga peoples.[13] Among the Kirghiz the use of beginning assonance has been preserved, as well as the repetition of identical or similar material in adjacent verses, expressed in varied but similar ways. The beginning verses of "Sirtbayding obonu" ("Sirtbay's Song," Ex. 43) can serve as an example.

> She, the white-faced one, is probably walking
> Glancing, chattering and laughing.
> Impatiently awaiting the return
> Of the one who went off to distant lands.
> With her rosy cheeks she is probably walking
> Glancing and suffering,
> Remembering her darling
> Who went off to distant lands.

As for the song forms of Kirghiz folk art, these usually consist of the simplest types of strophes.[14] The one–part or one–line form (A) occurs in songs of earlier origin and most often in those of the recitative type. Example 2, the Kirghiz cowboy's song "Sïrïldang," can serve as an example of this form.[15] The AB, or half stanza, two–part strophe,[16] is widespread in all genres of Kirghiz folk song. This form stems from the singing of two lines of text, *i. e.*, half of a verse, and consists of two structures which usually form a rising and falling melodic phrase. The songs "Selkinček" (Ex. 10) and "Kïzïl gül" (Ex. 7) can serve as examples of this form.

A richer melodic development of text lines leads to complex, whole stanza structures of the two–part strophe form, the textual basis of which is not half, but the whole strophe (a quatrain). For building this form it is necessary to have not two, but three or four, different melodic structures; together, they make the two–part strophe form with an internal structure more complex than the small AB form.

Example 6, "Jal-jal," is an example of the whole-stanza, two–part form, in this case having the common two–part reprise form ABCB. As another example, Example 11, "Ësimde," has a form made up of four different melodic structures, ABCD.

This does not exhaust the variety of strophe structures in Kirghiz folk songs. Some of them constitute transitional forms between the basic types listed above. Thus the uniqueness of Example 1, "Bekbekei," which is an AB type, rests in B, which is independent while also being a variant of the basic A structure. Similarly, in "Jal-jal" (Ex. 6), its structure (ABCB) stems from melodic alternation of A during repetitions, leading to the creation of C, which differs from A only in its cadence.[17]

It is noteworthy that in Kirghiz strophic song forms the refrains are only rarely well developed, *e. g.*. Example 44 ("Küydüm čok") and a few others. In Example 9 ("Küngötay") one finds a developed refrain which includes a repeat of one of the lines of basic text.[18] In addition, in the fourth line of this song there is: 1) the insertion of an opening call on the words "O, kurgur," 2) a repetition of the word "kïzdïng," and 3) the introduction of the concluding exclamatory syllable "ai." These additions to the line of text double the length of the melodic line (Ex. 21).[19]

Ex. 21.

O, kur - gur! Kü - ngö - tay!   kïz - dïng. kïz - dïng   ka - pas,   *ay!*

Scalar Basis of Kirghiz Folk Song. The scalar basis of many early work and ceremonial songs, as of tunes for epic recitation, is made up of the following grouping of pitches, related to major and minor scales. (Ex. 22).[20]

Ex. 22.

This is the basis for further development of Kirghiz scales (similar to the scalar basis of the music of Eastern Slavic peoples), which leads to wider ranging structures that form diatonic scales: a) major-like scales (Ionian, Mixolydian), and b) minor-like scales (Aeolian, Dorian, and Phrygian).[21]

Many songs show striking pentatonic traits, linking Kirghiz music culture to that of the Mongol peoples. The pentatonic element appears as a mixture of various pentatonic tone-rows in a single melody; this occurs in the music of several peoples employing this system. This can be seen in "Kïzïl gül" (Ex. 7, in which there is a clear mixture of two pentatonic scales at the opening (Ex. 23).[22]

Ex. 23.

In Kirghiz folk music there are, to be sure, a limited number of chromatic scales which may be called altered or mixed. Among these are the following: major scale with alternating major or minor seventh; minor scale with major or minor sixth; and minor-major scale with minor seventh and alternating minor or major third.[23] A mixed minor scale with two varieties of sixths (Aeolian and Dorian) can be seen in the song "Küigön" (Ex. 8).[24]

Kirghiz Epic Art[25]

Kirghiz Epic. Both in its time of origin and its stylistic characteristics the Kirghiz epic belongs to one of the oldest types of folk musical-poetic art. It is considerably older than the epic tradition of many other peoples of the USSR. It occupies an intermediate position historically between the earlier varieties of this art found among the peoples of the Soviet North [i. e., eastern Siberia—M. S.] and the later types, found among the peoples of Central Asia. Its content has undergone significant changes over the centuries. Like every other type of historical epic, the Kirghiz epic is basically heroic. The major Kirghiz epic centers on the legendary hero Manas, for whom the whole cycle is named.

The Kirghiz epic arose among the ancient forebears of the Kirghiz in a preclass society as a common heroic tale of all the people, projecting the ideas of the struggle against external and internal usurpers and calling on the scattered tribes to unite into a single people.[26] In the period of feudal relations the Kirghiz epic came under the strong influence of the feudal-tribal clique in terms of thematic content and the image of the hero . . . .

Due to the great significance of the *Manas* in the development of Kirghiz folk culture, its reciters were not just called storytellers (*jïrši*) but *manasči*, i. e., tellers of the *Manas*. They preserved a huge quantity of verses of the epic from memory and achieved outstanding popularity among the people. Performances of *Manas* were listened to with close attention and lasted for many hours, usually from evening until early morning.

Musical Structure of the Manas' Narratives.[27] The narration of Kirghiz epic tales consists of solo recitative without instrumental accompaniment, allowing the performer a wide range of expressive means from a tranquil reciting tone (for descriptive passages) to moments of great emotional animation in various moods: magnificent, threatening, stormy, accusatory, sad, among others.

The verse basis of the Kirghiz narrative is a seven-syllable trochaic line and its variants. The tale itself, *ïr* or *jir*, breaks down into varying numbers of verse lines. Rhyme is irregular; sometimes there is none, sometimes six to ten successive lines are unified by a single rhyme, often achieved by repeating a single word. Alliteration is widely used, both for the opening words of whole lines and for individual words.

Two types of recitative form the basis of musical expression for the Kirghiz epic. One of these consists of precise rhythmic declamation of seven-syllable trochaic tetrameter. The other consists of continuous, even, and more rapid declamation of several consecutive lines with speech accentuation and prolongation of the final syllables of long text phrases. The first type of recitative is used in narrative or tranquil episodes and the second during moments of great emotional animation.

The recitation of the *Manas* is built of short phrases and their variants, equal to one line of text. Usually every manasči employs his own phrase. These phrases do not generally exceed a third or fourth in range and have a cadential leap down a fourth from the tonic (Ex.24).[28]

Ex. 24.

The phrases are usually in triple meter. In this way epic singing differs radically from the meter of Kirghiz songs, which is basically duple.

Tales are performed without instrumental accompaniment. The manasči becomes carried away and usually raises the tessitura gradually. This rise cannot always be exactly regulated and brought into a given musical system. The transcription of an excerpt from the *Manas* by V. M. Krivonosov (see the anthology *Kirgizkii musykaľnyi foľklor*, Moscow-Leningrad, 1939) gives a good depiction of the musical development of the Kirghiz epic. It was taken from the manasči Saiakbai Karalaev (b. 1894). The excerpt begins with an even declamation of the text, based on the variation of the following short phrase featuring unstable intonation of the third at first (Ex. 25):[29]

Ex. 25.

17

This entire episode is tonally crystallized in A-flat major.[30] Next comes a free melody, sounding a whole tone higher and playing the role of tonal transition (Ex. 26).

Ex. 26.

Further, a new rise follows, a whole tone higher, with a prolonged variant of the basic tune (Ex. 27).

Ex. 27.

The whole excerpt is rounded out by a climax in e-flat minor with wide ranging phrases in free recitative form (Ex. 28).[31]

Ex. 28.

As a result of the emotional rising of the tessitura of the scale, the tonal plan of this epic excerpt is the following: A-flat major b-minor c-minor e-flat minor.

Aside from the *Manas* the Kirghiz have legendary heroic tales and novelistic poems of later origin. In these poems, prose, describing the conditions and circumstances of the action, alternates with poetry in a melodic-recitative style with *komuz* (lute) accompaniment to portray the speech of characters.

Art of the Kirghiz Akins

The Kirghiz Akins. Highly popular, talented musicians were selected from among the broad mass of people. This began the professionalization of the art and subsequent specialization in various aspects of music performance. In the area of vocal mastery the Kirghiz defined two specialists: the irči and the akins. The title *irči* is usually given to singers with good voice and knowledge of a wide repertoire. *Akins* are professional folk singers who also have a poetic gift, ability to improvise verses, and compositional talent (the craft of forming new melodies). However, there is no sharp line between these specialties, and the more common title irči is often applied to the akins. Both irčis and akins are masters of musical instruments, principally the *komuz*, the basic Kirghiz accompanimental instrument [a three-stringed fretless lute—M.S.].

The Art of the Kirghiz Akins.   The musical-poetic activity of the akins has enormous social significance in that the themes of the folk singer's output are usually topical and the genres of songs are connected to the social role of their art.

The following genres are basic to the akins' art: *maktoo*, a panegyric song, *sanat* and *nasiat*,[32] didactic and edifying songs, and *kordoo*, denunciatory songs, opposite in content to the maktoo.[33]

These compositions are cast in strophic forms or in the terme form (also widely used by the Kazakhs), which stems from epic recitation. *Terme* denotes a "composite" composition, built on improvisation with free transitions from one theme to another. The text does not fit the strophic mold; both the musical and textual form are closer to the structure of epic tales. Musical declamation of the terme is based on speech intonation and accentuation. Example 40, "Toktogul's Salutation to Alimkul," is a striking example of the terme form. Toktogul's derisive song "Beš kaman" ("Five Boars," Ex. 39) is an example of the akins' song in strophic form.

The akins' songs served as keen weapons in the class struggle. The akins sharpened these weapons in contests (*aytiš*), which were competitions for professional mastery as well as heated polemic jousts on ideological ground between singers of the democratic and aristocratic camps.[34] In the aytiš the akins took turns, and the singer who refused to continue the contest was the loser. Poetic-musical competitions in the mastery of rhyme and verse were called *alim sabak*.

The art of the Kirghiz akins of the prerevolutionary period reflected the struggle between the two classes of society. The akins who served the khans, *manaps* and *bais* ["Landowners" and "headmen"—M. S.] were obliged to praise their patrons, sing of their race horses, perform mourning songs at the death of "respected" people, and the like. Among their obligations was also the task of deprecating those singers, professional rivals, and rich people who were objectionable to the akins' patrons. The democratically inclined akins defended the interests and rights of the working masses . . . .

In the nineteenth century a pessimistic mood appeared in the work of some Kirghiz akins at the time of the conquest of Kirghizia by the backwards, feudal Kokand Khanate. In this period, called "the time of sorrow" (*zarzaman*) in the history of Kirghiz and Kazakh literature, some akins sought liberation from social inequality and a return to the old tribal structure of life . . . . Among these akins was the talented Arstanbek (*ca.* 1824-1874). In the years preceding the annexation of Kirghizia to Russia he stood against this union and called for a return to the age-old tradition of patriarchal-tribal life . . . .

Kirghiz Instrumental Music

Kirghiz Musical Instruments. Over the centuries of musical development, the Kirghiz created their instrumentarium, related to that of other Central Asian nomadic peoples.

The basic musical instruments of the Kirghiz are the following: 1) the *komuz*, a three-stringed fretless plucked lute; 2) the *kiak*, a two stringed bowed lute; 3) the *čoor*, an open end-blown flute; and 4) the *temir komuz* ["iron komuz" —M.S.] or jew's-harp. In the feudal period the military orchestra of the Kirghiz khans long included instruments designed for that purpose and used all over the Orient: the *surnai*, a large oboe; the *kernei*, or *kerinei*, a bass horn; and the *dool*, a drum.[35] These instruments of the Kirghiz military orchestra are mentioned in the *Manas*.

The čoor, sometimes called *sibizgi*,[36] is a pastoral wind instrument made of reed or, more rarely, of wood. In the former case, it is sometimes wrapped in a sheath of calf's intestines to guard against breakage. The čoor usually has three to five fingerholes, giving the following basic diatonic scale (Ex. 29):

Ex. 29.

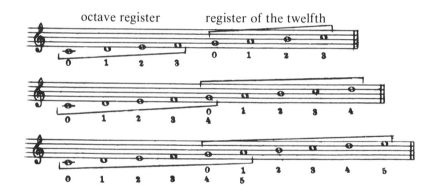

When the higher overtones are used, the range of the čoor can be considerably widened.[37]

The kiak is a bowed lute, similar to the Kazakh *kobiz*. It looks like a large wooden dipper, the handle of which serves as neck and the bowl as body. The bottom of the body is covered with a piece of camel skin acting as a lid. The kiak has two thick horsehair strings tuned to a fourth or fifth. In play the fingers touch the strings without pressing them to the neck.

The kiak is a solo instrument. One can play some types of sporadic two part music on it. Formerly it was also widely used as accompaniment for song, but now it has yielded this role to the komuz.

The komuz belongs to the lute family of instruments. It differs from similar lute-types of other Central Asian peoples in that it has three strings instead of two. This allows for three-voice play, which is an important characteristic of Kirghiz instrumental music. Komuz tunings are varied and unique: the highest pitched string is the middle string. The following are various types of fourth- and fifth-tunings. They are given in third-to-first string order (Ex. 30).[38]

Ex. 30.

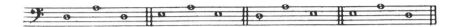

When tuned in fourths the two upper strings can be played in parallel fourths, while the third string yields a drone; when tuned in fifths, they can be played in parallel fifths. The technique of komuz playing is highly developed, and Kirghiz performers often play in one part, two parts, or three parts. The komuz is the solo instrument of professional performers, and can also be used to accompany song.[39]

The temir komuz is mainly an instrument for women and children. Players accompany jew's-harp performance with whistling.

The surnai was a melodic instrument in the Kirghiz military orchestra. The kernei held drones or played fanfare-like phrases. The dool furnished rhythmic accompaniment to the ensemble of surnais and korneis. Both the kernei and dool also served as military signaling instruments (they are described in the chapter on the music of Tajikistan).

Kirghiz Instrumental Music. Three manners of performance can be distinguished in Kirghiz instrumental music: 1) the pastoral, as in čoor music; 2) the "concert" manner, with a rich tradition among komuz and kiak players; and 3) the military style, connected with the surnai and its accompanying instruments.

We do not know of any special transcriptions of melodies for the čoor.[40] A. V. Zataevich in his anthology *250 Kirghiz Instrumental Pieces and Tunes* [see Zataevich, 1934—M. S.] includes three examples of melodies for the flute transcribed from performance on the kiak. Here is one of them (Ex. 31):

Ex. 31. "Sïbïzgïnïng kör tolgoo." A. Zataevich, *250 pesen*, #6.

Melodies for the temir komuz are of special interest. On this instrument the lower buzzing tone is a drone and a narrow ranging melody, consisting of overtones, is produced above. The following pitches are possible in such melodies (Ex. 32):

Ex. 32.

They form the basis of the pastoral melody "Kök muzoo" ("The Gray Calf," Ex. 33).

Ex. 33.

It is impossible to overlook the production, through whistling, of two-voiced vocal music by one person on this simple idiophone. This technique, called *khömei* among the Tuvins and *uzliau* among the Bashkirs, belongs to one of the oldest and most original ways of producing harmonics with simultaneous sounding of an extended fundamental pitch.[41]

Programmatic pieces take first place among compositions for the kiak, the instrument of Kirghiz master musicians.[42] As a typical example of complex pieces for this instrument, let us introduce "Koškayrïk" by Muratali Kurenkeyev; the title of this piece means "paired repetitions" of the basic melody, and indicates the variational nature of its make-up. The free rhythm of the piece is also of interest (Ex. 34).[44]

Ex. 34. "Koškayrïk" (Transc. Saks-shuv. *Kirgizkii fol'klor*).   Con moto.

23

In this piece multiple variations of a single theme are given. This leads to a form which is typical for the basic variety of Kirghiz monothematic instrumental compositions. The compositional and variational technique during performance is closely tied to the mastery of the musician and depends on it. Thus, this Kirghiz instrumental form foreshadows the development of thematic material which is embodied in such forms of free variation as the Azerbaijani mugam and other forms.[45] The kiak, now going out of use, includes in its repertoire small instrumental and song-like pieces as well as large forms.

Compositions for the komuz are always broad, varied, and interesting; it is a popular, but at the same time difficult, instrument to master. Pieces for the komuz, as those for the kiak, are largely programmatic. However, some of them have genre names, analogous to the names of compositions of [Western—M. S.] classical music, such as prelude, intermezzo, and the like. The terms "kambarkan," "kerbez," and "šingrama" are primarily connected to tunings of the komuz. The tuning in fifths is typical of the kambarkan; the tuning with a fourth and fifth is used for the šingrama, and (most often) the tuning in two fourths is used for the kerbez among others. The term *šingrama* specifies a bright shimmering character in piece and performance. The *kerbez* is an effective virtuoso piece. This term is also used for large vocal compositions. As for the term *kambarkan*, its origin is connected with the name of Kambar-ata, the mythical protector of horses and shepherds and the father of Kirghiz music.[46] All of these terms are used for pieces of varied theme and content.[47]

There are three types of komuz pieces. The first consists of long compositions in song style and related short instrumental pieces. The second consists of the monothematic, single tonality compositions of the variational type. The third variety consists of pieces in a broad three part form consisting of: 1) an exposition and variational development of the first theme, 2) a middle section on a new theme in a higher register, and 3) recapitulation of the first part, to which an independent coda may be added. The piece "Terme-kambarkan" of Toktomambet Orozov is a rich composition with a broad flight of creative fantasy; it can serve as an example of the three part form with rising mid-piece modulation (labelled II), free recapitulation of the main theme (III), and broad coda (IV, Ex. 35).[48]

Ex. 35. "Terme-kambarkan." Zataevich, *250 pesen*, #78,   Moderately quick and light.

accelerando

Quickly (♩ =208); this tempo until the end.

III.

IV. Fiery and agitated.

26

The themes of komuz pieces are quite varied. One finds artistic embodiment of lyric, daily-life and historical themes, as well as many others. Among the lyric komuz pieces cast in small forms, the *botoy* genre has been highly regarded by Kirghiz composers. The name of this genre derives from the word *boto* ("suckling camel"), used as a pet name for children. One of the best examples of this type is "Tilendening botoyu," ("Tilen's Botoy"), named for the nineteenth-century komuz player (Ex. 36).[49]

Ex. 36. "Tilendining botoyu." A. Zataevich, *250 pesen*, #56.

In the feudal period special forms of military music also developed, performed by orchestras of surnais, kerneis, and dools, which existed until the mid-nineteenth century. Zataevich transcribed several melodies for such orchestras, preserved in *contrafacta* for kiak. Among them the melody of the cavalry march "Kör ozon" can be given. It is typical of Kirghiz melodies in the variational development of a basic motive during repetitions and in the use of a leap to the fourth below tonic as a cadence (Ex. 37).

Ex. 37. "Kor ozon" (A. Zataevich, *250 pesen* No. 24).   Fairly quickly.

A little more softly.

Broad and heated, with energy, no ritard.

Kirghiz Music in the Last Quarter of the Nineteenth and First Half of the Twentieth Century

The Annexation of Kirghizia to Russia. The many-faceted Kirghiz folk and professional oral tradition provided soil on which Kirghiz music could grow. The annexation of Kirghizia to Russia in the last quarter of the nineteenth century began a new period in the history of Kirghiz music, which by that time had a fully formed and independent style . . . .

Kirghiz Music Culture of This Period. Accumulated and polished over the course of the centuries, the storehouse of epic, song, and instrumental art preserved orally by the Kirghiz people and enriched by national masters served as the basis on which Kirghiz music developed in this new period. The influence of progressive Russian democratic culture and the flowering of the revolutionary movement contributed to eradication of the dark aspects of the old way of life and the rise of class consciousness among the workers . . . .

The Art of the Kirghiz Akins

The Kirghiz Akins.[50] The greatest representatives of Kirghiz akins' art of this period, those who expressed progressive views, enthusiastically greeted the Great October Socialist Revolution. These were Togolok Moldo (the pseudonym of Baimbet Abdrakhmanov) and Toktogul Satilganov. Both of these outstanding poets and thinkers were the fathers of contemporary written Kirghiz literature and attained great popularity in the Soviet period.

Togolok Moldo (1860-1942). Togolok Moldo, a pupil of the great akin and komuz player Muzook, came out against the cruelty and greed of the bais and manaps in courageous satire and stood up for the oppressed Kirghiz woman, protesting against the payment of the bride price. To save himself from continuous persecution by the manaps and bais, Togolok led a difficult life, moving from one place to another.

Togolok Moldo basically used the traditional forms of the akins' art in his social and artistic work, but, having had an elementary education and being a well read man, he wrote out the texts of his songs and created works in new forms which were closer to those of prosody. In his poem of this genre, "The Earth and Her Children," the akin tried to explain the forces of nature, thus striking a blow at religious and antiscientific notions . . . . Only a few examples of his writing are available. "Žaštïkka" ("To Youth") already dates from the Soviet period (Ex. 38).

Toktogul Satilganov (1861-1933). Toktogul Satilganov was the most popular and talented representative of democratic thought among the akins of the period described above.

Ex. 38. "Žaštïkka." (V. Vinogradov, *Toktogul*, p. 27)   Smoothly, singingly.

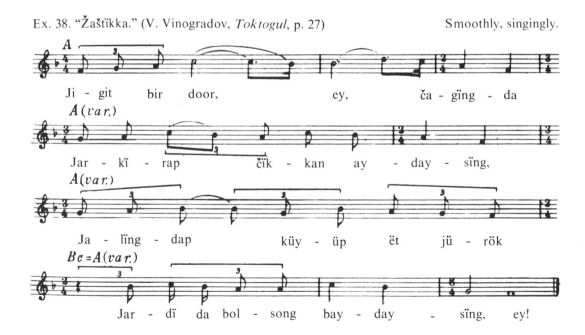

When a jigit is young
He is like the full moon.
Be kindled, my heart;
Even if you are poor,
You are still richer than the rich.

Toktogul was born into an impoverished family in the settlement of Sasik
Žide on the territory of the present Toktogul village soviet in the Toktogul district
of the Jalalabad region of the Kirghiz SSR. Toktogul's father, Satilgan, was noted
for his independent and brave character; his mother, Burma, was a famous košokči,
or [professional—M. S.] mourner, who composed košoks, or laments. She knew
many tales and songs which she transmitted to her son, who showed unusual
musical talent at an early age. At twelve Toktogul became a transient worker and
started as a koyču, a shepherd for a bai. By this time the boy had already mastered
the komuz and tried to write songs on the theme of the unjust and hungry life of
the poor. The eighteen-year-old Toktogul appeared at a large folk gathering with
a vehement denunciatory song against the well known akin Arzimat, who was a
client of the powerful manap Dikanbay. Having achieved great fame after his
attack on Arzimat, Toktogul turned down a proposal of patronage by Dikanbay,
who had tried various promises to gain the allegiance of the young akin in the class
struggle . . . .

Dikanbay and his four brothers, among whom Kerimbay (a former local administrator) was known for cruelty, fiercely persecuted Toktogul. They did not
even stop at trying to take the life of the "obstinate" akin. These persecutions intensified in 1894 after Toktogul wrote the highly popular, angry song "Beš kaman"
("Five Boars") against them [the four brothers—M. S.] (Ex. 39).

Toktogul's enemies took advantage of the weakness of the czarist administra-
tion during the Andijan uprising of 1898[51] to gain satisfaction. The akin was
sentenced to death by a military court in Namangan, and the sentence was com-
muted to seven years of hard labor. These years, spent in a circle of Russian political
exiles, served as a school of political education for Toktogul, and had a decisive
effect on the development of his world view and his revolutionary ideas . . . .[52]

Toktogul's sentence was lengthened due to an attempted escape, and he
returned home only after twelve years through a second escape. There sorrowful
experiences awaited him: his wife had married another man, his only son had
died, and his eighty-year-old mother was living in poverty. However all of this
personal unhappiness did not shake the steadfastness of Toktogul's spirit and his
will to struggle with the oppressors of the people. He colorfully expressed his ideas
about the social significance and the lot of the akin in his song "Greetings, Longed-
for People!"

Why grieve about the past?
Why mourn the dead?
Rejoice now, Toktogul,
Since you see your people again!

31

Ex. 39. "Beš kaman" (V. Vinogradov, "Toktogul," p. 179). Decisively (♩ = 152).

Ak - mat, Dïykan al - dam - čï, Aktan, Mingbay jal - gan - čï

Ë - gem - ber -di _ Bak - tï - yar Ël - je - gen - ge jar - dam - či.

Kol ku - ra - dï beš ka - man, Mu - run - ku - day čap - mak - ka

Ko - roo do - gu koy tur - mak, Kor - gool ber - beyt jet a - ta.

The traitor Akmat and Dïykan
The liars Aktan and Mingbai
Ëgemberdi-Baktïyar —
The lackey, robber of the people:
You, the gang of five boars
Rob the people as before.
But the people will keep you from taking not just
    sheep from their flocks,
But even sheep dung!

32

Having reentered his homeland illegally, Toktogul had to hide from czarist officials, but he did not cease his public activities, writing new songs in a revolutionary spirit. His enemies persecuted him and again tried to do away with him. They succeeded in imprisoning the akin in Namangan, but now the whole people came to his defense. The akin's pupils (Eshmambet and Kalik) went from settlement to settlement and gathered a defense fund of twenty thousand rubles and much livestock for Toktogul. Under the prevailing conditions of popular prerevolutionary ferment, the authorities decided not to take harsh measures against Toktogul, and after a half-year's confinement they were forced to release him.

Toktogul lived to see the liberation of his people . . . . He triumphantly met the Great October Socialist Revolution and greeted it with fiery songs, opening a new stage in the development of Kirghiz poetry, literature, and music. Toktogul died in 1933 and was buried in his homeland. His memory, like his songs, lives on among the Kirghiz people, for whose liberation he selflessly struggled all his life.

Toktogul's Work. Toktogul's creative and performing talent was exceptionally versatile and embraced all the genres of Kirghiz folk music, aiding its development.

The akin genres occupied an especially important place in his music . . . . He created some remarkable compositions on the basis of the maktoo genre . . . . The kordoo genre became a method for abusing the oppressors of the people. The akin used the sanat and nasiat genres for educational goals, arousing the people to creative work and moral perfection. Toktogul's creative interests also extended to the area of the Kirghiz epic. He worked out a version of the legend about Kedei-khan (the pauper khan), well known among other peoples of the Altai and Central Asia . . . .

The transcriptions of Toktogul made by A. V. Zataevich [see Zataevich, 1934—M. S.] testify to the akin's broad grasp of creation and performance in various Kirghiz genres.[53] Among these transcriptions are the instrumental genres (šingrama, kerbez, and kambarkan), programmatic pieces, *contrafacta* of songs, and others. Toktogul's mastery of performance was outstanding. Zataevich speaks of Toktogul's striking originality, subtle musicianship, breadth of phrasing and melodic freshness, and of the "decidely inspired and captivating performance of some of his works at certain moments." Toktogul did not exclude merry joking from his work.

The art of Toktogul is closely connected to the traditions of Kirghiz folk and akin artistry. He used the age-old forms broadly, filling them with new content. Thus, his salutation to Alimkul (a young akin) upon first meeting him,[54] is constructed in the manner of early Kirghiz recitative with a basically seven-syllable, free-rhythm verse line close to Kirghiz speech rhythm. The text of this salutation approximates the structure of epic narrative: free rhyme, wide use of assonance and rising motion at the beginning, succeeded by falling motion (Ex. 40).

"Beš kaman" (Ex. 39) can serve as an example of Toktogul's use of the strophic form with a seven-syllable verse line. In this song an attempt has been made to transcribe the free improvisational manner of performance of the first strophe with added grace notes and text underlay.[55]

Ex. 40. "Toktogul's greeting to Alimkul" (V. Vinogradov, *Toktogul*, p. 90).

O! Kar - kïl - dap uč - kan kar ör - dek,

Kay - rï - lïp kon - so köl - mïn - da

Ka - rï ᴵ - sam da - gï Ta - las - ka

Kay - rï - lïp, ba - lam, köl - dim - da

Ka - dim - ki To - kom köl - di dep

Ka - lïng kïr - gïz ël - mïn - da

Ka - ba - rïm u - gup ke - lip - sing

Ka - čïp - jür - böy ta - laa - ga

Kar - ga - day, ba - lam, köl - mïn - da!

Ka - rip ket - ken ke - zim - de,

Ba - lam, sen ke - lip - sing - da kaš - ma.

If the black duck, crying and flying, returns
    and alights,
Come to me, my son!
I returned to the Talas
Although I am quite old.
Know that Toktogul returned
And that here the Kirghiz people gathered
Having heard about me, and you came
Don't flee into the steppe, come to me, my son!
You returned to me, my son,
When I was already quite old.

Toktogul's art was widely spread not only in Kirghizia, but also in Kazakhstan. He himself speaks of this in his song "Having Missed You, I Greet you!"

In all the Kirghiz steppes,
In all the Kazakh steppes,
I was a young race-horse,
I was the wished-for native singer.

This facilitated a rapprochement between the music cultures of the two peoples, thanks to which Kirghiz songs spread among the Kazakhs, and *vice versa*. Toktogul's musical perspective was quite broad. He knew well the famous Kazakh songs and instrumental works, and also Russian folk and workers' revolutionary songs, with which he became closely acquainted during his exile. "The Russians have the source of knowledge," he said about the importance of Russian culture. He was very interested in the music of neighboring peoples. His meeting with the famous Uzbek singer Molla Toichi Tashmuhammedov (1866-1943) is a case in point.

The outstanding pupils of Toktogul were the akins Kalik Akiev (b. 1883) and Alimkul Usenbaev (b. 1894), whose work extends into the Soviet period. Alimkul holds dear the precept of his teacher: "Serve eternal truth, akin!" In 1938 an artistic meeting took place at which Kalik, Alimkul, and the composer Abdilas Maldibayev met the famous Kazakh akin Jambul. As a present they brought him a komuz on which and to whose accompaniment Toktogul Satilganov had performed his inspiring songs.

Instrumental Artistry

Muratali Kurenkeyev (1860-1949). If Toktogul was the greatest Kirghiz akin of the prerevolutionary and early postrevolutionary years, then Muratali Kurenkeyev must be named as the most outstanding exponent of instrumental artistry of those years.

35

He not only mastered two of the basic Kirghiz instruments (the komuz and kiak) but played on the čoor and the Kazakh *dombra* [a two-string fretted lute —M. S.] and was a great composer of national instrumental music. Inheriting compositional and performing talent from his father, Kurenkei (1826-1907), who was a widely known composer and performer, Muratali further developed his heritage. Muratali possessed great strength of imagination and a striking personal style. His repertoire was exceptionally extensive. He performed not only his own works and those of his father, but numerous folk genres widespread in Kirghizia. Both as creator and performer he mastered the great diversity of form in Kirghiz folk music to perfection, from vignettes to complex compositions.

Some of Muratali Kurenkeyev's works have already been introduced: "Kör ozon" (Ex. 37), the delicate miniature "Tilendening botoyu" (Ex. 36) and the highly developed monothematic variational piece "Koškayrïk" (Ex. 34). In his "Kerbez" for komuz the same variational principle is connected to wider melodic development and more complex polyphonic accompaniment. Muratali gives the central presentation of the theme in a three-voiced setting, but the final coda-like section includes a broad rise to the upper register, making a melodic culmination to this entire gay piece (Ex. 41).

Ex. 41. "Kerbez" (A. Zataevich *250 pesen*, #65).   Tranquilly and freely.

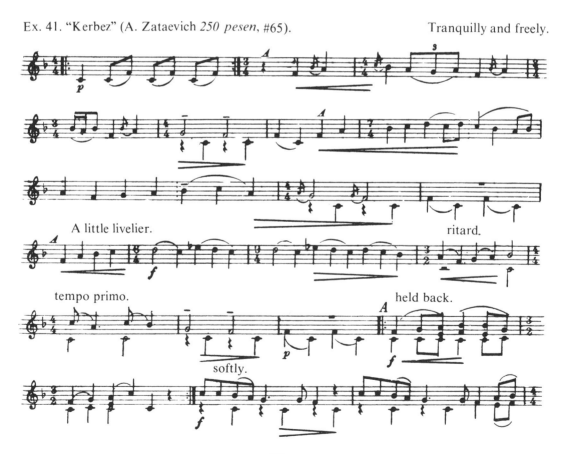

Muratali Kurenkeyev's output is closely tied to the way of life, history, and aspirations of the Kirghiz people and reflects their psychological make-up. Muratali did not remain within the bounds of his own national art, but also knew Kazakh and Russian music well. He said: "Our music and Kazakh music are sisters." In one piece for kiak (titled "Russian Echoes" by Zataevich) Muratali uses the melodic turns of Russian folk dance music in an original way (Ex. 42).

Ex. 42. "Russian echoes" (A. Zataevich, *250 pesen*, #41).　　　Bravely and decisively.

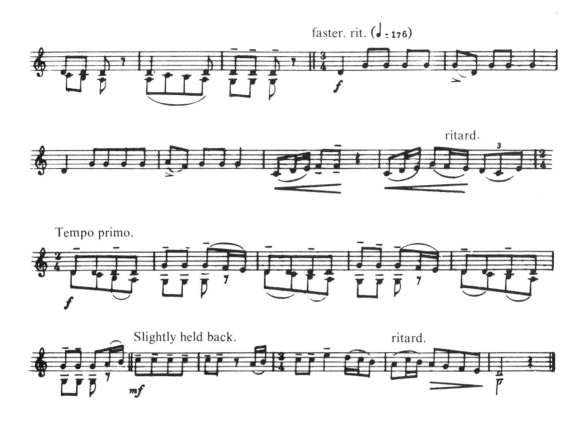

Zataevich, who transcribed a great number of Muratali's pieces, characterized him as a "storehouse" of musical talent, experience, and knowledge, as the most typical representative of Kirghiz music, and as an artist "with a wealth of folk humor and keen observation." In the postrevolutionary period, Muratali wholeheartedly participated in the building of Soviet Kirghiz music culture, working in the Philharmonia and the Kirghiz theater from their inception. Kirghiz society solemnly marked the eighty-fifth birthday celebration of Muratali Kurenkeyev in 1945.

Toktomambet Orozov (Karamoldo). Toktomambet Orozov (b. 1888), called Karamoldo (*i. e.,* "the black mullah," in the sense of a specialist or authoritative representative of his profession) for his mastery, belongs to the group of outstanding instrumentalists who were contemporaries of Muratali. Karamoldo is a great master of the komuz. His repertoire yields nothing to Muratali's in richness and variety. It consists of programmatic pieces with lyric, daily-life, and humorous content, as well as compositions of satiric and social wit, pieces of military and historic character and the like.

A. V. Zataevich spoke of Karamoldo as a very serious musician with a decisive and reserved manner of performance, through which a hidden temperament shines, and with irreproachable technique on the komuz.

Epic and Song

Epic Artistry. Kirghiz epic tales of both the heroic style (including the *Manas*) and novelistic style were preserved in the period under discussion by many tellers, and attracted a broad audience. This facilitated the preservation of the tales down to our times through oral tradition. The greatest representative of the Kirghiz epic tradition in the prerevolutionary years and in the Soviet period are Sayakbay Karalaev (b. 1896) and Moldobasan Musulmankulov (b. 1893).

Development of Song. Melody was considerably enriched in the work of Musa Baetov (1902-1949) and Atay Ogonbaev (1904-1950), who developed in the Soviet period. Both of them were itinerant shepherds at an early age and experienced the full weight of servitude under the bais. In the last prerevolutionary years these musicians underwent all the adversity which fell to the lot of young singers of little means. They had to work their talent for a crust of bread while not selling their gifts to the manaps and bais. The talents of both of these men developed and achieved full flowering in the Soviet period. They won a place among the leading performers of the Kirghiz Philharmonia from its inception in 1937.

Musa Baetov had a broad repertoire of Kirghiz folk songs. He also composed songs and performed them masterfully to his own accompaniment on the komuz. One of the best loved songs popularized by Musa Baetov, "Sïrtbaydïng obonu" ("Sïrtbay's Song"), is a striking example of the developed Kirghiz lyric song. Its author was the singer Sïrtbay, whose talent was marked by lyricism and profundity, and whose character was frank and independent. Inherent in this song are typical national traits (Ex. 43).

Ex. 43. "Sïrtbaydïng obonu" (Transc. A. Zataevich in Orozov's *Muzykal'naia gramota*).

39

Akkuba bolgon tügöngür,
Anggeme süylöp külgöndür,
Alïska ketip kaldï dep,
Amalsïzdan jürgöndür.

Kïp kïzïl bolgon tügöngür,
Kïlčaktap basïp jürgöndür,
Kïzïktüüm alïs ketti dep,
Kïynoo taptïp jürgöndür.

Alïškan kolüng bek bolso,
Aytïlgan sözüng ëp bolso,
Asïlsa ëčen köp baldar,
Aytbagïn maga dep koyso.

Karmaškan kolün bek bolso,
Kaalgan sözüng ëp bolso,
Kat jazsa dalay čït kursak,
Katïlba maga dep koyso.

She, the white-face one, is probably walking,
Looking back, chattering and laughing
Impatiently awaiting the return of
The one who went to distant lands.

With rosy cheeks she is probably walking,
Glancing back and suffering
My darling went far away,
He is probably suffering there.

And if your handclasp is strong,
And if your word is spoken firmly,
And if she is bothered with youths,
And if she tells them to leave;

If her extended hand is firm,
And her word is strong,
Then, if the jigits write to her,
Let her not answer them.

Atay Ogonbaev was an outstanding Kirghiz folk singer and komuz player who composed famous songs and interesting instrumental pieces. He was a pupil of Toktogul's and learned the techniques of both the komuz and composition. The song "Ësimde" (Ex. 11) and "Küydüm čok" ("I Burn from Love" Ex. 44), in which the traditional Kirghiz lyric song (the küigön) undergoes rich artistic development, testifying to his outstanding poetical gift.

In the examples given, Atay Ogonbaev appears as a striking creative individualist who developed on the basis of Kirghiz folk music and is closely connected to it.

Ex. 44. "Küydüm čok" (Transc. A. Zataevich, transl. Beliaev).   Fairly quickly.

41

Kaizhallo, o-o, grief, akh!
High, akh!
I wait with this, o-o, grief, akh!
    for a breeze.
For the black-eyed one, akh! I wait,
    akh! akh!
And my heart is consumed, akh! by grief!

The appearance of this entire constellation of highly talented musicians (both composers and performers) during the late nineteenth and first quarter of the twentieth centuries is connected with the development in the prerevolutionary period of a progressive democratic tendency in the area of the akins' art, reaching a high revolutionary pathos in the works of Toktogul. This prepared the way for the further development of Kirghiz Soviet musical artistry.

Notes to Chapter I

1. *Narodnaia muzyka* can be translated as "folk music" or "national music"; I have used both possibilities, depending on context. In many cases the word *narodnaia* can simply be omitted in English without damaging the meaning.

2. *Rechitativnyi* is an adjective translated here as "recitative," or "recitative-like," and is applied to folk song or epic chant sung syllabically in a measured way. Sometimes the term comes close to the *parlando-rubato* concept used by non-Soviet writers.

3. Beliaev, like other Soviet ethnomusicologists, presupposes an evolutionary approach to folk song based on Marxist theory, particularly on Engels' theory of cultural development (*see* his *Origin of the Family, Private Property and the State*). Thus, phrases like "early type of song" appear frequently and naturally in Soviet writings.

4. "Daily-life" is a possible translation of *bytovyi*, a standard term for all genres of folk song not definitely classed as work songs. "Lyric songs," a standard subgroup of daily-life songs, appear to include all types of daily life song not directly connected to age-grade, sex, humor, or songs for specific occasions; however, it is certainly not a consistent or well defined category.

5. "Means of expression" refers to type or degree of musical expressiveness, as defined by Western observers.

6. Here is a clear expression of Beliaev's view on the evolution of song genres: songs not directly related to the means of production or not connected to family life (lullabies, chidren's songs) emerged at a later stage of musical development in every culture.

7. Also typical is the heterometric shifting in measures 10-13.

8. According to the basic Soviet ethnographic survey of the Kirghiz (Abramzon, 1963:318), "One of the best loved entertainments of the youth is swinging on swings (*selkinček*) of rope attached to trees or stalks. They swing in pairs, singing." Example 10 is taken from *Altin qiz*, an opera of Soviet Kirghizia, composed by Vlasov and Fere. However it should not be assumed that the melody is not typically Kirghiz in structure; a folk song may well be quoted in its original form in a Central Asian opera and, further, many Kirghiz folk tunes are remarkably "Western" in structure.

9. In Kirghiz music, the "tonic," or tone above which most melodic activity occurs, shares importance with the pitch a fourth below, a situation which led me to use the terms "upper" and "lower" tonics for these two poles of Kirghiz melodies (Slobin, 1969a).

10. *Protiazhnaia pesnia*, or "extended, drawn-out, or protracted" song is a term of Soviet ethnomusicology adopted from Russian folk song, and in non-Russian contexts generally refers to songs of greater-than-average length in a slow tempo.

11. This sort of extended melodic sequence is less common in Kirghiz music than, say, in Uzbek music, which is more in contact with the Near East.

12. "Caucasian," as used in the present edition, refers to the three major peoples of the Soviet Caucasus: Georgians, Armenians, and Azerbaijanis.

13. By "Volga peoples" Beliaev means the Finno-Ugric and Turkic peoples (*e. g.*, Udmurt, Chuvash peoples) living along or near the upper Volga.

14. Beliaev's evolutionary approach to strophic structure follows. His basic tenets are: 1) songs with varied settings for different strophes of text are more advanced than strophic songs, and 2) within each strophe, songs which contain melodic differentiation of all the lines of text (usually in a quatrain, for Central Asia) are "richer" than those which have one or two melodies for the four lines of text.

15. In Example 2, the line marked A (*var.*) hardly seems melodically identical to the other lines.

16. "Strophe" is my translation of *kupletnaia forma*. The latter implies the regular melodic repetition for successive differing stanzas of text which we use in English when referring to a "strophic" setting of a song.

17. Here the reader may differ with Beliaev on the criteria for similarity and uniqueness of short musical lines; those criteria are not defined.

18. For Beliaev's use of the term "refrain," *see* note 5 to the Preface.

19. This improvisatory modification of lines of text is typical of Central Asian Turkic music in general, and relates (at least in the Kirghiz context) to the type of variation which is a hallmark of the solo instrumental style, of which more below.

20. Example 22 is an excellent schematization of the double-tetrachord basis of Kirghiz scale structure, including 1) overall range of a seventh, 2) melodic activity above upper tonic *(g')*, and 3) gap of a fourth, often left melodically unfilled, between upper *(g')* and lower *(d')* tonics.

21. Soviet ethnomusicologists, like their Western colleagues, have consistently applied the octave-species "Greek" church modes to non-European folk musics with tetrachordal and/or pentachordal bases. *See* note 22.

22. Example 7 affords a useful opportunity for inspecting the Kirghiz tonal system which, I feel, involves more than "clear mixture" of two pentatonic scales. The piece is built around two opposing sets of thirds. Third chain #1 includes the pitches *f-sharp'-a'-c-sharp"-e"*, while the smaller, "alternate" set (#2) includes *b'* and *d"*. Such structures are typical of Kirghiz tunes.

The melody of Example 7 consists of two phrases (marked A and B by Beliaev). In phrase A, the pitches of third-chain #1 occupy most of the attention, save for passing *b*'s and the important, isolated *d''.* Note that this key pitch is stressed by accent and duration, as well as by its location in the melodic line. Following the climactic *d''*, the melody turns back to the *e''-c-sharp''-a''* of third-chain #1, the basic melodic material. Even casual listening to a performance of a Kirghiz song will acquaint the listener with the letting-up of the voice which occurs after the high point of a melodic line has been reached.

It is my argument that *d''*, with its associate *b'*, serve as tonal alternating points, providing the slight tension and release which make the melodic line move forward. Let us look at the second line of the song for confirmation: here, the *d'-b'* complex is more clearly defined than in line 1, and the same release follows (what Beliaev calls "cambiata-like" release) from *b'* to the *c-sharp''-a'-f-sharp'* chain.

Examination of other examples in this chapter will provide the reader with closer acquaintance with Kirghiz tonal thinking. Perhaps my analysis (detailed in Slobin, 1969a) is not the only approach to the tonal material, but simple decisions based on terms like "pentatonic," "major-like," "Mixo-lydian," and the like do not seem to cover the matter. This terminology is often similarly applied in Euro-American ethnomusicology. Recently, at least one scholar (Cazden, 1969) has suggested that our quick categorizations of Anglo-American ballads by "Greek" or "church" modes are hasty and presumptuous; *see* note 16, Chapter 2, for a similar recent Soviet view.

As for the general subject of pentatonicism, it is not often extensively discussed in Soviet ethno-musicology, as the pentatonic is still felt to be an early, underdeveloped forerunner of the Western diatonic scale (*see* Kulakovskii, 1962). One exception to this trend, relating to Tatar music culture, is Ia. Ghirshmann's *Pentatonika i ee razvitiia v tatarskoi muzyke* (Moscow, 1960).

23. The "alternation" of major and minor intervals referred to by Beliaév at times reflects the presence of unstable intonation of the given interval, *i. e.,* "non-tempered" performance; the third seems to be the least stable interval among the Kirghiz.

24. Unstable sixths are found across northern Afghanistan and in several regions of Central Asia.

25. For extensive Soviet commentary on the *Manas, see* Manas (1961), or the excellent discussion in English in Chadwick and Zhirmunsky (1969).

26. This and the following passage are indicative of the standard Soviet approach to the epic.

27. For more thorough discussion of this subject, *see* V. Vinogradov's essay "Kirghiz National Recitative" in Vinogradov (1961b) or Chapter 6 of Vinogradov (1939).

28. Here again is the basic Kirghiz tonal pattern of upper tonic (melodic basis; *a-flat'*) and lower tonic (cadential; *e-flat'*) separated by an empty fourth.

29. Here again is the unstable Kirghiz third, apart from which the Kirghiz epics sound surprisingly "well tempered."

30. Beliaev does not literally mean here that the tune is in Western A-flat major, but that it fits the outline of our scale. However, earlier Soviet writings (notably those of A. V. Zataevich) consistently placed Central Asian tunes into a Western framework through key signatures which did not match the actual tonal content (*see* Zataevich, 1934, the classic collection of Kirghiz music).

31. If one conceived the piece to conclude in e-flat minor, one would have to postulate an ending on the dominant (*b-flat'*), an uncomfortable westernization of the tonal material.

32. Doubtless from the Arabic (through the Persian) *nasihat,* "advice."

33. Vinogradov also lists the *arnoo,* a dedicatory song, and *kuttuktoo,* a congratulatory song (Slobin, 1969a:6).

34. For a Western study of Central Asian singing contests, *see* Emsheimer (1956). As far as I can judge, such contests generally split along clan or tribal lines rather than class affiliation. The discussion of the role of Kirghiz bards given by Beliaev is the classic Soviet interpretation of the place of such performers in various cultures. Similar passages in *Essays* relating to other Central Asian music cultures have been deleted due to redundancy.

35. For details of the construction, ranges, tuning, and manner of playing of all the instruments used by peoples discussed in the present volume (along with copious illustrations), see Vertkov's useful *Atlas of the Musical Instruments of the Peoples of the USSR* (1963), henceforth cited as *Atlas.*

36. These military instruments were adopted from the neighboring Uzbek and Tajik kingdoms, who, in turn, imported them from the Near East.

37. *Sibizgi* is also the Kazakh term for a similar end-blown flute; *see* Chapter II. Among the Uzbeks, the *Sibizik* is a short single reed pipe (*see* Karomatov, 1972).

38. Beliaev's works, like the *Atlas*, provide clean-cut scales for the aerophones of Central Asia. Fieldwork among the Central Asian peoples in northern Afghanistan has led me to believe that such ideal scales give very limited information about the full range of pitches produceable, due to lipping, half-holing, and other techniques.

39. For more thorough discussion of komuz tunings, including terms for each, *see* Vinogradov (1968:53). The same chapter has extensive details concerning komuz construction.

40. This holds true for the jew's-harp in most of Central Asia and Afghanistan. However, the playing of the jew's-harp among the Kirghiz and Kazakhs is considerably more complex than among other peoples, as shown in Beliaev's mention of simultaneous melodic whistling and jew's-harp twanging, which can be heard on Soviet recordings of Kirghiz folk music.

41. Beliaev's remark is in accordance with the general tendency among Soviet ethnomusicologists to ignore the flute repertoires of Asian peoples. Few of the major flute traditions are well represented in published works. This state of affairs is probably due to the Soviet evolutionary belief that flutes, as pastoral instruments, must of necessity have died out as a consequence of the modernization of life and music in Soviet Asia.

42. For an extensive and extremely lucid account of this extraordinary vocal style among the Tuvins, *see* Aksenov (1964:54-62). On the other hand, *see* Lebedinskii (1965:82-90) for a lengthy, if unconvincing, rebuttal of both Aksenov and researchers among the Bashkirs on the subject of solo two voiced singing. At any rate, it is clear that the Bashkirs hum a fundamental and whistle a tune while playing on their flute (the *kurai*), as do other Central Asian and Near Eastern peoples, *e. g.*, the Baluch of Iran and Afghanistan, which certainly qualifies as a type of solo two part voice production. Certain Mongolians also indulge in solo two part singing (Wolcott, 1970; Smirnov, 1971); the connection between this vocal technique and that of Tibetan monks, who are reputed to sing three tones simultaneously, is unclear.

43. Here Beliaev does not take up the ramifications of the term "programmatic," which is an essential concept in Kirghiz and Kazakh (*see* Chapter 2) instrumental music. This basically involves the existence of a story line for each instrumental piece, either so well known to the audience as to need no announcement or specially provided for listeners by the performer through a verbal introduction.

44. "Koškayrik" is a splendid example of kiak variational style, which is carried out in more complex fashion in the komuz repertoire.

45. There seems to be little connection between the improvisatory variational style of Kirghiz instrumental music, a purely indigenous Central Asian approach to musical structure, and that of Azerbaijan, an offshoot of Arabic-Persian classical modal style.

46. He is usually called Kambar Khan (hence kambarkan for the genre), and is said to have invented the komuz by imitating the actions of a monkey plucking stretched intestines.

47. The exact meaning of the genre names has yet to be clarified; it is certainly true that the same genre label can cover a wide variety of pieces.

48. Noteworthy in Example 35 as characteristics of many komuz pieces are: 1) frequent change of texture (one to two to three voice play); 2) frequent dynamic change; 3) stable *vs.* heterometric passages rhythmically; 4) change of tempo from slower to faster for segments of a piece. Many of these features seem more typical of earlier performers (Example 35 was transcribed *ca.* 1930) than of today's komuz players, who have been influenced by European ideals of sound, structure, and technique. The mid-piece rise cited by Beliaev as characteristic of komuz pieces appears much less frequently in recent transcriptions. Beliaev's section III, "free recapitulation," seems to me to be stretching the point a bit; Kirghiz style leans more toward continual variation than toward sonata form.

49. This is a fine example of the simpler komuz style, in which monophonic play predominates, and the melody is "set" chordally in a manner familiar to Western ears, yet it is perfectly Kirghiz.

50. For thorough discussion of the lives and work of Kirghiz akins, *see* Vinogradov (1952) or Chapter 7 of Vinogradov (1958). Beliaev's discussions provide some interesting glimpses into the lives of prerevolutionary musicians, though the discussion proceeds from postrevolutionary hindsight at times.

51. "Of all the popular uprisings in prerevolutionary Central Asia, disregarding the great 1916 revolt, which really belongs to the history of the 1917 revolution, the most serious and most significant was that of 1898" (Carrere d'Encausse, 1967:167).

52. "Socialist ideas penetrated the area [Central Asia—M. S.] from the end of the nineteenth century onward thanks to the czarist political deportees, whose numbers kept on swelling" (*ibid.*, 181).

53. These transcriptions can be found in Zataevich (1934) and Vinogradov (1961a), and are reproduced in part in Slobin (1969a).

54. Greetings by the roadside were apparently often sung in traditional Kirghizia, and "Vinogradov has been able to substantiate this practice among present-day Kirghiz *kolkhoz* workers" (Slobin, 1969a:5).

55. That Beliaev felt called upon to emphasize the grace notes and text underlay in this example indicates the bareness of most transcriptions of Kirghiz (and Kazakh) music.

Beliaev's Bibliography

Beliaev, V. M. "Kirgizskaia narodnaia muzyka." *Sovetskaia muzyka,* no. 6, 1939.
—— and Smirnov, M. "Tvorchestvo Murataly Kurenkeeva (1860-1949)." *Sovetskaia muzyka,* no. 2, 1949.
Kirgizskii muzykal'nyi fol'klor. Sbornik kabineta po izucheniiu muzyki narodov SSSR pri Moskovskoi gosudarstvennoi konservatorii, Moscow-Leningrad, 1939.
Kirgizskaia SSR (Kirgiziia) in Bol'shaia Sovetskaia Entsiklopediia, vol. 21, 1953.
Toktogul. *Izbrannye proizvedeniia* [translated from the Kirghiz] Frunze, 1950.
Vinogradov, V. *Muzyka Sovetskoi Kirgizii.* Moscow, 1939.
—— *Kirgizskaia SSR, Seriia Muzykal'naia kul'tura soiuznykh respublik.* Moscow, 1954.
—— *Toktogul Satylganov i kirgizskie akyny.* Moscow-Leningrad, 1952.
Zataevich, A. *250 kirgizskikh instrumental'nykh p'es i napevov.* Moscow, 1934.

For further Kirghiz bibliography, see the bibliography at the end of the present volume and that in Slobin (1969a). Between Zataevich (1934); Vinogradov (1961a); and Vinogradov (1958) all the basics of Kirghiz music discussed to the present can be found.

The Music Culture of Kazakhstan

The Development of Kazakh Music in the Pre-Soviet Period. The music of the Kazakhs, like that of other Central Asian peoples, existed as an unwritten art in the pre-Soviet period. It is most closely related to the music of the Kirghiz as a result of the ethnic and linguistic ties and historical similarities between the two peoples. The culture of both Kazakhs and Kirghiz was strongly marked by their nomadic way of life. In the pre-Soviet period Kazakh music attained great diversity and elaboration of styles and genres. Melody was especially well developed, marked by tunefulness, expressiveness, and rich subtlety in transmitting feelings and moods. This trait of Kazakh folk music has been noted by many authors since the earliest times of contact with the way of life and culture of the Kazakhs . . . .

THE BASES FOR THE DEVELOPMENT OF KAZAKH MUSIC CULTURE

Kazakh national musical art reached a high stage of development in the pre-Soviet period. Its basic styles were folk songs, epic, instrumental music, and the rich art of professional singers and instrumentalists, who were also composers. In all styles Kazakh music makes use of developed musical forms. The application of simple forms is mostly limited to daily-life songs (such as lullabies, humorous songs and the like), to the early work and ceremonial songs, and to epic recitation, along with the related recitative style song called *terme*. The basis of pre-Soviet Kazakh music was the art of the proto-Kazakhs, long settled in the area of Kazakhstan. The formation of original styles of musical art was closely tied to the process of ethnic formation.

47

Kazakh Folk Song

Genres of Kazakh Folk Song. For the Kazakhs, "song" has two names: *en* and *oleng*. The first term is used for song as music and the second for song as poetic-literary composition. Hence, the term *enši* is given to master performers of Kazakh folk songs, and the word *olengši* is used for singers who compose songs, *i. e.*, first the texts, then the melodies. In performing their songs, the Kazakhs often use the *dombra* [a two-stringed fretted lute—M. S.] for accompaniment; it is the indispensable instrument of professionals and is also widespread for domestic music making.

Authors who have written about Kazakh folk music have remarked on the rich musical and poetic talent of the Kazakhs and their facility in improvising new texts to popular melodies.[1]

Kazakh music arose and developed under the conditions of pastoral nomadic life, with which it is closely tied and which it fully reflects. In a general way this is expressed in the basic genres of Kazakh folk songs: work, ceremonial, and daily-life songs, as well as in historical songs, songs of social protest, and the like. All of these genres, which are more or less widespread among all peoples, have special national form and content among the Kazakhs, connected with the conditions of their life, the characteristics of their psychic make-up and that of their music culture.

Work songs, accompanying the work process, reflect the thoughts and hopes of the workers, who were exploited in the prerevolutionary period. The basic type of work for men among the Kazakhs was livestock herding. Thus, the main types of men's work songs were pastoral, divided into the songs of cowboys, who pastured herds of horses (*jïlqïš ëni*), and songs of shepherds (*qoyši ëni*). Domestic and subsidiary pastoral work fell to the women's lot. Women's work songs were connected to milking domestic animals, preparing dairy products, weaving and spinning, making felt and carpets, working with a hand mill or mortar and pestle to prepare grain. The construction and dismantling of tents during transhumance, another duty among Kazakh women, was also accompanied by singing. Both men and women took part in agricultural work such as melon growing, gardening, and field work, which was also reflected in song. "Jïlqïši ëni" ("Cowboy's Song," Ex. 1) displays the practical significance of Kazakh pastoral songs.

Ex. 1. "Jïlqïši ëni" (Transc. Suleimanova). Broadly, unhurriedly.

I have driven horses since childhood with loud songs.
Who is dejected living by honest work?
When I sing a song for entertainment in the steppe,
The one-year old colts chime in with their neighing.

Another "Cowboy's Song" is based on the social theme of the burden of involuntary transient work, linked to the lyric theme of remembering the beloved. Each verse has a whistled refrain, as a sign of its being a work song (Ex. 2).

Ex. 2. "Jïlqïši ënï" (Transc. A. Jubanov).　　　　　　　　　Slowly.

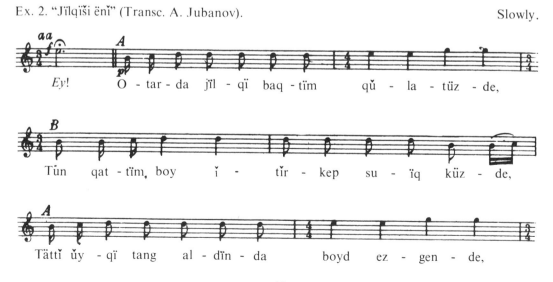

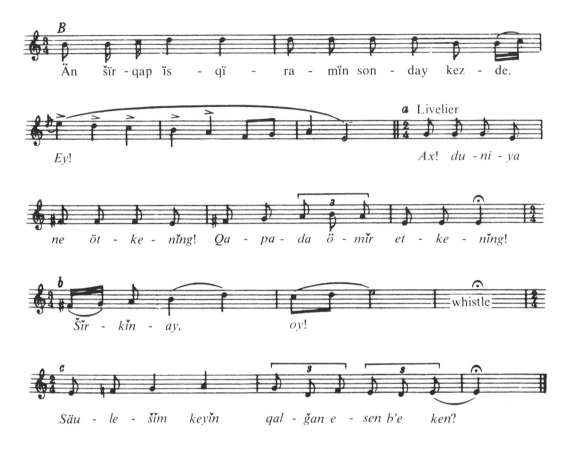

Otarda jïlqï baqtïm qŭlatüzde,
Tün qattïm boy tïtïrkep suïq küzde.
Tättï üyqï tang aldïnda boydï özgende,
Ën šïrqap ïsqïramïn sonday kezde.
Ax, duniya, ne ötkening!
Kapada ömïr ötkenïng!
Šïrkïn-ay, oy!
Säulešïm keyïn qalğan esen be eken?

Tüsedï eske säulem sonday kezde,
Kelgendey özï elestep közbe-közge.
Jetetïn tïlegïme kün bar ma eken,
Qayğï otï jas jürektï janšïp ezbey.
Duniya ay, šïrkïn-ay!
Armanğa jeter bïr kün-ay!
Axau-ay, oy!
Talqandap adïranï ketsem be eken?

I led the horses to pasture far in the steppe
In cold autumn nights I froze.
I would like to have slept sweetly before dawn;
In order not to sleep, I whistle a melody:
Ah, a bitter fate! What have you done to me!
My life passes in suffering!
O my dear one!
O dear one, how does she live far from me?

And when I remember my dear one,
It's as if she stands before me.
When will my hopes be fulfilled?
Sadness and sorrow burn my heart.
Ah! My dear one, how bitter is my fate!
When will my dreams be fulfilled?
Akhau-ai, oi!
When will my suffering be over?

In "Qoyšï ëni" ("Shepherd's Song," Ex. 3), both the social and lyric themes are more deeply expressed.

50

Ex. 3. "Qoyšĭ ёñ" (Transc. B. Erzakovich).   Sadly.

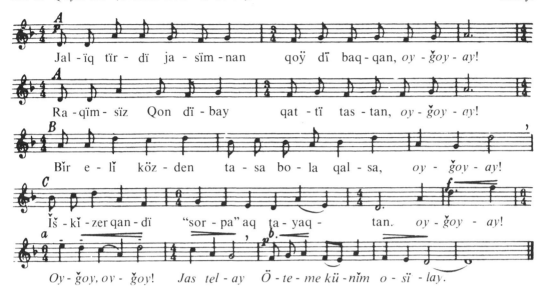

Jalïqtïrdï jasïmnan qoydï baqqan
Raqïmsïz Qondïbay qattï tastan.
Bïr elĭ közden tasa bola qalsa,
Ĭškĭzer qandï "sorpa" aq tayaqtan.
Oy-ǧoy-ay! Oy-ǧoy!
Jas tel-ay,
Öteme künĭm osïlay!

Men de bĭlem jar süye janïmmenen,
Qïz Eljan qálay jürsĭn menĭ menen.
Qoy jün šekpen denemdĭ qotïr etken,
Magan qarap külgendey ötken-ketken.
(last 3 lines same as last 3 lines of first stanza)

It is tiresome to herd sheep from childhood on;
The pitiless Kondybai is more cold-hearted than a stone.
And if even one head is lost,
He'll make you eat bloody soup with a stick.
Oi-ghoi-ai! Oi-ghoi!
Is this really
The way my whole life will pass?

I also know how to love with my whole soul,
But how will the girl Elzhan go out with me?
The coarse shirt rubbed me raw,
And all the passers-by laugh at me.

51

The title of the song "Ri qoyïm" is taken from the refrain, a sheep call. The song paints the picture of the unhappy life of a boy working for a bai (Ex. 4).

Ex. 4. "Ri, qoyïm" (Transc. B. Erzakovich).   Sadly.

Qozï jayǧan jerïm bar Mätï bŭlak,
Ri, qoyïm!
Šešemdï oylap zarlanam künde jïlap.
  Qasqïr qoydan šülaysïn,
  Ri, qoyïm!
  Qoraǧa kep topalam qïrïl,
  Qoyïm, ay!

Tängertennen dïrdektep men jürgende,
Šešesï bar balalar jarïr sülap.

Qozïnï aydap, orgïzïp sayǧa barsam,
Talqan šeker tatidï šaynap qalsam

Qozï iesï quadï "qu jetïm" dep,
Šešemdï aytïp än šïrqap ayǧay salsam.

52

I herd lambs for Mati-bulak; Oh, my lambs!
Remembering my mother, I cry every day.
Refrain:
Somewhere wolves howl, oh my lambs!
I wish you wolves would croak! Oh my lambs!

I walk and freeze from morning to evening
And children with mothers still sleep. (Refrain)

I went with the lambs to the river;
Even fodder seems sweet to me (Refrain).

The owner of the flocks drives me, calling me a sly orphan,
When I sing a song about my mother (Refrain).

One of the earliest transcriptions of Kazakh work songs is the song of a Kazakh coachman working along the Orenburg-Tashkent route before the introduction of the railroad. The transcription was made in the 1880s.[2] This song is of the improvisatory type in which the singer conveys his spontaneous impressions of nature and passers-by and his thoughts about them (Ex. 5):

Ex. 5. "The Coachman's Song" (Transc. A. Eichhorn).   Lively, happy.

Sko - ro bu - det stan - tsi - ia,

Tam zhi - vet moi drug, Zhu - sup.

A station is coming up;
There my friend Zhusup lives.
Two officials are listening in the carriage
To how I while away the time with a song.
There go two eagles—
One is white and the other black.
If I were an eagle
I would fly to Bukhara.
Our elder has two rifles and a wife
And I have neither wife nor children.
A colt can't support a rider.
The back wheels of my carriage turn quickly
And the front wheels even more quickly.
If an old man marries a young girl
He's a fool.

The ceremonial songs of the Kazakhs, like those of other peoples, can be divided into two basic groups: family songs and practical songs, reflecting group work activity. Among the first group, the most important types are wedding and funeral songs. Among the second major group are calendric songs, marking transitional moments in the work year, and also invocations to the forces of nature, giving thanks for the success of man's work, e. g., calls for rain during drought among others. Healing songs also belong to this group.[3]

The Kazakhs have the following types of wedding songs: *jar-jar*, or guests' song, *sïnsu* or *qïz sïnsu*, or the bride's farewell to her parents and childhood home, and *betašar*, or "unveiling the face" for the greeting of the bride at the bridegroom's tent.

The jar-jar song takes its name from the repeated affectionate refrain, which means "dear one" (masculine or feminine). It is sung at the wedding feast by alternating groups of men and women. Its content is quite varied, ranging from serious congratulations and exhortations to merry jokes. Sometimes it contains a battle, or competition, of wits between the bride's and groom's relatives. This type of song is typically made up of alternating seven and six-syllable lines with the inclusion in the last line of the two-syllable refrain "jar-jar." Its melodic contour is nearly declamatory, as can be seen in the following example (Ex. 6):[4]

Ex. 6, "Jar-jar!" (B. Erzakovich, *Narodnye pesni kazakhstana*, p. 22). Lively.

Qara nasar zamandas,	Esïk aldï qara su
Qara nasar, jar-jar!	Maydan bolsïn, jar-jar!
Qara maqpal säükeleng	Aq jüzïmdï körgendey
Šašing basar, jar-jar!	Aynam boldïn, jar-jar!
Münda äkem qaldï dep	Qayinatasï bar deydï
Qam jemegïng jar-jar!	Köp jïgïtter, jar-jar!
Jasqsï bolsa qayïnatang	Aynalayïn äkemdey
Orïn basar, jar-jar!	Qaydan bolsïn jar-jar!

Boy: Black cloth, girls!
Black cloth, jar-jar!
Velvet *saukele* (=traditional women's headgear)
Holds the hair well, jar-jar!

Don't grieve
Because your father remains here, jar-jar!
If your father-in-law is good,
He will replace your father.

Let there be a black lake
In front of the door, jar-jar!
Let there be a mirror before me
So I can see my fair face, jar-jar!
Many youths say
That I have a father-in-law, jar-jar!
He will never replace
My dear father, jar-jar!

Ex. 7. "Qïz sïnsu" (Transc. B. Erzakovich).   With grief, sobbingly.

Qayranday aulïm qaladï,
Qarasam közïm taladï.
Erkeletken aulïm-ay.
Zamanïm qanday boladï?

Jürüšï edïm ağalap,
Ağayïnda panalap,
Panalap jürgen basïmdï
Malğa da sattï bağalap.

Aq üyge salğan düdege,
Aq tüyğïn ïlgen bedene,
Öz elïmnen ketken song,
Körgende künïm nemene.

Taqïya tïktïm šïm keste
Šïm keste emes sžm keste,
Erkeletken ağa eken,
Jetkïzbey berdïng on beske.

55

I am leaving my beautiful settlement.
My eyes are weary, and I have no strength to look at it.
O, my settlement, where they spoiled me!
What does the future hold?

Here I lived, respecting the old,
My kinfolk cared for me.
But now they have sold me, their beloved,
For cattle.

Felt bands decorate the white tent;
The white falcon caught a quail on the fly.
O how will I live
When I leave my own native soil?

I sewed bright patterns on my hat,
But they have become dark for me.
My older brother, who was fond of me,
Gave me in marriage before I reached fifteen.

The Uzbeks and Turkmens have wedding songs similar to the jar-jar type. The bride's lament (*sïnsu*) is performed in the spirit of a lament for the dead and is sung when she parts from her parents and leaves for her husband's settlement. In their content these songs often reflect the constraints of marriage for Kazakh girls in prerevolutionary times. This occurs in the example below of the bride's farewell song. Each verse of text begins with a call with moans, and finishes with its repetition, now used as a refrain (Ex. 7).[5]

The terme style (of which more below) is typical for the betašar type of wedding song, performed when the bride leaves for the groom's tent. It consists of advice to the bride concerning behavior upon coming into her husband's family (Ex. 8).[6]

Funeral wails and laments (*joqtau*) are similar in musical content to the bride's lament. They also begin, are interrupted by, and conclude with sorrowful exclamations and sobs, and are made up of short expressive tunes, often more melodious than recitative-like. The example of joqtau below belongs to the type of lament performed by professional mourners, as can be seen from the regular and elaborated strophic structure of the text (Ex. 9).

Ex. 8. "Betašar" (B. Erzakovich, *Narodnye pesni Kazakhstana*, p. 24).   Jokingly.

A!   Ayt ke - lĭn,   ayt ke - lĭn!   Ö - zïng ja - tïp bay - ï - nga

Tŭr - tŭr - la - ma, ke - lĭn - šek, Qap - tïng au - zï   bos tŭr   dep,

Ëy,   ayt   ke   lĭn!   Qŭrt ŭr - la - ma, ke - lĭn - šek.

56

Öžïng jatïp bayïnga	If you haven't gotten out of bed,
Tŭr-tŭrlama, kelïnšek,	Don't tell your husband to get up, bride!
Qaptïng auzï bos tŭr dep	If a bag is left open,
Qŭrt ŭrlama, kelïnšek.	Don't steal curds from it, bride!

Jŭrt aldïnda sïmpangdan	Don't put on airs
Qaqangdama, kelïnšek,	In company, bride!
Uyge tüsken tüyenï,	If a camel strays into the house,
Baqandama, kelïnšek.	Don't tie it up there, bride!

Auzï-basïng süyrengdep	Don't enjoy yourself with gossip;
Ösek aytpa, kelïnšek.	Respect the old, bride.
Ulkenderdïng aldïnan	Don't put on airs
Attap ötpe, kelïnšek.	In front of your elders, bride.

Ex. 9. "Joqtau" (B. Erzakovich, *Narodnye pesni Kazakhstana*, p. 25).   Mournfully.

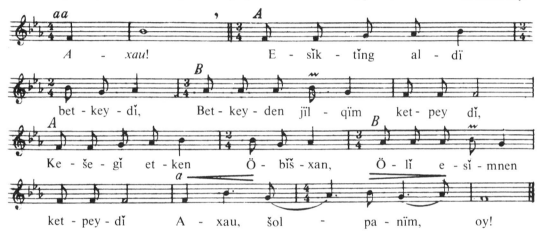

Esïktïng aldï betkeydï	A plain is before my door;
Betkeyden jïlqïm ketpedï	My horses won't leave the plain.
Kešegï ötken Äbïšxan	Abishkhan, who died yesterday,
Alï esïmnen ketpeydï.	Lives on in my memory.
A-xau, šolpanïm, oy!	Refrain: Akhau, o my star!

Äbïšxan kettï-au bel asïp,	Abishkhan went along life's path.
Belïne belbeu jarasïp.	The belt which bound his waist suited him well.
Jarasqanï qŭrsïn-ay,	But what use is this belt
Külïmxan qaldï-au adasïp.	If Kulimkhan remains alone!
A-xau, šolpanïm, oy!	

Esïktïn aldï kürke edï,	A hut stood before the tent
Kürkenï jauïn bürkedï.	And the rain poured down on it.
Kešegï ötken Abïštïng,	The earth swallowed up
Topïraq betïn bürkedï.	The deceased Abishkhan.
A-xau, šolpanïm, oy!	

The enumeration of Kazakh ceremonial songs above does not exhaust the repertoire. One can also mention New Year's congratulatory songs (like carols), performed during the spring New Year's holiday *nauryz*, which is widely celebrated by the peoples of Central Asia and the Near East,[7] and those sung at the time of Ramazan, the Muslim holiday.[8] *Bedik* can be cited among the old Kazakh curing ceremonies. It was accompanied by the singing of incantations by girls and young women who sat near the patient in two rows facing each other.[9]

Daily-life songs, constituting a major segment of Kazakh folk song, consisted of lullabies, children's songs, lyric songs (love, family, and nature songs), humorous songs, and other types. They relate closely in content to songs of other genres, which enrich the daily-life songs. As among other peoples the richest and most important type of Kazakh daily-life song is the lyric song. Here there is a particularly broad development of melody and verse form in many aspects, *i. e.,* those basic traits which distinguish lyric songs from epic songs and related recitative forms. Lullabies and children's songs are among the earliest type of Kazakh daily-life songs, and in this respect are close to work and ceremonial songs. Here, for example, is a lullaby, "Bešik jïrï" (Ex. 10):[10]

Ex. 10. "Bešik jïrï" (B. Erzakovich, *Narodnye pesni Kazakhstana*, p. 20.). Fairly quickly.

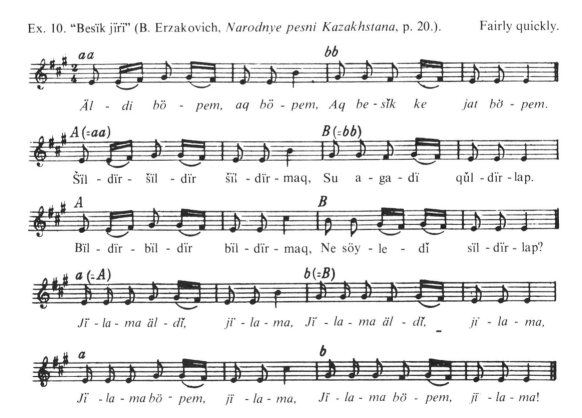

Rock-a-bye baby, rock-a-bye
Lie in your white cradle.
The water gurgles in the brook.
It sings in the brook.
The rattle is rattling.

What is it saying?
Don't cry, rock-a-bye, don't cry.
Don't cry, rock-a-bye, don't cry.
Don't cry, little one, don't cry.
Don't cry, little one, don't cry.

"Bal xadiša" ("Khadisha's Melody") can serve as an example of the simplest type of lyric song. In it the youth complains about the hopelessness of love for his chosen girl due to domestic and family obstacles (Ex. 11).

Ex. 11. "Bal xadiša" (A. Zataevich, *500 pesen*, #234).　　　Calmly, with soft sadness.

Degen sen Bal Xadiša, Bal Xadiša
Kuyeuïng seksen beste-šal, Xadiša.
Ökenge ol ölgenše rïzasïng,
Berïptï tengïn tauïp, bar Xadiša.

Japanga jalğïz bïtken sen bïr šïnar,
Qonuğa men aq süngqar bolğan qŭmar.
Arada talay kezeng tolïp jarïr,
Ey qalqa! Ğašïq köngïlïm qašan tïnar.

59

You are well-known, honeyed Khadisha, honeyed Khadisha.
Your husband is eighty years old, he is an old man, Khadisha.
Thank your father to your dying day
For finding you such a husband, Khadisha.

You are a lonely plane-tree in the steppe
On which I, the white falcon, thirst.
On our path we have many obstacles.
My dear, when will my enamoured soul find rest!

As an example of a more developed lyric song, let us take "Ardak," named for the girl in whose honor it was composed. The content of this song is quite picturesque. It is connected to the broad scene of a hunt on horseback with falcons and hounds on the steppes. In the development of the subject a basic image is repeated threefold, with new light cast on it in each verse. In this one can see a link between the poetic techniques of the Kazakhs and the Kirghiz. The text of "Ardak" is beautiful and expressive, as is its music (Ex. 12).

"Qïzïl biday" ("Red Wheat") has a moral exhortation along with strong lyrical feelings. Its images are connected to agricultural work and gardening (Ex. 13).[11]

The song "Qorlan" was transcribed from its author, Estay Berkimbayev (1863-1946), who gained great fame from it. This popular lyric song is an example of an especially well developed verse form. In this song, celebrating the beauty of the girl Qorlan, the author uses images of nature and of Kazakh pastoral nomadic life. One also finds the names of distant lands, gleaned from literary sources (Ex. 14).[12]

Ex. 12. "Ardak" (A. Zataevich, *500 pesen*, #102).   Slowly, with great poetry

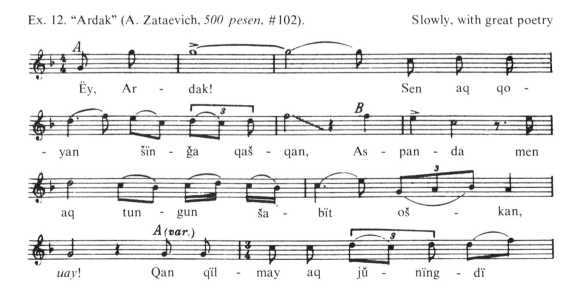

men ĭ - ley - ĭn, A - ra - da tŭr -

- sĭn qar - ap dos pen dŭš - pan ,

a (=A var.)
uay! Ay uy, er - kem! Ay uy, er - kem! Ay uy,

er - kem! Xa - li - lya - li - lyay - au!

Xa - li - lya - li - lyay, au! Xa - li - lya - li -

- lem lya - li - lyau! I - lya - lya - li - lyay,

lyau!

Ëy, Ardak! Sen aq qoyan šĭnǧa qašqan,
Aspanda men aq tungun šabĭt oškan.
Qan qilmay aq jŭnĭngdĭ men ĭleyĭn,
Arada tŭrsĭn qarap dos pen dŭšpan!
  Ay-uy, erkem! Xalilyali-lyay, au!

Ëy, Ardak! Sen aq qoyan sekektegen,
Qolĭmda bĭr tazĭm bar jestektegen.
Qönglĭmde üš ŭyqtasam barmay menĭng,
Ayrĭlĭp sen qalqadan keted degen!
  Ay-uy, erkem! Xalilyali-lyay, au!

Ëy, Ardak! Sen aq qoyan jŭmarlanǧan,
Bŭldĭrap köz šĭnde mŭngarlanǧan.
Jolĭngda janĭm qŭrban eter edĭm,
Könlĭmde bĭr tĭngdĭrsang kŭmarlanǧan!
  Ay-uy, erkem! Xalilyali-lyay, au!

O Ardak! You run into the valley like a white rabbit.
I flew into the cloud like a falcon.
I won't stain your white fur with blood, but take you carefully.
Let friends and enemies love one another!
Refrain: O you! My naughty girl! Trala-la.

O Ardak! You white rabbit, little leaper!
I take my hound with me on a leash.
In a deep dream I believed
That you won't leave me, my dear one!
(Refrain)

O Ardak! You are a little round white rabbit
Hardly seen in the unclear distance.
I am ready to sacrifice my life
If you yield to the wishes of my heart for a moment!
(Refrain).

Ex. 13. "Qïzïl biday" (B. Erzakovich, *Narodnye pesni Kazakhstana*, p. 46.).   Broadly.

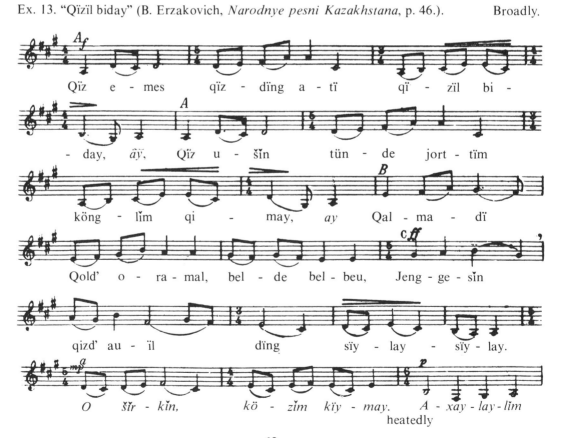

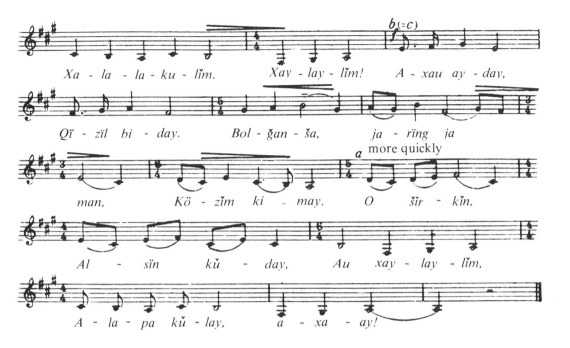

Xa - la - la - ku - lĭm. Xav - lay - lĭm! A - xau ay - day,

Qï - zïl bi - day. Bol - ǧan - ša, ja - rĭng ja

man, Kö - zĭm ki - may. O šĭr - kĭn,

Al - sïn kŭ - day, Au xay - lay - lĭm,

A - la - pa kŭ - lay, a - xa - ay!

Qïz emes qïzdıng atï qïzil biday,
Qïz üšĭn tünde jorttïm könglïm qimay.
Qalmadï qolda oramal, belde belbeu,
Jengesĭn qïzdï auïldïng sïylay-sïylay.
   O, šĭrkĭn, közĭm qïymay!
   Axaylaylĭm, Xalala kulĭm,
   Xalaylĭm. Axau ayday
   Qïzïl biday.
   Bolǧanša, jarĭng jaman,
   Közĭm qimay.
   O, šĭrkĭn, alsïn qŭday,
   Au xaylaylĭm,
   Alapa kŭlay, axa-ay!

Qïz emes qïzdïng atï qïzil alma,
Jamanǧa teng bolmaytïn közïng salma
Tüyeše boyga senïp bosqa qalǧan,
Uyrenbey öner-ǧĭlĭm keyĭn qalma.
   O, šĭrkĭn, közĭm qimay!
   Axaylaylĭm, Xalala kulĭm,
   Xalaylĭm. Axau ayday
   Qïzïl biday.
   Bolǧanša, jarĭng jaman,
   Közĭm qimay.
   O, šĭrkĭn, alsïn qŭday,
   Au xaylaylĭm,
   Alapa kŭlay, axa-ay!

They call this girl red wheat.
For her sake I galloped at night
My heart couldn't stand it.
I am left without belt or shirt;
I gave it all to the girl's sister-in-law.

[no translation]

They call the girl the red apple.
Don't join the bad one, and don't look at him
Don't be deceived like a camel, relying
   on his size,
Aim at knowledge, don't lag.

Ex. 14. "Qorlan" (B. Erzakovič. *Narodnye pesni Kazakhstana*, p. 41).   Calmly.

Bïr kïz bar Maraldïda Qorlï-ğauïn,	In Maraldy lives the girl Qorlan-ghayin.
Tabïğat bergen eken kün men auïn,	Nature gave her the beauty of sun and moon.
Mŭratka ïzdegen jan bärï jetken,	He who seeks his happiness always finds it there.
Darïğa armanïm köp ne qïlauïn.	I have many desires, o fate!
Axau arman,	O, fate!
Qüsni, Qorlan!	Khusni and Qorlan
Ekï-au bağlan	The two of them
Ekeyï tuğan eken bïr anadan.	Were born of the same mother.
Bozbala qalma qapï bul jalgannan,	O youth don't be deceived,
Jïgittïng armanï jog süygendï alğan.	You must wed your favorite.
Özïngdey bop jan tumas,	There is none like you
Tusa tuar, artïlmas,	Perhaps one has been born, but not better than you
Bar ğalamdï šarïqta,	I read all the books,
Ua darïğa läulïk tas.	But my fate is like a stone.
Bağdad, Mïsïr, Sïn-Mašin	You can't find a girl like Qorlan, certainly,
Ïzdesem Qorlan tabïlmas!	In Baghdad or in Egypt.

The song "Sïrïmbet," remarkable for its poetic description of mountain scenery, can serve as an example of a lyric song about nature (Ex. 15).

Dialogues (*aytis*) are popular as a form of daily-life song among the Kazakhs, as among many other peoples (Kirghiz, Uzbeks, Tajiks, Armenians, and Azerbaijanis). These are songs in which the performers alternately "converse," trying to outdo each other in wit and resourcefulness. These songs have varied content.

Ex. 15. "Sïrïmbet" (Transc. B. Erzakovich.).　　　　　　Broadly.

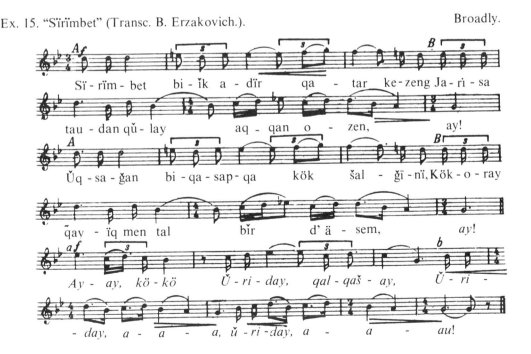

Sïrïmbet biïk adïr qatar kezeng,
Jarïsa taudan qŭlay aqqan özen.
Ŭksağan biqasapqa kök šalğïnï,
Kökoray qayïng men tal bïr de äsem.
    Ay-ay, kökö ŭriday, qalqaš-ay,
    ŭriday, ŭriday!

Möp-möldïr sïnapqa ŭsar bŭlaq aqqan,
Mangïnda üš türlï köl šalqïp jatqan.
Topïrağï beyne maqpal egïnge jay
Šïrayï ädemï jer külïp jatqan.
    Ay-ay, kökö ŭriday, qalqaš-ay,
    ŭriday, ŭriday!

Sïrïmbet is a chain of high hills.
A quick stream winds between them.
A meadow like a multicolored robe
How beautiful are the shrubs, birches and
    a rose willow! (Refrain)

Pure water runs in the brook
Nearby are three broad lakes full of water.
The black earth, like black velvet, is ready
    for plowing,
The beautiful earth smiles to me (Refrain).

Among the youth they usually have the character of love lyrics, sometimes including jokes and derision. Among *akins* [professional bards—M. S.] they become competitions for mastery in poetry and struggles with a social and ideological basis between representatives of progressive and reactionary trends.

The texts of Kazakh dialogue songs are often improvisatory folk quatrains. Musically speaking, dialogues are half melodic, half recitative in nature and are cast in simple verse forms. Both performers usually employ the same tune, varying it during manifold repetitions. Here is a transcription from the 1880 s of such a dialogue song between a boy and a girl (Ex. 16):

Ex. 16. "Aytis" (Transc. A. Eichhorn).   Happy, lively.

O beautiful girls, your laughter rings
You are lovelier than the dawn.
Oh my dear!

One of the earliest transcriptions of an entire dialogue song text was published in the 1830s (A. Levshin, *Opisanie kirgiz-kazach'ikh ili kirgiz-kaisakskikh ord i stepei*, St. Petersburg, 1832, 137-38):

Boy: Your eyebrows are not painted;
They have tied me to them.
I love you truly,
You drive me away.

Girl: Go give oats to the horse
So you don't remain a pedestrian.
Give away your cattle for a girl
So that you'll never part from her.

Boy: I am deeply in love with you.
Let me play with you.

Girl: You're too young for playing.
Let a horse fall on your neck.
A hawk pounced on the ducks,
On a whole large flock.

Boy: I'm sick all over
And can't even think of food.

The dialogue form is exceptionally popular in Kazakh song. We have the following evidence for it, from the 1870s (N. Gotovitskii, "O kharaktere kirgizskikh pesen." *Zapiski Turkestanskogo otdela obshchestva liubitelei estestvoznaniia, antropologii i etnografii*, vol. I, Tashkent, 1879):

Its content (dialogue song—V. B.) takes the form of a competition in wit, usually between a man and a woman. Someone asks a riddle and various clever questions, and the other has to reply to them; sometimes the person replying escapes from the difficulties with remarkable agility . . . but sometimes he is caught unawares and is confused. The latter type is usually a *khoja* ("learned man") who, as shown in songs, has studied in Bukhara and strikes up conversations with a girl he likes. Genuine comedy is fully expressed in the anger of the khoja, who doesn't know what to answer at the end of the quarrel and begins to curse; it is also expressed in the girl's ridicule of his gravity, hypocrisy, white turban, *etc.*

Kazakh humorous and satirical songs are close to the aytis in a general way. They are simple in form and measured in rhythm. Their text is made up of short lines of verse. The song "Kŭlbay bay" of the famous akin Jaiau-Musa (1836-1929) is a striking example of the satiric song; it ridicules the stinginess of the bai Kŭlbay (Ex. 17).

Ex. 17. "Kŭlbay bay" (Transc. B. Erzakovich). Quickly, with humor.

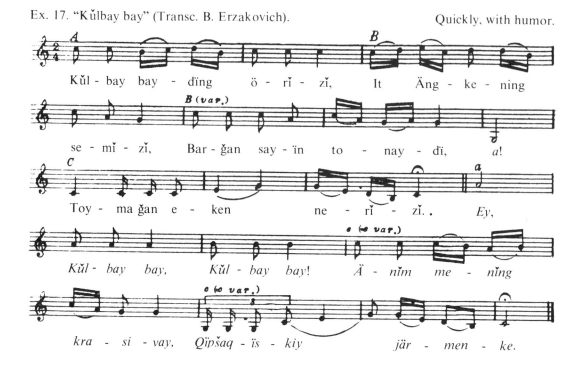

Kŭl - bay bay - dïng ö - rĭ - zĭ, It Äng - ke - ning
se - mĭ - zĭ, Bar - ğan say - ïn to - nay - dĭ, a!
Toy - ma ğan e - ken ne - rĭ - zĭ. . Ey,
Kŭl - bay bay, Kŭl - bay bay! Ä - nĭm me - nĭng
kra - si - vay, Qïpšaq - ïs - kiy jär - men - ke.

Kŭlbay baydïng ögĭzĭ,	Kŭlbay bai is like a bull.
It Änkenĭng semĭzĭ.	The fat Anka (=K's daughter-in-law) is like a bull.
Barğan sayïn tonaydï,	If you go to them, they steal everything.
Toymağan eken negĭzĭ.	They've never yet eaten themselves full.
	Refrain:
Ey, Kŭlbay bay!	O Kŭlbay bai!
Änĭm menĭng krasivay!	My song is beautiful!
Kïpšakïskiy jarmenke!	The Qipchaq market!
Kŭlbay baydïng ïrgesĭ,	Into Kŭlbay bai's barn
Bŭzauning sïrgesĭ.	Goes the calf, including the muzzle.
Bitteri tïyïn bolsa.	Although their lice are quiet,
Šïdatpaydï bürgesĭ.	There's no rest from their fleas.
	(Refrain)
Kŭlbay baydïng eškĭsĭ	Kŭlbay bai has goats;
Kŭyeŭĭ keldĭ bes kĭsĭ.	Five sons-in-law came to him.
Šešesĭ ittĭk etse de,	His daughters are all smart,
Qïzdarïnïng estĭsĭ.	But their mother's like a dog.
	(Refrain).

The theme of social protest permeates the prerevolutionary Kazakh folk song in various genres . . . . In the recitative style song "Güldaray!" ("O, My Flowers!") a protest is expressed against the forcible marrying-off of girls. It is close to the bride's lament in structure (Ex. 18).[13]

Ex. 18. "Guldaray!" (B. Erzakovich, *Narodnye pesni Kazakhstana*, p. 163.).

Slowly, expressively (♩ =72).

Gül - da - ray - men qïz   be - lïn   qï - nay - tŭ - gïn,   *ay*

ay!   Mal - ǧa   ke - tïp   qïz   sor - lï

ji - lay - tŭ - gïn,   *Gül - da - - ray!*

Güldaraymen qïz belïn qïnaytŭgïn,
Malǧa ketïp qïz sorlï jïlaytŭgïn,
Güldaray!
Auzï qïysïq bolsa da malïm bar dep.
Bay balasï arudï suraytŭgïn,
Güldaray!
Men de bïrï jïlaǧan köp äyeldïng,
Qašan ǧana özgerer gŭrpï eldïng,
Güldaray!
Jatqa malša satïlïp ketïp baram,
Tek bŭyïrsïn topïraǧï tuǧan jerdïng,
Güldaray!

Sometimes girls would tightly belt themselves
   with flowers!
Sold for cattle, many of the poor girls wept,
   O flowers!
Although his mouth is crooked, he is a bai's son/
He prides himself on his money and
wants to choose the most beautiful one.

I was one of those many women who wept.
When will this old custom change?
I must go to a stranger, like bartered cattle;
If only I am buried on native soil when I die!

The song "Berdïbek," named for its author, contains a protest against the hard conditions of life of the Kazakhs under prerevolutionary feudalism, when the workers could expect poverty and could not speak out freely. The song cries: "If at all possible—don't give in to anyone!" (Ex. 19).[14]

Ex. 19. "Berdïbek" (B. Erzakovich, *Narodnye pesni Kazakhstana*, p. 27).   Sadly.

Bas - tay - ïng söz - dïng basïn, *ay,* jïy - ïl - ğan köp, *äy,*

Joq - šïlïk bas - ka tüs - kän, *ay,* men mü - ge - dek, *a - ay!*

A - dam - mïn qo - lïm qïs - qa, *ay,* oy - ïm a - lïs, *äy,*

Ba - sïm - dï ma - lï, bar - ğa, *ay,* i - mey - mïn - tek, *a - ay!*

I - ğa - ğa - ğa - ğa ğa - ğa - ğa ğa - ğa - ğa - ğa i ğay.

Bastayïng sözdïng basïn jïyïlğan köp,	Let me tell you, people,
Joqšïlïq basqa tüsken men mügedek.	I became as poor as a powerless cripple.
Adammïn qolïm qïsqa, oyïm alïs,	I'm generous, but constrained;
Basïmdï malï barğa imeymïn tek.	If I had the strength, I would go far away.
Šïrqayïn änge salïp jüz kübïltïp,	I'll sing you a song in different scales,
Seyleyïn išaratpen suday tïnïp.	And let me tell you quietly and figuratively,
Jamanğa aytqan sözïng bolar šïğïn,	Don't waste words on unworthy people,
Ondayğa šamang kelse bïlme sïnïq.	And if you possibly can, don't give in to anyone!

The Kazakh people always knew the true value of the hypocritical . . . mullahs, and expressed their contempt for them in denunciatory songs. One of these is the song "Bağdad," which speaks of the moral emptiness of followers of Islam (Ex. 20)[15] . . . .

Acquaintance with the genres of Kazakh folk art provides us with concrete examples of its high development from earlier, simpler types (mostly ceremonial and work songs) to highly developed forms of lyric song, connected with the characteristics of the Kazakh song text.

Ex. 20. "Bağdad" (Transc. B. Erzakovich).   Tranquilly.

What mullah, who says he is devoted to religion, is better than us?
A thoughtful woman is better than a careless man.
As much as I've traveled in Baghdad, Mecca and Egypt,
There's no better life than at home.

Development of Prosody in Kazakh Folk Song. The basic verse lines of Kazakh
folk song are seven or eleven syllables long. The former is used in the early work,
ceremonial, lullaby and children's songs, as well as in rapid humorous or satiric
songs. The latter appears in lyric and other songs with deep meanings. Both types
of verse line are often complicated by insertions of additional syllables, exclamations and whole words, which augment the syllabic content of the lines and actually
lead to the creation of new forms of prosody. We have seen an analogy to this in
the case of Kirghiz song.

The seven-syllable verse line of the Kazakhs is usually trochaic, with a division into two groups of 4+3 (Ex. 21).

Ex. 21

We can see augmentation of the seven-syllable line through the addition of exclamations in the following example, where the first line is broadened to nine syllables (4+1)+(3+1), and the second to eight syllables (4+1+3) (Ex. 22).

Ex. 22

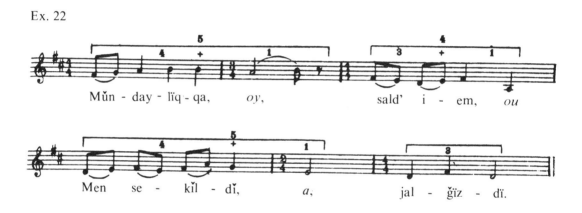

The eleven–syllable verse line is the most common variety. Whereas most peoples organize their eleven–syllable lines into trochaic trimeter of 4+4+3, or in two groups of 6+5, the Kazakhs divide theirs into three groups (3+4+4), which provides a strong national flavor to the metrics of Kazakh folk song texts (Ex. 23).

Ex. 23

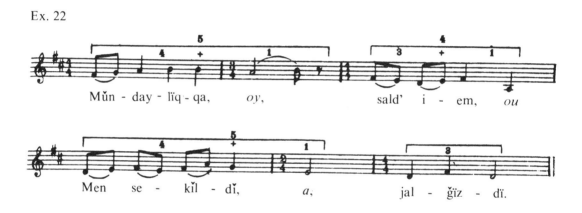

As is evident from Example 23, the last syllable of this line structure usually falls on a weak beat. In order to conclude this line on a strong beat, which is very important for the final shape of the verse, a concluding exclamatory syllable is usually added, as in the following example (Ex. 24):

Ex. 24

Qiz e - mes   qïz - dïng a - tï   qï - zïl bi - day,   *ay!*

One also finds cases of a 4+3+4 structure of the eleven–syllable line (Ex. 25).

Ex. 25

Bosk' e - ser - lĭk   kŭr - bïm - ning,   je - lĭ - gĭ - ne.

The "jar-jar" wedding song (Ex. 6), as noted above, typically has a rhythm which arises from the alternation of seven-and six-syllable lines, grouped into 4 and 4 and 3 syllables respectively (Ex. 26).

Ex. 26

Qa - ra na - sar za - man - das, Qa - ra na - sar, *jar - jar!*

The varieties of meter of Kazakh songs cited above, as applied to melody, furnish rich possibilities for the development of musical rhythm. Exceptional rhythmic and melodic freedom can be observed in refrains, which are linked to free syllabic text structure and the use of the techniques of virtuoso vocalise.

In Kazakh, as in Kirghiz folk poetry, elision occurs in the case of the last vowel of a word if the following word also begins with a vowel; thus, "kolda oramal" is sung "kold' oramal."

Melodies of Kazakh Folk Song. The textual basis of Kazakh folk song including both long and short lines, creates rich possibilities for the free development of melody, from short recitative phrases to broad melodic structures. The melody of Kazakh songs arises from the emotional, agitated declamation of the song text, drawing its turns of phrase from colloquial speech. It reaches a high degree of expression in its melodic lines.

Two basic types of melodic motion characterized Kazakh folk songs: 1) descending and 2) ascending-descending. These two types of melodic motion are most often found side by side, as in the song "Ardak" (Ex. 12); its melodic curve is given here (Ex. 27):

Ex. 27.

As for melodies of the descending type, they usually begin with a loud, prolonged introductory exclamation in the upper tessitura (as much as an octave or a ninth above tonic), after which a gradual fall to the concluding tonic ensues.

Scalar Basis of Kazakh Folk Song. The basis of Kazakh folk song is a system of diatonic scales: major (Mixolydian, Ionian) and minor (Aeolian, Dorian, Phrygian and, in some cases, pentatonic scales).[16] Narrow scales with the range of a sixth or less predominate in the early types of Kazakh songs, such as ceremonial songs. One can also rarely find narrow pentatonic scale structures in these songs, *e. g.*, in the wedding song "Betašar" (Exs. 8, 28).

Ex. 28.

In developed strophic songs the scale and melody reach the compass of an octave or ninth above the lower tonic. In individual cases even wider ranges are used.[17] A "leading tetrachord" of the pitches 5, 6, and 7 below the tonic may be included, as in the song "Qïzïl biday" (Ex. 13), composed in the Ionian scale (Ex. 29).

Ex. 29.

Sometimes one finds highly developed pentatonic structures in melodically developed songs. Most Kazakh folk songs are in one scale, but in several cases chromatic scales appear, arising from the modulation from one scale to another with a common tonic. Thus, for example, the modulation from Ionian to Mixolydian introduces the change from major to minor seventh. In Mixolydian melodies the seventh step may be raised in the lower octave while the minor seventh is preserved in the upper octave (Ex. 30).[18]

Ex. 30.

In minor scales the following cases of chromaticization of the basic scale can occur: 1) raising of the third in Aeolian scale (Ex. 31); 2) replacement of the Dorian scale by Aeolian (Ex. 32); and 3) replacement of the Aeolian scale by the Phrygian (Ex. 33). The last case usually occurs in cadences of natural minor and is expressed in the lowering of its second step, as in both "Cowboy's Songs" (Exs. 1, 2).

Ex. 31.

either

Ex. 32.

either

Ex. 33.

either

Along with the aforementioned examples of scalar modulation on the basis of a single tonic there are also examples of true scalar modulations, *i. e.*, a number of transitions from one scale to another with a change of tonic. This type of modulation can be seen in "Šašubaydïng ënï" ("Šašubai's Song"). Here is the basic content of the verse is given in G-major Mixolydian and the refrain in G-major Mixolydian (Ex. 34).[19]

Ex. 34. "Šašubaydïng ënï" (A. Zataevich, *500 pesen*, #85).   Broadly and grandiosely.

My name is son of Košhkarbai, Šašubai.
I am poor in cattle, but gifted with the word.
If I were given a thousand rubles instead of a hundred,
I would still not become rich
Since I have a hole in my pocket.
O fate! The bad has gone, passed by.
O my ancestors: Uysun, Argin, Naiman.

Forms of Kazakh Folk Song. The basic strophe of Kazakh folk song is the quatrain with *aaba* rhyme scheme, *i. e.*, the same type of stanza which is widely used among the peoples of Central Asia, the Caucasus, and some of the Volga peoples. The even number of lines in this strophe allows for two-part strophe forms, for the most part, such as 1) the half-strophe two-part form (AB), 2) the whole strophe two-part form, including the more common variety, the "two-part reprise form" (ABCB) and other types. The predominance of two-part strophic forms in Kazakh folk songs does not preclude the use of the one-part or one-line form with numerous repetitions (A).

Basic to Kazakh song forms is the extensive development of refrains, which usually contrast structurally with the verse.[20] Refrains may attain great length, and can then constitute whole strophes. Let us look at some examples. In Example 34 ("Šašubaydïng ëni") a basic one part structure (AAAA) is complicated by the addition of a melodic refrain with two part structure (ab). In "Qïzïl biday" (Ex. 13) the refrain has a three part form (aba). In "Ardak," (Ex. 12) the refrain displays the whole-strophe two-part form (abcd).

Let us also take note of some other common structures of Kazakh songs. Their appearance. is connected to the development and enrichment of melody in full-strophe two-part forms. Among the possible types of such forms which appear in Kazakh folk songs, the following should be noted: 1) AABC, *e. g.*, "Qoyšï ëni" Ex. 3) and "Qïzïl biday" (Ex. 13); 2) ABBC, as in "Kŭlbay bay" (Ex. 17); and 3) ABCC, as in "Boz torgay" ("The Woodlark," Ex. 58).

Kazakh verse forms are not necessarily made up of only one stanza., In some cases, broader two part forms arise, uniting two whole strophes of song text into one musical unit. One of these broad verse forms is the structure AABC + DEBC + abcd, as in "Qorlan" (Ex. 14). Two of its sections, concluded by a refrain, represent two independent strophes with common melodic content.

In addition to refrains one also finds opening calls in Kazakh songs. They usually consist of long, loud tones in the upper register sung to a short exclamation, and seem to call the attention of the listeners to the beginning of the song (Exs. 2, 7, 9, among others).

Regional Kazakh Song Styles. The huge territory occupied by the Kazakhs, the variety of living conditions, and the abundance of dialects . . . all facilitate the appearance of regional song styles. The develop on a single national basis and express the traits of national character as a whole.[21]

In addition to a variety of regional styles, Kazakh song is distinguished by special area-wide characteristics: wide melodic development, a wealth of expressive nuances, and ties to colloquial speech. The songs of southern Kazakhstan (the Semirechie, Aral region, and the banks of the Syr-Darya) are marked by simplicity of form, regularity of rhythm, and clarity of emotional make-up. In the West (the trans-Urals region and the Caspian shores) lyricism, with wide ranging melodies, is developed on the one hand, and the *terme*, or recitative forms, on the other. Finally, in central Kazakhstan one must mention a special wealth of melodic means of musical expression, breadth of melody, and complex structure of verse forms. All of this testifies to the huge and rich treasure house of song constructed by the Kazakh people over the ages.

Kazakh Epic Art

The Kazakh Epic. Born in the depths of antiquity among the Kazakhs' ancestors as heroic stories transmitted by oral tradition, the epic of the Kazakh people changed and developed over many centuries, becoming enriched by new historical occurrences. In original form it was a vocal narrative without instrumental accompaniment, as among the Kirghiz. Later it became performed to the accompaniment of the kobiz [a horsehair fiddle—M. S.] and then the dombra. It is in this form that we know the Kazakh epic (since the early nineteenth century). It is not unified, like the Kirghiz *Manas* cycle, but falls into a series of tales about individual heroes. Romantic love plays an important role in these stories, which are permeated with details of daily life. Sometimes love even becomes the main theme, and the tale takes on the characteristics of a lyric or lyric-dramatic poem, or novella or novel, far from its epic origins.

A transition from the early epic to the later, and to romantic tales, leads to changes in the form of the narrative itself among the Kazakhs. The regular recitative declamation of the epic story is replaced by an alternation of narrative in prose and musical performance in verse, with instrumental accompaniment of characters' lines. Sometimes this performance is enlivened by the insertion of instrumental interludes. Verse episodes are given in the terme form, as well as in the more developed strophic forms.

The historical basis of the Kazakh epics belongs mostly to events of the fifteenth century, the period of formation of the Kazakh nationality, and to the seventeenth century, the period of intense struggle against the Jungar-Kalmucks . . . . Among the epics with a democratic ideology was the folk version of the tales about Kambar-batir, the poor hunter and defender of the working people, provider for sixty households, and conqueror of the Kalmuck khan Karaman. Among the epic-novelistic tales, or lyric poems, the story of "Kozï-korpeš and Bayan-slu," "Kïz-jïbek" and Aiman and Solpan" were very popular among the Kazakhs. [2 2]

The story of the lyric poem "Kozï-korpeš and Bayan-slu" was transcribed for

Pushkin when he was working on materials of the peasant wars led by Pugachev (1773-1775). Here is the story: Bayan-slu's father (Karabay) and Kozï-korpeš's father (Saribay) meet while hunting and swear to marry off their children if one has a son and the other a daughter. Saribay dies and Karabay changes his vow, promising Bayan-slu to the athlete Kodar, who had saved his cattle from disease. Bayan, never having seen her bridegroom Kozï-korpeš, awaits him. When they finally meet and recognize their common interests, Karabay and Kodar treacherously kill Kozï-korpeš. Bayan cannot stand this and kills Kodar, finally stabbing herself on Kozï-korpeš's grave. Kodar's supporters bury him between Bayan and Korpeš, hoping even in death to divide them. A prickly thorn from Kodar's grave grows among the plants placed on the lovers' grave and serves as a fence between them.[23]

The poem "Kïz-jïbek" ("The Silken Maiden") portrays a Kazakh bride who is true to her obligations to the bridegroom and faithful to established customs. The youth Tulegen, having long searched for a bride, finds her in the beautiful Kïz-jïbek. To prepare for the wedding, Tulegen goes home, where his father, who opposes the marriage, restrains him. Using the absence of Tulegen, the youth Bekejan entreats Kïz-jïbek. Rejected by her, he treacherously kills Tulegen, who is hurrying toward his bride, on the lonely steppes. Wild geese witness the murder and inform Kïz-jïbek; her brothers, at her demand, kill Bekejan. Jibek, having lost her bridegroom, remains faithful to his memory and transfers her love to his younger brother Sansïzbay, who, according to custom, should take her after the older brother's death. The Kalmuck khan lays siege to Jibek's settlement and demands the girl from her parents. Jibek nevertheless refuses to marry the khan, awaiting Sansïzbay. Sansïzbay murders the khan with her help, and Jibek, having overcome all obstacles through her idealistic faithfulness, is united with him . . . .[24]

The poem "Ayman i šolpan" tells of the struggle of the beautiful Ayman for her personal freedom and for her right to marry for love. The ruling elder Kotibar, chief of one of the Kazakh clans, seizes the settlement of the chief of a neighboring clan, Maman, and forcefully takes his daughters, Ayman and Šolpan, as prisoners. He wants to make Ayman his wife against her will. Ayman decisively, cleverly, and subtly struggles against the claims of Kotibar. She is victorious in this struggle, forcing the old man to give her her freedom, and she marries Alibek, whom she loves.

Musical Basis of Kazakh Epic Narrative. The musical basis of Kazak epic narrative is steady declamation of seven- or eleven-syllable trochaic lines with prolongations of the last syllable of each line. Finished sections [*Absatz*, a German term —M. S.], as is the case with epics of other peoples, do not have a regular strophic structure and consist of varying numbers of lines. The performance of sections of tales usually begins with introductory exclamations in a high register, after which text is declaimed with gradual descent to the lower register and the tonic. All excerpts usually conclude in a slower tempo, sometimes based on the broad singing of words of the refrain. Free rhyme is characteristic of Kazakh epic tales.

Ex. 35. "Kïz-jïbek" (B. Erzakovich. *Narodnye pesni Kazakhstana*, p. 15). With fortitude.

A! Ba - zar - bay dïng Tö - le - gen, Sek - sen jï - gït qosš' alïp,

On bes jï - gït basš' a - lïp, Aq Jay - ïq - qa je - nel - gen,

Ay - dïng öt - ken ne - še - si, Ay qa - rang - ǧï ke - še - si,

Pa - dï ša - dan kem e - mes, Er Tö - le - gen mü - še - si,

Ar - tï - nan - ku - ïp ke - le - dï, Ö - zï - nïng tu - ǧan še - še - si.

Bazarbaydïng Tölegen,	Tulgen, son of Bazarbai,
Seksen jïgït qosšï alïp,	Having gathered eighty youths
On bes jïgït basšï alïp	Left for the white Yaiku (=Ural River)
Aq Jayïqqa jönelgen	With fifteen youths.
Aydïng ötken nešesï,	How many days passed—no one knows.
Ay qarangǧi keśesï,	How many moonless nights—no one knows.
Padïšadan kem emes,	Tulegen's appearance
Er Tölegen müšesï,	Is no worse than a king's.
Artïnan quïp keledi,	Someone is chasing him:
Özïnïng tuǧan šešesï	It is his own mother.
Kelgende söyley beredï,	
Seylegende büy deydï:	Having caught up with him, she says,
Mïngen de atïng alasïng,	She says this to him:
Menen de tuǧan balasïng.	Mount this dapple horse,
Adal bala tastayma	My dear son.
Atasï men anasïn.	Does a good son
Qal degende qalasïng	Really leave his father and mother?
Aytqan tïldï alasïng,	I say: stay, don't go farther.
Qal degende qalmasang	You can't disobey me.
Aytqan bïr tïldï almasang	And if you don't stay
Aytqan bïr tïldï almasang	And don't heed my words,
Qǔrttïng bïr anang šarasïn!	You will have killed my last hope.

A fragment from "Kïz-jïbek" can serve as an example of a small concluding excerpt of a Kazakh epic tale with a seven-syllable line. It contains the description of the hero Tulegen's farewell to his mother (Ex. 35).[25]

Kazakhs call the epic tale *jir* and storytellers *jirši*.

Terme and Jeldirme. The narrative form is used by the Kazakhs not only for epics, but it was also used for early types of song and for the musical-poetic compositions of akins on social (and other) themes; its use is widespread even in Soviet times.

When applied to recitative songs, the jir form is called *terme* or *jeldirme*. The latter term literally means "horse's gallop," and is tied to the lively rapid-fire tempo of its performance. In addition, the terme typically uses the seven-syllable verse line, and the jeldirme the eleven-syllable line. Example 35, from "Kïz-jïbek," can serve as an example of terme. The development of the terme and jeldirme forms sometimes influences the strophic song, since both terme and jeldirme, which preserve a recitative character in melody, may be cast in strophic form when their text is in that form.

Musical Formation of Epic-Novelistic Tales. As noted earlier Kazakh epic-novelistic tales and lyric poems consist of prose narrative and poetic sung episodes with instrumental accompaniment, representing the speech of characters. Instrumental interludes are sometimes performed in pauses of the story.

Solo episodes in these tales use either the terme form or strophic songs for musical expression, depending on the emotional content of the song. Example 35, from "Kïz-jïbek," is an example of an episode in terme form. We can also include the touching lament of Bayan-slu over Kozï-korpeš's body from the poem "Kozï-korpeš and Bayan-slu." In this excerpt the joqtau genre of funeral lament or the *zar* type of sad song, with a deeply expressive broad melody like a sorrowful lyric song, is used (Ex. 36).

Ex. 36. "Bayanïng zarï" (B. Erzakovich, *Narodnye pesni Kazakhstana*, p. 13).　　Slowly.

Ja - tïr - mï - sïng ey ja - rïm, jer ba - yïr - lan,

Ja - ra sa - lïp jau o - ği at - qan ŭr - lap,

Qŭ - day qos - qan qo - sa - ğïng Ba - yan kel - dï

81

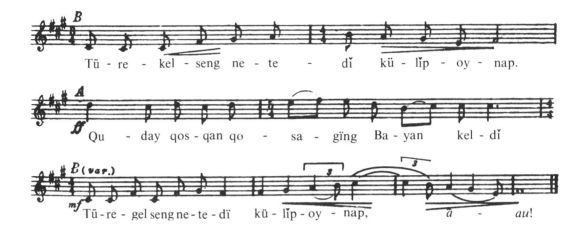

Tü - re - kel - seng ne - te - dǐ kü - lǐp - oy - nap.

Qu - day qos - qan qo - sa - gǐng Ba - yan kel - dǐ

Tü - re - gel seng ne - te - dï kü - lǐp - oy - nap, ā - au!

Jatïrmïsïng, ey jarïm, jer bauïrlap,
Jara salïp jau oğï atkan ŭrlap.
Qŭday qosqan qosağïng Bayan keldǐ,
Türegel'seng netedǐ külǐp-oynap.

Kǐskeneden atadan jetǐm edïng,
Tǐlǐn almay jŭrtïngnan ketǐp edïng.
Sen kǐsǐge bǐr ezǐm deuši edïng goy.
Qapïlïsta Qodardan netǐp öldǐng?

Altïndï er aq boz at mïne almadïm,
Men büyterǐn Qodardïng bǐle almadïm.
Özǐng qosqan jarïngdï aldï tängǐrǐ,
Bǐr armansïz oynap ne küle almadïm.

There you lie, my dear, spread out on the ground.
Pierced by the stealthy enemy's arrow
Baian, promised to you by God, has come;
Why don't you arise with a smile on your lips?

You were an orphan since childhood;
You parted unwillingly from your parents.
You told many people you were lonely.
How did you die at the hands of worthless Qodar?

O, now I cannot jump into the white horse's golden
    saddle,
And I couldn't know that Qodar would be so base.
O God, you gave me this promised one, and took him
    away yourself.
I am gripped by sorrow; farewell my dreams, fare-
    well, my happiness!

Let us also add the monologue of Ayman from the poem "Ayman i Šolpan," in which the heroine describes her happy girlhood years. The monologue consists of a small strophe in a song of simple structure (Ex. 37).

Ex. 37. "Ayman-šolpan" (Transc. B. Erzakovich).   Slowly.

Qïz' e - dïm Ma - man - bay - dïng a - tïm Ay - man, *au,*

Sur jorg' at jï - bek ar - qan,

Du - ni - ey bïz jay - la ǧan, *au.*

I am the daughter of Mamanbai, called Aiman.
I always rode on a gray pacer with a silk bridle.
I rode around many places.
I rode in wind-blown fields in a luxurious caftan,
And rode my pacer to holiday festivals.
I am the daughter of Mamanbai, called Aiman;
I always rode on a grey pacer with gold reins.
Stop the horse, Koteke (= nick-name for Kotybar)
I hear my mother calling "Aiman, Aiman."

As noted earlier Kazakh epic artistry moved from heroic epics to the genres of novels and romances, and from historical themes to daily-life subjects, remaining unwritten and relying on methods of oral transmission suited to the new content. On this basis, epic-novelistic compositions were enriched by various genres of songs.

Kazakh Instrumental Music

Kazakh Musical Instruments. The kazakh musical instrumentarium is small. It includes the *dombra, kobiz, sibizgi* and *šan kobiz.* [26]
The Kazakh dombra (a lute) has two strings, usually of gut, tuned to a fourth (or, less frequently, to a fifth), and tied-on frets. The scale of the dombra varies regionally in Kazakhstan. It is basically diatonic, with a Mixolydian sequence

of tones in the range of an octave with two or three tones above, up to a tenth or eleventh. Fretless play can extend this scale somewhat. This basis is complicated by the introduction of chromatic frets in the following order: first, the minor third, then, a minor sixth, and finally, a minor second. This complication gives the following, most common scale of the instrument, in which the chromatic notes are indicated with black note-heads, as are the tones in the upper register played without frets (Ex. 38).[27]

Ex. 38.

In performing some pieces the frets for major and minor thirds are pushed into an intermediate position, giving a neutral third.[28] The dombra is played with a strum, i. e., striking both strings simultaneously.[29] The Russian domra is close to the Kazakh dombra. This is borne out by similarity in both structure and name. The body of the Kazakh dombra, however, varies from oval to pear-shaped to a prolonged barrel shape or triangular form.

The kobiz is a fiddle, analogous to the Kirghiz kiak. Its body and neck are made of one piece of wood in the shape of a huge dipper. A piece of camel skin serves as lid, fastened only to the lower portion of the instrument.[30] A high bridge stands on this skin, across which two thick horsehair strings extend from the neck, tuned to a fourth or fifth in the small octave.[31] During play the strings are shortened by the fingers without pressing the strings to the neck. The kobiz is a solo instrument, also used for accompanying vocal performance. It is usually played monophonically. Its scale is basically similar to that of the dombra.[32]

The sibizgi, a type of end-blown flute, is a pastoral instrument. The sibizgi is usually made from the stalk of an umbellate steppe plant and has four or five fingerholes. It is similar to the Kirghiz čoor and to open end-blown flutes of other peoples in construction, scale, and range. Here is the basic scale of the sibizgi with four or five fingerholes (Ex. 39):[33]

Ex. 39.

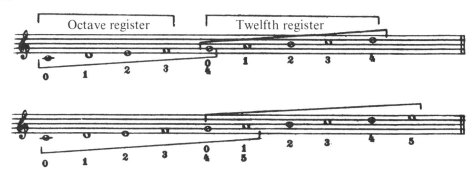

The jew's-harp, or šan kobiz, is used as a domestic, primarily children's instrument among the Kazakhs.[34]

The military orchestra of the feudal period was an ensemble of *surnai*s (oboes), *karnai*s (large bass horns) and *daulpaz* (copper kettledrums attached to the saddle).[35] The daulpaz was also used during falcon hunting to summon the falcons.

Kazakh Instrumental Music. There are three basic styles of Kazakh music, in both the compositional and performing senses: 1) the practical wind style, connected with the sibizgi; 2) the domestic and concert style of the kobiz and dombra; and 3) the military style, related to the instruments of the Kazakh military orchestra.

Sibizgi pieces can be divided into three types.[36] The first type is that of pastoral pieces, directly connected with shepherd's work. There are no transcriptions of such pieces. The second type consists of folk songs arranged to suit the sibizgi. "Estek" and "Zaureš" can serve as examples of this type of piece, as performed by Iskhak Valiev (1902-1944), (Exs. 40, 41).[37]

Ex. 40. "Estek" (Transc. G. Jubanov).   Moderately.

Ex. 41. "Zaures" (Transc. G. Jubanov).   Moderately.

Finally, the third variety of sibizgi compositions consists of arrangements of dombra pieces cast in large forms and complex original compositions.

The richest area of Kazakh instrumental music is the repertoire of the dombra. It is mostly programmatic and broadly reflects the way of life, history, psyche, and hopes of the Kazakh people. Among dombra pieces, usually called *küi*,[38] we can find works with historical, epic, social, military, autobiographical, and daily-life themes, as well as descriptions of nature—all of which express human feelings and spiritual experiences. Aside from serious, artistic pieces there is also a sizeable body of works with comic, humorous, and satiric content.

Dombra pieces can be seen as the height of Kazakh professional art, outstanding examples of which earn the title of instrumental classics. They demand mastery of instrumental technique, for they require many years of practice under the guidance of great teachers.

Dombra pieces are cast in continuous two-part style by Kazakh composers, with parallel motion in fourths or fifths, depending on the tuning used.[39] Another type of polyphony occurs through playing the melody on the upper string and accompanying it with lower-string drone. In some cases the melody is played on the lower string with the drone above.[40]

It is important to note that the quartal and quintal basis of parallel voice-leading in dombra music allows for the use of other intervals as well, which significantly enrich the harmonic means of two-voice play. Thus, a tuning in fifths, sixths, and fourths can be produced (Ex. 42), and, similarly a tuning in fourths, fifths and thirds may arise (Ex. 43).

Ex. 42.

Ex. 43.

Kazakh dombra music is marked by broad, masterful development of musical forms. The major genre is a large three-part form, consisting of the following sections: 1) exposition of the basic theme, which itself may have a complex internal structure; 2) middle section with new theme in a higher register (fourth, fifth, or octave higher); 3) recapitulation of the first theme. An introduction and conclusion, or coda, may also be included.[41]

Dombra music may depart from this typical form in the direction of internal broadening and toward creation of more complex structures. The piece "Hunting" is typical of a form widely developed for dombra music; it paints a picture of hunting on horseback, with hounds or falcons, on the steppes (Ex. 44).

Ex. 44. "Hunting" (A. Zataevich, *1000 pesen*, #307).   Moderately.

88

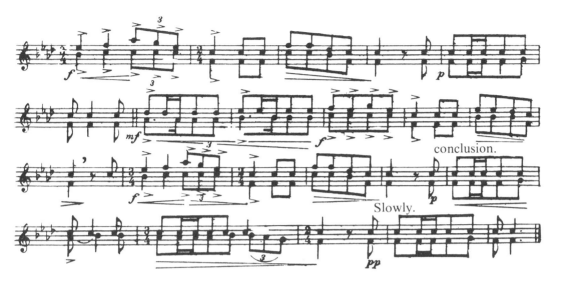

The küi "Aqsaq qulan" ("Lame Wild Ass"), based on a semilegendary figure of the thirteenth century, is a striking example of the programmatic style in Kazakh dombra music. A. V. Zataevich transcribed this piece and relates its content.[42] Chingis-khan's son Juči had a favorite son, his oldest, who was a passionate hunter of qulans (wild asses). Once he went off with his followers deep into the steppes without telling his strict and gloomy father, who forbade him to go out on dangerous hunts. Following a herd of qulans, they caught up with them and wounded the leader in the leg. But misfortune followed. The wounded qulan succeeded in kicking the hunter right in the heart and killed him on the spot. Juči, disquieted by the long absence of his son, was in the grip of an evil premonition. He threatened to pour a dipper of molten lead into the ears of the one who brought him fateful news. No one wanted to earn this terrible reward from the grim khan. Finally the khan's favorite dombra player, an old man, felt called upon to rectify the situation, and told the khan what had happened without words. He composed a piece which was later called "Aqsaq qulan." The khan wept when he learned through the music of what had transpired. Remaining true to his word he ordered the dipper of molten lead to be poured into the resonance holes of the dombra, which was the first to tell him of the fate which befell him. And the dombra was silenced forever.

In structural terms this küi is made up of: 1) an introduction; 2) presentation of the main theme (I), which has a complex three–part structure (AA + B + AA); 3) introduction of the second theme (II), based on the subdominant of the fundamental tonality and with a return to the main theme in the ·basic register; 4) introduction of the third theme (III) in the octave register with a new return to the main theme; and 5) a short conclusion, based on the material of the introduction. The introduction of a third theme with subsequent repetition of the first theme converts the three-part structure into a rondo-like form.

89

The piece "Aqsaq qulan" is made up of three themes, presented twice in the following order: ABAC+ABAC+A. Here is the transcription of this famous küi (Ex. 45):

Ex. 45. "Aqsaq qulan" (A. Zataevich, *1000 pesen*, #583).   Calmly, seriously and grandiosely.

softly and tenderly. (♩=96)

Greatly strengthening.

Heatedly, as if

groaning in desperation. (♩=132)

Rit. Tempo I.

Tempo I, sadly, gradually

fading

Sadly, morendo. *p*

Always p. Rit.

Zataevich is inclined to think that the first theme of the küi, as introduced in the basic lower and higher octave registers, characterizes the images of the father and son. He looks on the second theme as an expression of the youth's anxiety on leaving the world so early. And finally he sees the third part as the cry of despair of the father after hearing the news of his son's loss.[43] In this interpretation of the program of the piece we find no reflection of the image of the "lame qulan" given in the title itself, and of the description of hunting. However, no matter how we interpret the piece, its basic content is a deep affirmation of the wondrous powers of music, which is artistically embodied in the myths and legends of many peoples.

Kobiz pieces, written for an instrument of earlier derivation than the dombra, are marked by less highly developed forms.[44] Today, kobiz playing is not very widespread, but its past role in the development of Kazakh music culture was great. It accompanied epic tales and the performance of songs by akins. It was also used as a solo instrument with a rich repertoire, differing from that of the dombra by those expressive traits which are inherent to bowed lutes and which are inacessible to plucked instruments.[45]

The piece "Ixlas," named for its author Ixlas Daukin (1843-1916), is a colorful programmatic kobiz piece of an autobiographical nature. Its content is connected to an incident in the life of the composer. A horse thief attached to a certain bai steals Ixlas' last horse. Using a situation when he is playing for that bai, Ixlas improvises a küi in which he expresses his anger and helplessness due to the loss of his horse. The bai, under the influence of the music, orders the horse thief to return the horse to Ixlas. Thus, we see a legend arising around the name of the famous Kazakh kobiz player the theme of which is basically related to that of the "lame qulan" song: the strength of music's influence upon man (Ex. 46).[46]

Ex. 46. "Ixlas" (Transc. G. Jubanov). Quickly.

In musical structure, "Ixlas" belongs to the group of monothematic, monotonal compositions which are also quite characteristic of music for the Kirghiz kiak.

The old Kazakh military orchestra, which went out of use in the eighteenth century, was similar to the feudal military ensembles of the Kirghiz and other Central Asian and Near Eastern peoples. It included oboes (surnais), horns, and percussion instruments; however, we have no transcriptions of this orchestra among the Kazakhs.

Art of the Kazakh Akins

The Kazakh Akins and Their Art. Since earliest times the main role in the development of a social side to Kazakh art has been played by the *akin*s, professional singers who have the gift of versification and poetic improvisation, can compose song tunes, and also master the dombra as an accompanying instrument.

The basic genres of the Kazakh akins, like those of the Kirghiz singers, are full of social and publicistic content: panegyric songs (*maktau*) and didactic and denunciatory songs (*tolgau*).[47] The didactic songs are more general in character, being a sort of musical-poetic lesson in folk wisdom. They existed in well defined, stable musical forms. As for the genres of denunciatory and panegyric songs, they were more occasional, being improvised for specific polemic appearances of the akins. These songs were usually cast in the recitative forms (Terme and jeldirme). The akins also composed songs in different genres (lyric, historic), using developed strophic forms. They often attained great mastery in this area and created works which became widespread among the public and turned into popular songs . . . .

KAZAKH MUSIC FROM THE FIFTEENTH TO THE MID-EIGHTEENTH CENTURIES

Kazakh Music of This Period. The fifteenth to eighteenth centuries laid the groundwork for Kazakh folk and professional musical art. In the area of song, those genres were worked out which have lasted to the present day, preserving traits of old but valuable images of various phases in the life of the Kazakh people. Melody, rhythm, scales, and forms developed; in short, all of the characteristics of folk song.

As noted earlier the best known types of epic art are connected with events of the fifteenth to seventeenth centuries, and reflect the struggle of the people for independence, especially against the Jungar-Kalmucks. The development of epic-novelistic genres, a more advanced form basically in the epic tradition, also belongs to this period.

Basic types of instrumental music also appeared, and the Kazakh military wind ensemble was created, an indispensable accessory of the military way of life brought about by the continuous clashes which characterized the feudal epoch.

The art of the Kazakhs became greatly developed and the struggle between two orientations intensified: the popular-democratic and the feudal-reactionary. This provided soil for the growth of written literature and poetry in the next period, the progressive representatives of which carried on a struggle against the reactionary akins. Thus the founder of the new Kazakh literature, Abay Kunanbayev, in one of his poems, derides the akins Bukhara-jirau (*ca.* 1693-*ca.* 1787), Shortambay (1808-1871) and Dulat, who spread the ideas of disillusionment in life and called for a return to old ways among the Kazakhs.

> Shortambay, Bukhar-jirau, and Dulat;
> How many stains and patches are in their work!
> If I could only have found one expert,
> I could have exposed all those flaws in an instant!

At the same time, the best representatives of the progressive, democratically oriented akins not only called the working people to battle with the oppressors in songs, but, like Makhambet Utemisov (1804-1846, of whom more below) even directly led that struggle.

KAZAKH MUSIC FROM THE MID-EIGHTEENTH TO THE LATE NINETEENTH CENTURIES

Vocal Artistry. Having achieved a high level in the mid-eighteenth century, Kazakh musical art underwent further development, permeated with new content drawn from the life of the people and perfected in the work of progressive professional Kazakh composers. . . . At the same time as the akins who served the feudal rulers and bais never left the sphere of mendacious flattery surrounding their patrons, the popular singers not only denounced the supporters of the feudal rulers, but also introduced highly moral songs into their work.

Here is an example of the type of song sung by akins who grovelled before their patrons. It was transcribed by A. A. Ivanovskii (*Etnograficheskoe obozrenie* III, 1889, 217-18) and is a panegyric sung before the performance of singers at a feast:

> You, Sarsenbay, are an honorable man, rich and a warrior since your youth; you are always generous, expansive and judicious. I will praise you and grow rich. Then I will sing day and night.
> Sarsenbay is a respected man. Your money lies in full sacks. I consider you a marvelous person. "There is no one better than Sarsenbay"—thus will I praise you in my songs. Sarsenbay is very rich. In the whole world I could not find anyone as generous as Sarsenbay.
> Sarsenbay, you like to ride on a pacer. Your saddle and harness are silver, your clothes are all valuable. Your generosity is great. You are a man of great fairness. You have been wealthy since childhood. If I praise you, you will give me a present.

The preceding text of shameless and crudely mendacious praise honoring a bai is taken from Ivanovskii's essay "The Kirghiz (*i. e.*, Kazakh—V. B.) National Poet-Singer Nogoibay." The author also portrays the striking image of Nogoibay, a highly popular akin among the Kazakh working masses, who grieved deeply over the bitter fate of the workers and the oppressed and who denounced social injustice. At the same time that the khan's and bai's singers

> Compose and sing songs about military heroes, khans and sultans, about feasts which they gave out on the steppes for entire Kirghiz [*i. e.*, Kazakh—M. S.] hordes, you will hear nothing of the sort from Nogoibay. The grief, complaints, and endless sighs of the people can be heard in his songs. For this reason every song of Nogoibay reaches the depths of his listeners' souls, penetrating to its innermost secrets, and touches the heartstrings themselves [presumably *ibid*—M. S.].[48]

Ivanovskii also says that:

> Nogoibay also sings other songs, full of hatred, malice and curses toward those who, in one way or another, do harm to the welfare of his people. He mercilessly and threateningly castigates all those who leave such deep tracks in one trip across the steppe that even whole years cannot erase them.

Similar content permeates the work of such progressive Kazakh singers of the nineteenth century as Makhambet Utemisov, Birjan Kojagulov, Jaiau-musa Bayjanov, and many others.[49]

Maxambet Utemisov (1804-1846). Maxambet Utemisov was an outstandingly talented akin. He came from a poor family, and came out sharply against the extortion and autocracy of the khans and sultans. During the popular uprising of 1836-1837, Maxambet joined and became the closest military advisor to the leader, Isatay Taymanov, and appeared at the same time as a poet and a singer who, as a fiery ideologue of revolt, inspired the people with his songs. Calling the Kazakh workers to war, he sang:

What use are golden thrones to the people?
What use are extortionist khans to the people?
If there is no justice from them,
For the powerless and the poor.

The hopes and aspirations of the people in revolt were strikingly expressed in his poems.

How I would love to bare my sword
And see a pile of skulls,
To hear the camel-like death cry
Of the khans who torment the poor people,
Of bais who grow themselves bellies.
How I would like to settle a crowd of free men
    among the meadows of the Volga.
How I would like to drive my livestock
Along your spacious banks, Volga!

He bitterly denounced the despised Kazakh sultan Baymaxambet Ayčuvakov.

You are a perfidious wolf, not a khan.
Let Satan strangle you.
Let your friends ridicule you
And your enemies beat your skull!
You are a venomous snake,
You were born with a black infection!
You are cruel and fierce on the throne.
You are a crooked-tailed scorpion!

After the defeat of the rebellion Makhambet did not stop his denunciatory activity and in 1846 was treacherously murdered by men sent by Sultan Ayčuvakov, who thus satisfied his desire for vengeance against the poet who had denounced him. Makhambet Utemisov entered Kazakh literary history as a talented poet. His work influenced the progressive akins of the following generations.

A transcription exists of the music of a small excerpt from the concluding section of the historical poem "Isatay," dedicated to Isatay Taymanov. In it Isatay has gone the road of supporting the khan's rule, has been abandoned by his military following, and has lost his support among the people, and turns to Makhmabet Utemisov with a premonition of imminent death. The excerpt is in the form of an agitated terme with an inconsistent seven-syllable verse line, which testifies to the improvisational nature of the text (Ex. 47).

Ex. 47. "Isatay" (B. Erzakovich, *Narodnye pesni Kazakhstana*, p. 18).
Invocatory, majestically.

99

Ey, Maxambet joldasïm,	O my friend Makhambet,
Aš arïstan jolbarïsïm!	My lion, my tiger!
Jolïmning bïldïm ongbasïn,	I know that misfortune awaits me
Ongbağan emey nemene,	But I believed lies
Ötïrïk sözge aldanïp,	And therefore am being punished.
Baqïtïm auïp basïmnan,	Happiness has deserted me
Ëskerim ketïp qasïmnan,	My warriors are not alongside me
Japanda jalğïz qalğan song.	I am left alone in the depths of the steppe.

Birjan Kojagulov (1825-1887). Birjan Kojagulov was a major composer of very popular songs to his own texts and to some texts of Abay Kunanbayev (of whom more below), whose close friend he was. His lyric songs are very melodious, and his satiric songs are expressive. In the latter Birjan came out as a defender of the worthiness of human individuality and as a denouncer of the bais and mullahs, which brought him continuous persecution. Pronounced mad he spent the last few years of his life bedridden.

Birjan knew Russian peasant songs well. One of his most popular songs is the fiercely denunciatory song "Janbota," named for a local administrator, in whose presence the poet had been subjected to insults and injury. The song is deeply dramatic (Ex. 48).

Jaiau-Musa Bayjanov (1835-1929). Having learned to write from a mullah, Jaiau-Musa Bayjanov left his home at an early age and went to Petropavlovsk, where he worked for a Tatar merchant. There he learned Russian. Moving next to Omsk,

Ex. 48. "Janbota" (B. Erzakovich, *Narodnye pesni Kazakhstana*, p. 236).

Heatedly, espressivo.

Janbota, osïma edï ölgen jerïm,
Kökšetau boqtïğïna kömgen jerïng?
kïsïsïp bïr bolïstïng bïreu sabap,
Barma edï statiyada körgenderïng.
   O-xo-xo, darida
   O-oy, sabap kettï au!

Janbota, özïng bolïs, eken Qarpïq,
Üstïnen segïz bolïs jürdïng artiq.
Özïndey Azanbaydïng poctabayï,
Bïr qoyïp dombïramdï aldï tartïp.

Janbota, didn't you die
And aren't you buried in rubbish under Kokshetau (a town)
Where did you find a clause
Allowing you to torture the people of a whole region?
Refrain:
O-ho-ho, da-ri-da
O-oi, he was beating me.

Janbota, you are the administrative official, son of Qarpyq.
You are esteemed above eight other local administrators by the government.
The postman Azanbai is a tyrant like you;
Having beaten me, he took my dombra. (Refrain).

Musa entered a Russian school, having earned his way through work. Being musically talented, knowing Kazakh folk music, and mastering the dombra, he became closely acquainted with Russian and Tartar songs as well in Petropavlovsk and Omsk and even learned to play the violin and accordion.[50] Later, he used the violin along with the dombra to accompany his own songs.

Having defended the rights of the Kazakh working people in his songs, Musa Bayjanov brought persecution upon himself, was arrested and underwent long imprisonment in Tobol'sk. He went from Omsk to Tobol'sk on foot.[51] which brought him the nickname "Jaiau-Musa," or "Musa the Walker," which stuck to him all his life. This nickname sounded ridiculous to the bais, but to the Kazakh people it was indicative of Musa's stance as a fighter, willing to sacrifice everything for the happiness of the people. In his autobiographical song "Aq sitsa" ("White Cotton") Musa tells of the origin of his nickname and of his enemies: the bai Šorman and his son Mustaf, who sent Musa into exile (Ex. 49).

Musa escaped from exile and returned to his homeland, continuing to hide from his pursuers for many years. Jaiau-Musa's songs are similar to terme in style, but have a strophic structure, of which Example 17 ("Kŭlbay bay") can serve as typical. Jaiau-Musa lived a long life and died at the age of ninety-one. In his songs he reflected his love for nature and his people, for whose rights he struggled lifelong. Musa was one of the first Kazakh composers to write songs on Soviet themes.

Ex. 49. "Aq sitsa" (B. Erzakovich, *Narodnye pesni Kazakhstana*, p. 34). Not hurriedly, with anger.

Aq sit - sa, qï - zïl sit - sa, sit - sa, sit - sa,

Qal - may - dï kĭm - der ja - yau zor - lïq qil - sa.

Šor - man - nïng Mŭ - sta - fa - sï a - tïmd' a - lïp,

A - tan - dïm sol se - bep - tĭ Ja - yaü Mŭ - sa, ay!

Gek - kay gik - kay gik - gik - kay gi - gik - gi gik - kay gi - gi

gik - kay! Gi - gi - gi gi - gi gi - gi - gi - gi kak - gay!

Gi - ga - ga - ga gau - gi gau - gi - gi - gi ga - ga, au!

Aq sitsa, qïzïl sitsa, sitsa, sitsa, sitsa,
Qalmaydï kĭmder jayau zorlïq qïlsa.
Šormannïng Mŭstafasï atïmdï alïp,
Atandïm sol sebeptĭ Jayaü Mŭsa.

Janïma batqandïqtan ašïnamïn,
Men nege jayaumïn dep basïlamïn.
Malïm joq Šorman aydap alatüğïn,
Qïlïğïn Mŭstafanïng paš qïlamïn.

103

Üš jüzge bolǧan maǧlŭm atïm Mŭsa
Jïgïtter šešen bolsang, maǧan usa.
Sïrtïmnan menĭ qazaq qašqïn deydĭ,
Körer em qašqïndïqtï, kunĭm tüsa!

White cotton, red cotton, cotton, cotton.
Who will not walk on foot after being subjected
   to violence?
Mustafa Šormanov took my horse;
That's why they call me "Musa the Walker."
I suffer because I'm in pain.
The thought of why I'm walking won't leave me
I have no livestock, so that Šorman could steal it
Now I will denounce the crime.
My name, Musa, is known to all three Hordes.
Youths, if you are witty, be like me;
Everywhere the Kazakhs call me a fugitive.
May the day come when I can show what kind of
   fugitive I am!

Instrumental Art. In the period under discussion instrumental music developed alongside vocal art . . . . The dombra, as the most popular musical instrument, had the leading role in instrumental music. Kobiz and sibizgi playing were less widespread.

Dombra Music. The repertoire for the dombra became filled with "concert" pieces of Kazakh composers who were also masterful performers. Two great artists stand out: Dauletkerei Šagayev and Kurmangazi Sagirbayev, founders of the two leading trends among Kazakh dombra players. Each in his own way developed the musical tradition of western Kazakhstan.

Dauletkerei Šagayev (d. 1870s) was considered the unequaled master dombra player of his day. He belonged to the feudal elite and received an unusually thorough education for his day. His work was connected with epic, historic, and daily-life themes: lyricism, nature imagery, hunting subjects, portraits of folk entertainment (wrestling) and holidays, epic heroics (the Korogli cycle)—this was the basic sphere of his art.

Dauletkerei's compositions were marked by compactness and well proportioned forms, and his performance by great mastery. His sons, Salavat and Alikei, were also outstanding composers and performers on the dombra. "Qonǧïr yok-šek" ("Two-Stringed qonǧïr"), a piece in three-part form with melodic exchange between the two strings of the dombra, can serve as an example of Dauletkerei's art (Ex. 50).

Ex. 50. "Qonggir yok-šek" (A. Zataevich, *500 pesen*, #20).

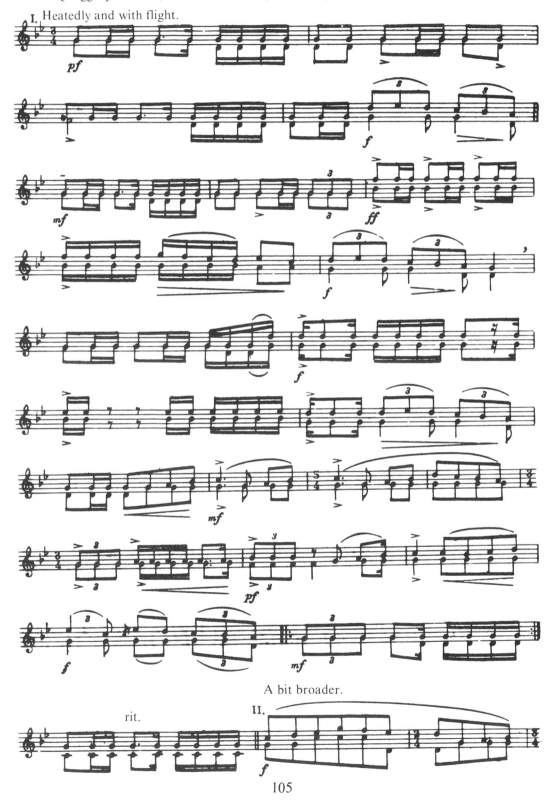

Kurmangazi Sagirbayev (1806-1879) was the son of a poor nomad and worked as a bai's shepherd from childhood. Showing great love for music as a child and possessing great talent, he made himself a dombra from which he never parted.

106

Kurmangazi achieved great technical mastery and displayed unusual compositional talent in his early years. He led the wandering life of the Kazakh musician, for whom his profession is his only means of existence, and lived for the interests of the working masses, reflecting deep social problems in his art.

He was persecuted by the bais and feudal rulers for his social-artistic activity and unbending character, and was imprisoned in Orenburg, but escaped, having cut off his fetters.

The deeply democratic themes of Kurmangazi's works were closely connected to national liberation ideas. Thus the content of the küi "Kiškentay" is dedicated to the popular uprising led by Isatay Taymanov; the küi "Kobïk šaškan" ("The Raging Billows") reflects the misery brought by flooding. In "Sarï-arka," carrying the name of a locale of Kazakhstan, he gives the picture of the broad Kazakh steppe. Some of his works portray episodes of his confinement and flight. We can use "Serper" ("The Gust") as an example of Kurmangazi's style. Zataevich called it "a masterpiece of two-voiced music in Kazakh instrumental art" (Ex. 51).

Ex. 51. "Serper" (A. Zataevich, *500 pesen* 26).
Quickly; sounds two octaves lower than written.

energetically.

Kurmangazi created a school of performers, one of the most outstanding representatives of which was Dina Nurpeisova (1861-1955). Both of these dombra players [Dauletkerei and Kurmangazi—M. S.] commanded a huge repertoire and performed Turkmen küis. They sometimes even introduced the characteristic Turkmen instrumental device of playing a middle section of a work above a lower string drone. The output of Dauletkerei and Kurmangazi can justly be ranked as an important component of classical national music.

Kobiz Music. The kobiz, once a widespread instrument among the nomadic Turkic peoples, was much less popular in the period under discussion than the dombra. However some outstanding performers were well known up to recent times. To this group belongs, above all, Ixlas Daukin (1843-1916), whose work has already been cited (Ex. 46) . . . .

Sibizgi Music. Basically pastoral in origin and use, the sibizgi, an aerophone, began to be used for the performance of serious music as well, such as in küis similar to those for dombra, but adapted to the capabilities of the sibizgi as a legato wind instrument. Transcriptions of sibizgi music are still rather rare. Among the pieces already given, Example 40 ("Estek") belongs to the küi type of piece, while Example 41 ("Zaureš") is the melody of a folk song. Two famous virtuosi on the sibizgi were Sarmalay (1835-ca. 1895) and Iskhak Valiev (1902-1944).

KAZAKH MUSIC IN THE LAST QUARTER OF THE NINETEENTH CENTURY

. . . *Abay Kunanbayev (1845-1904).* Abay (Ibrahim) Kunanbayev was born into the family of the autocratic steppe ruler Kunanbay. He received his elementary education in Semipalatinsk in a *medrese*, or Muslim religious school. Abay felt a calling for poetry at an early age and began to write verse in his school years. He studied the classic writers of the East with great interest: Firdausi, Hāfez, Sa'adi, Nizami, Fizuli, and Navai. His father intended Abay to become a judge (*bi*) . . . . But . . . Abay thought that the Kazakh people might be able to rid itself of poverty, ignorance, injustice, and inter-tribal warfare through education. This trend of thought brought him to a complete break with his father and to friendship with the representatives of the Russian nongentry intelligentsia. They helped him to study the Russian language and literature, and aided in the formation of his views as a democrat and enlightener. Abay saw the road to the salvation of the Kazakhs from age-old darkness in a rapprochement of Kazakh and Russian culture. He translated a number of works of Pushkin, Krylov, and Lermontov into Kazakh, choosing those works he considered most valuable for his goal of enlightenment. As a poet and democrat, Abay Kunanbayev was deeply tied to Kazakh folklore in his artistic work. He strikingly characterized the role of song in folk life in the following quatrain:

> Song opens the doors of the world to you,
> Song opens the doors of death to you.
> Listen, Kazakh, grasp its wisdom.
> Song accompanies your whole life.

Abay, as a profound master of Kazakh folk song and of the art of the akin, became very popular. His settlement was a constant gathering place for singers demonstrating their works and learning the poet's new works, then spreading them across Kazakhstan.

Abay knew well the songs of the Russian democratic intelligentsia as well as the romances of Russian composers. He made a number of translations into Kazakh of the texts of Russian songs and romances and created his own settings for them, which showed the way toward the development of a new style of Kazakh song, which can be called urban democratic song.[52] This style prepared the way for the further development of Kazakh mass songs and romances.

Abay's Songs. Abay's songs are lyrical in the broadest, richest, and most varied meanings of the word. In creating song texts, Abay used Kazakh folk poetry and verse structure, as well as types of poetry and verse new to Kazakh prosody. In his melodies he introduced the intonation of Russian urban songs. The melodic structure is marked by expressive laconicism, closely connected to the meaning of the text. The same laconicism is a basic trait of the strophic forms of his songs.

Abay usually used a two-part strophic form with repetition of the second half, which is also characteristic of the songs of the Russian democratic intelligentsia. His popular lyric song "Ayttim sëlem, qalamqas" ("I Send You Regards, Thin-browed One") has a wide melody in which Kazakh folk poetry is combined with a striking and expressive melody of a new type (Ex. 52).

Ex. 52. "Ayttïm sëlem, qalamqas" (B. Erzakovich, *Narodnye pesni Kazakhstana*, p. 278, transl. Shubin).

Broadly, with deep feeling.

Ay - tïm së - lem, qa - lam - qas, *oy,*

sä - ğan qŭr - ban mal men bas. Sa - ğïn - ğan - nan

se - nï oy - lap, Ke - ler köz - ge

ïs - tïq jas. Sa - ğïn - ğan - nan se - nï oy - lap,

Ke - ler köz - ge ïs - tïq jas.

I send you greetings, thin-browed one.
There has never been anything like you!
When I pine for you, my tears darken the world.
You are better than all the rest.
The world has not been kindled by one like you for a century.
My love belongs to you alone; your image has long been celebrated.

In the song "Közïmnïng qarasï" ("You Are the Apple of My Eye") a new anapest meter, reflected in the melodic structure, is given in the framework of the Kazakh folk strophe with *aaba* rhyme scheme (Ex. 53).[53]

111

Ex. 53. "Közïmnïng qarasï" (Transc. L. Xamidi, trans. Petrov).

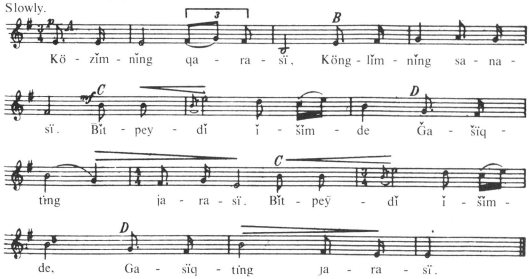

Kö - zïm - nïng qa - ra - sï, Köng - lïm - nïng sa - na -

sï. Bït - pey - dï ï - šïm - de Ğa - šïq -

tïng ja - ra - sï. Bït - peÿ - dï ï - šïm -

de, Ğa - šïq - tïng ja - ra - sï.

You are the apple of my eye,
The flame of golden souls.
My heart cannot be rid of suffering,
So deep are its scars.

Using the admonitory and denunciatory genres of the akïns' songs in an original way, Abay created his remarkable "Segïz ayaq" ("Eight-Liner"), exhorting the people to moral perfection. He based this extensive verse form on a unique strophe of eight lines with different syllable numbers, the structure of which is preserved even in Russian translation.[54]

The syllable structure and rhyme of this verse can be expressed in the following scheme:

$$558 + 558 + 88$$
$$aab \quad ccb \quad dd$$

Abay created a melody for this poem which reflects the structure of the strophe of this "eight-liner," opening new roads for the artistry of Kazakh poets and composers (Ex. 54).[55]

Ex. 54. "Segïz ayaq" (B. Erzakovich, *Narodnye pesni Kazakhstana*, p. 282).
Unhurriedly, singingly.

A voice calls from afar.
It comes from the soul.
It makes us thrill.
It is sharper than everything.
It is quicker than everything.
It can keep a deer rooted to the spot.
O great supple language,
You are great in the mouths of the people!

Striving to renew Kazakh folk song style, Abay made translations of the texts of popular Russian songs and romances from the repertoire of the democratic intelligentsia and composed melodies for them. Among these songs are "Men kordim uzïn kayïn kulaganïn" ("I Saw the Birch Tree, It Was Broken"), text by Krylov; "Surgïlt tuman" ("Not an Autumn Shower"), a folk version of a text by Del'vig; and "Karangï tunde tau kalgïp" ("Mountain Tops,") by Lermontov after Goethe. Abay made a series of translations of excerpts from Pushkin's "Eugene Onegin," and wrote a melody for "Tat'iana's Letter" [from "Onegin"—M. S.] which became extremely popular throughout Kazakhstan. In translating the letter, he used Kazakh folk poetry and connected the textual content to the hopes of Kazakh girls for freedom in their feelings and choice of husband, in opposition to the hard conditions of domestic and family oppression. The melody of "Tat'iana's Letter" has an elegaic character (Ex. 55).[56]

Ex. 55. "Tat'iana's letter" (Transc. L. Xamidi).
Slowly, singingly.

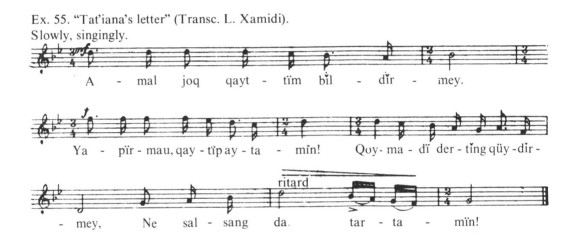

I don't know where to begin
I would like to hide my heart's passion!
But I can keep silent no longer;
I cannot cool my soul's ardor.

The songs of Abay, responsive to the new needs of the people, became famous in Kazakhstan.

The Study of Kazakh Music. Data concerning Kazakh music have been published since the early nineteenth century in connection with the interest of Russian researchers in Kazakhstan and its people. Some of these works contain transcriptions of folk melodies.

The first transcription of Kazakh melodies was published in the *Aziatskii muzykal'nyi zhurnal* [Asiatic music journal] put out by I. Dobrovol'skii in 1816-

1818. Next, A. I. Levshin gave two sibizgi melodies in his *Opisanie kirgiz-kazach'ikh ili kirgiz-kaisakskikh ord i stepei* [Description of the Kirghiz-Kazakh or Kirghiz-Kaisak hordes and steppes]. A. Pfennig included a series of transcriptions in his essay "O kirgizskikh i sartskikh narodnykh pesniakh" [On Kirghiz and Sart folk songs], published in the journal *Etnograficheskoe obozrenie* [Ethnographic review], of 1889.

The greatest work of the nineteenth century on Kazakh and, partly, Kirghiz folk music was the still unpublished[57] work of A. Eichhorn *O muzyke kirgizov* [On the music of the Kirghiz (*i.e.*, Kazakhs—M. S.)] finished in 1888. The materials for this work were collected by the author, starting in the early 1870s. This work represents special research into Kazakh music with a series of valuable observations and a significant number of musical examples. Two of Eichhorn's transcriptions were included in the present work (Exs. 5, 16).

In the twentieth century a whole new body of research appeared with transcriptions of Kazakh folk melodies, such as S. G. Rybakov's essay "Liubov' i zhenshchin po narodnym pesniam inorodtsev" [Love and women in the folk songs of foreign peoples] in the *Russkaia muzykal'naia gazeta* [Russian musical gazette] of 1901. Extensive study of Kazakh music culture began only in the Soviet period, as reflected in the works of A. V. Zataevich (1925 and 1931).

The First Arrangements of Kazakh Folk Songs. In his work "On the Music of the Kirghiz," Eichhorn gives several arrangements of Kazakh folk melodies he transcribed. Here is a lyric dialogue between a boy and a girl (Ex. 56):

Ex. 56. "Aytis" (Harmonization by A. Eichhorn).
Moderato.

More artistically significant were the arrangements of two Kazakh folk songs done by N. S. Klenovskii after the transcriptions of Pfennig. They both have advanced orchestral accompaniment. The first is performed by solo voice and the second by a mixed choir. Whereas the national color is missing in Eichhorn's arrangements, in Klenovskii's the melodies are given in a "general Oriental" harmonic and orchestral arrangement. Klenovskii made his arrangement for a grand ethnographic concert he organized in Moscow in 1893. He published the pieces on that program in an anthology of songs of different nationalities. This "Ethnographic Concert" went through five printings.[58]

Several Kazakh tunes were included in the "Asiatic Potpourri" for the band of F. V. Leisek, performed at the Turkestan exposition in Tashkent in 1890. There is also evidence for a number of concerts of Kazakh folk music in various cities of Russia. Among them, let us note two lectures of Rybakov in the Ethnographic Division of the Russian Geographical Society in St. Petersburg in 1897 and 1909, which were accompanied by demonstrations of Kazakh compositions.

KAZAKH MUSIC IN THE PREREVOLUTIONARY YEARS

. . . *Jambul Jabayev (1846-1945).* Jambul Jabayev was born into a poor family in the Semirechie. His name comes from that of Mt. Jambul. He showed an exceptional predilection toward music and versification in his early years. His first teacher was the akin Süyumbay, whom Jambul remembered with warmth to the last days of his life. He began to lead an independent life as a folk singer at the age of fourteen, when he left his father's settlement and started wandering from place to place. In 1881, at the age of thirty-five, Jambul met and defeated the hitherto invincible akin Kulmambet at an *aytis* (singing contest). . . . Having annihilated his opponent with caustic verses, Jambul gained fame as the leading akin of the Semirechie. The feudal lords tried to attract Jambul to their side with all manner of promises . . . .

The work of Jambul is quite broad in scope and theme. The major part consists of works which reflect the ongoing events in Kazakh life which Jambul, as a poet-democrat, commented on in lively and immediate fashion. His works fall into the terme style in poetic and musical make-up. They are recitative narratives with dombra accompaniment of a pure and consistent manner. Here are examples of his basic melodic phrases (Ex. 57):

Ex. 57. "Jambul's tunes" (Transc. G. Jubanov).

Jambul composed poems about Kazakh folk heroes ("Suranši batïr," and "Utegen batïr" among others) in a style approaching the epic. Jambul was a great artistic figure who united the living traditions of Kazakh epic and akin artistry and directed them toward the education of the people and the defense of human rights. The real flourishing of the great talent of Jambul was reached in the Soviet period, when the work of this Kazakh poetic genius received recognition in all corners of the Soviet Union.

Jambul was illiterate, but his information about poetry and literature was exceptionally extensive. He memorized works (read to him) by Navai, Nizami, Abai, Pushkin, Nekrasov, Shevchenko, Gorky, Lakhuti, Suleiman Stal'skii, and others. His output is marked by exceptional wealth of poetic imagery, high level of feelings, great simplicity, and deep content. The works of Jambul have been translated into many languages of the peoples of the USSR. Many songs have been set to his texts by Soviet composers. The city of Aulie-ata, the center of the Jambul district, was named for Jambul in honor of his ninety-ninth birthday.

Songs of the Early Twentieth Century. One of the great singers and song writers of the early twentieth century was Kenen Azerbayev (b. 1884),[59] who masterfully developed Kazakh folk song traditions and created many beautiful compositions in the Soviet period. "Boz torğay" ("The Woodlark"), characterized by virtuoso style and picturesque content, can serve as an example of his style. In this lyric song Kenen expresses the feelings of the prerevolutionary itinerant shepherd, suffering from the burden of forced labor for the bai (Ex. 58).[60]

Ex. 58. "Boz torǧay" (B. Erzakovich, *Narodnye pesni Kazakhstana*, p. 28).　　　Broadly.

Boz torğay šïrïldaysïng jerge tüspey,
Men jürmïn keške deyïn tamaq ïšpey.
At qïlïp aq tayaqtï qolïma ŭstap,
Sandalïn qoy artïnda erte-keške.
  Boz torğay šïrïldaysïng, šïrkïn-ay,
  Qŭtïlar kün barma eken,
  Qoy jayudan bïr kün-ay,
  Boz torğay!

Otïrsa qoy küzetïp tang atpaydï,
Jürgende maldï jayïp keš batpaydï.
Qaraytïn qabağïma bïr adam joq,
Bel šešïp jïlï tösekke bïr jatpaymïn.

Woodlark, you sing without alighting.
I walk on the steppe, hungry, until evening.
I have a white stick instead of a horse.
I herd the flocks day and night.

Refrain: Woodlark, full-throated woodlark.
          Will the day come when I can stop herding sheep?
          My woodlark.
If I guard the flocks at night, I can't wait for morning;
If I tend the flocks during the day, evening never comes.
No one cares that I
Go to sleep without undressing.

We see a new type of professional singer and composer, the female Kazakh artist, in the person of Mayra, or Magira Šamsutdinova (1896-1929), who sharply broke with old customs.[61] She appeared at fairs and bazaars, in teahouses and *kümis* [fermented mare's milk—M. S.] houses, performing Kazakh songs to the dombra as well as Russian and Tatar songs to the accordion. The song "Mayra", named for her, is similar in form and content to "Šašubaydïng ëni" (Ex. 34); in "Mayra" the songstress gives her artistic autobiography, telling how she appeared in defense of the rights of Kazakh women for equality in artistic activity (Ex. 59).

Ex. 59. "Mayra" (B. Erzakovich, *Narodnye pesni Kazakhstana*, p. 52).   Lively.

Qïz' e - dïm   U - a - li - dïng May - ra a - tïm,

Tar - ta - dï   boz - ba - la - nï ma - gni - tïm.

119

Qïzï edĭm, ualding Mayra atïm.
Tartadï bozbalanï magnïtĭm.
Qŭrbĭlar jastïq šaqta oyna da kül,
Qarayïp külkĭ qašar uakït jetĭp.
  Mayra, Mayra qïzïl tĭlĭm sayra,
  Mayra, Mayra, šïrqa osïndayda.

Degende atïm Mayra, atïm Mayra,
Otïz tĭs kömekey pen tĭlĭm sayra.
Qolǧa alĭp dombïra men än šĭrkasam.
Ĭleser sonda bĭzge jĭgĭt qayda.

I am Vali's daughter, named Mayra.
My magnet attracts youths.
O age-mates, dare and play in your youth.
For you won't be able to when you're old.
Refrain:

Mayra, Mayra, mellifluous Mayra,
Mayra, Mayra, play, here

My name is famous: Mayra, Mayra
Speak, tongue, lips and throat!
When I take up the dombra and sing,
No youth can compete with me.
(Refrain).

The long coexistence of Russian peasants with Kazakhs led to a mutual acquaintance of songs and musical works. In addition to the examples cited above of Kazakh singers acquainted with Russian songs (Mayra, Jaiau-Musa), we can also cite the famous example of one of the most popular songs of Kazakhstan, "Dudar-ay" ("O, My Dudar"). This song was composed by a Russian girl, Maria Egorova (d. 1951), the daughter of a fisherman, who earned the title of Honored Worker in the Arts of the Kazakh SSR. This song is composed in a good Kazakh folk lyric style and stands as a remarkable artistic document of the friendship between the Kazakh and Russian workers. Maria, or Mariiam Egorova, speaks of her love for the Kazakh youth Dudar (Ex. 60).[62]

Ex. 60. "Dudar-ay! (A. Zataevich, *500 pesen*, #235).
Bravely, loudly, with marked rhythm.

121

Mariiam, the daughter of Egor, is a Russian girl
When she was sixteen or seventeen
She fell in love with a youth named Dudar.
And then Mariiam said:
My dear Dudar, I was born for you.
My dear Dudar.

Kazakh Revolutionary Songs. Russian revolutionary songs, calling for a struggle against autocracy, became quite widespread in connection with the revolutionary movement. Under its influence Kazakh revolutionary songs arose, forming a basis for postrevolutionary mass songs . . . .

Notes to Chapter II

1. The Kirghiz are credited with similar talents, which Vinogradov (1958: Chapter 2) feels are connected to a general evolutionary pattern for Central Asian Turkic prosody and music.

2. This transcription by August Eichhorn can be found in Beliaev (1963), a Russian edition of Eichhorn's field notes (originally in German) from Central Asia. Eichhorn (1844-sometime after 1909) was an Austrian who served as *Kapellmeister* for the czarist military orchestra in Tashkent from 1870-1873 (for more on Eichhorn, *see* Chapter 5). His were the first field transcriptions of Central Asian music by a musician, and they contain much valuable information. His attitude was that of the nineteenth-century romantic observer of the Rousseauian "sons-of-the-steppe" school. Eichhorn wrote about Kazakh and Kirghiz music, as well as about music of urban Uzbeks and Tajiks, and we are deeply indebted to Beliaev for editing and presenting this valuable ethnomusicological document.

3. Shamanistic rituals involving music played a large role in prerevolutionary Kazakh life. For transcriptions of shaman's music, *see* Castagné (1930) and Erzakovich (1967).

4. Also given in Erzakovich (1966: 39, Ex. 28), where it is transcribed from Kenen Azerbayev (1948): is termed a "male *jar-jar*" and is given an MM of 116.

5. Oddly enough, this song is said by its transcriber (Erzakovich, 1966: 63) to have been collected in 1963, a year after Beliaev's *Essays* was published; the text of both transcriptions is identical.

6. In Erzakovich (1966: 66, Ex. 35) the same song is given with *c"* instead of *e"* as the first note. Erzakovich transcribed it from Kenen Azerbayev in 1948.

7. The holiday referred to is the New Year's of the Persian solar calendar, *nowruz*. The spread of the nowruz celebration among the Kazakhs is indicative of the extent to which most of Central Asia can at least partially be considered an Iranian-influenced region.

8. The Kazakhs were nominally Muslims, but maintained a considerable faith in shamanism and animism as well, as did the Kirghiz and even some Uzbeks and Tajiks.

9. Women's shamanistic curing ceremonies have been observed as far south in the Central Asian area as northern Afghanistan (Centlivres and Slobin, 1971).

10. Erzakovich (1966: 38, Ex. 8) transcribed the song from Kenen Azerbayev in 1948 and gives MM=92 as the tempo.

11. A variant of "Qïzïl biday" is given in Erzakovich (1966: 81, Ex. 42), as transcribed from Kurmanbek Jumarkbekov in 1963.

12. Erzakovich (1966: 84, Ex. 43) gives "Qorlan" with different barring and structural analysis. He transcribed the song from Estay Berkimbayev in 1938.

13. Erzakovich (1966: 112, Ex. 60) attributes this song to Janbope Erzazin from whom it was transcribed in 1932.

14. Erzakovich (1966: 126, Ex. 67) attributes this song, transcribed in 1937, to Jalpar Kalambayev.

15. For a variant of this song, *see* Erzakovich (1966: 27, Ex. 1).

16. Here the tendency to not only group Central Asian tunes by "Greek" scale types and to subsume the latter under major and minor occurs, but even the (anhemitonic) pentatonic is included in this system of categorization, a rather unusual step for Beliaev. Recently this approach to Central Asian scale structure, specifically that of the Kazakhs, has come under review by at least one Soviet ethnomusicologist. P. Aravin (1968: 109), reviewing Erzakovich (1966), writes: "It is completely obvious that this type of analysis of the particularities of Kazakh melody, with application of scalar norms suited to another style [*i. e.*, Western music—M. S.] does not facilitate the understanding of the internal logic of scalar intonational formation in the specific conditions of development of national music genres." In other words, Aravin feels that applying the terminology of Western scales to analyses of Kazakh music is unsuited to explaining Kazakh tonal thought.

17. A sample of one hundred six of Zataevich's (1925) 1000 Kazakh songs, weighted according to Zataevich's regional breakdown, gives the following table of ranges:

5th	m6	M6	m7	M7	8ve	m9	m10	M10	11th
6	6	6	18	0	38	12	5	2	5

The table indicates: 1) a decided preference for the range of an octave (roughly one-third of the total) and adjacent ranges of a seventh or ninth; 2) complete lack of the M7 range, showing the strong anhemitonic bias of Kazakh song as reflected both in pentatonic structures and in the conjunct tetrachordal skeleton shared by Kirghiz and Kazakh folk melodies. To judge by Zataevich's data, pentatonicism is regionally distributed over the vast area of Kazakhstan, perhaps most concentrated in the Eastern area, though the evidence is too scanty for well founded generalizations. One should not overlook the influence of such neighboring, pentatonically oriented music cultures as those of the Tatars and Bashkirs in discussing Kazakh pentatonicism. The Kirghiz, though otherwise close to the Kazakhs musically, display markedly less pentatonicism; they are perhaps sheltered by their mountains from the northern "pentatonic belt" of Central Asia, to offer a diffusionist explanation.

18. This is a widespread phenomenon in Central Asian music, extending to the music of the Central Asian peoples of northern Afghanistan.

19. This example reminds one of the transposition of melodies by a fifth pointed out by many writers as characteristic of some Central Asian musics, usually in connection with a similar phenomenon in the folk music of Hungary (*e. g.*, Szabolcsi, 1935). I have used the term "range-shifting" (Slobin, 1969a) for this type of melodic shift in discussing related occurences in Kirghiz music.

20. For an extended discussion of Kazakh refrains, stressing the role of nonsense syllables, *see* Tleubaeva (1967).

21. It is probably only in the Soviet period that songs have developed on "a single national basis," through the building of a unified national style disseminated by the schools and the mass media.

22. For a discussion of "Kozï-korpeš" and Kïz-jïbek," *see* Chadwick and Zhirmunsky (1969: 51-53) and for a general discussion of the Kazakh epic, *see* Chapter 3 of Winner (1958).

23. This resolution of the plot of "Kozï-korpeš" is an interesting variant on the motive "twining branches grow from graves of lovers" (E.631.01) in Thompson's listing of folk tale motives (Thompson 1955-58).

24. As Winner (1958: 75) has noted, "It is interesting to note that in the epics not only of the Kazakhs, but of all the Turkic peoples of Central Asia, the heroine is depicted as equal in moral worth and intelligence to her husband or lover, and that she is always highly idealized."

25. For a recorded example of a "Kïz-jïbek" fragment taped in northern Afghanistan, see Anthology of the World's Music, AST-4004, "Afghanistan II" (edited by Slobin).

26. There is also evidence (Sarybaiev, 1967) that the Kazakhs formerly played a zither called the *jetigan* or *iatigan* related to Siberian (and Far Eastern ?) zithers.

27. Beliaev's scale differs sharply from that in the *Atlas* (1963: 132), which shows a simple major scale for both Western and Eastern Kazakh dombras. Zhanuzakov (1964: 18) gives a major scale for the Eastern lute, but a scale like Beliaev's (except for the flat second scale degree) for the Western dombra.

28. This corresponds to the neutral third cited earlier for Kirghiz music, and is a common feature of many Central Asian musics.

29. An interesting feature of the Kazakh strum is that the middle finger may do the work, thus differentiating the dombra from neighboring Central Asian lute-types such as the Uzbek and Turkmen dutars and Uzbek and Tajik dambura, for which index finger strumming is basic.

30. For an account of the kobiz as a case of marginal survival in northern Afghanistan, see Slobin (1969b: 145ff).

31. A distinctive feature of the kobiz' bridge, as compared to that of other neighboring fiddles, is that it stands vertically on one side, but slopes off gradually at a 45-degree angle on the other side.

32. Since the kobiz is fretless it is hard to speak of its "scale"; furthermore, basic kobiz style involves many glides and harmonics which are hard to assimilate into such a "scale."

33. The *Atlas* (1963: 132) also gives the major scale as the basic sibizgi scale; however, as the examples here and elsewhere show, few sibizgi tunes are in major.

34. As noted in Chapter I this feature of the jew's-harp is nearly universal in Central Asia.

35. This is the same basic ensemble as noted for the Kirghiz earlier, and stems from the same Near Eastern source *via* the Uzbek.

36. Among Central Asian flute-types, the sibizgi has received the best documentation in print. Zhanuzakov (1964: 197-213) includes no fewer than sixteen flute pieces in his anthology of Kazakh instrumental music whereas, for example, there are no transcriptions whatever for the Kirghiz čoor.

37. Valiev, who was killed in World War II, was from the Ural region of Kazakhstan; some of his pieces are also found in Zhanuzakov (1964), but not the two included here by Beliaev.

38. *Küi* is also used to refer to instrumental pieces by the Kirghiz, and is sometimes in use among some Uzbeks.

39. This is one of the major differences between the style of the Kirghiz komuz on the one hand and the Kazakh dombra and Turkmen dutar on the other. The Kirghiz lute is usually played with a variety of textures, which are part of the variational style of komuz music, while the Kazakh dombra and Turkmen dutar are generally played continually in a two-voice manner. The structural basis of the music varies widely among the three styles.

40. Kazakh lute music exploits the possibilities of two-string play more thoroughly than perhaps any other related Central Asian style (Uzbek, Turkmen, and Karakalpak dutars; Uzbek and Tajik damburas).

41. Here Beliaev tends to oversimplify the structure of dombra pieces for textbook presentation; as he himself notes below, many dombra pieces are highly episodic in nature, due to their programmatic content, *i. e.*, the segments of the piece relate to events or descriptions in a specific plot, and there is often no clear musical form of the AB . . . *etc.* type. Erzakovich (1966: 203-17) has presented the full program of a fourteen-part küi, giving the whole text of the story between the segments of the piece, thus tying together for the first time the narrative and musical aspects of a dombra piece. He has also treated a sixteen-part kobiz küi similarly (*ibid.*: 191-201); in this way, we can perhaps eventually arrive at the musical semantics of Kirghiz and Kazakh instrumental music. Beliaev does not provide a specific reference to Zataevich in his text.

42. Beliaev does not provide a specific reference to Zataevich in his text. The story which follows is exactly that cited by Vinogradov in connection with Kirghiz instrumental music (1939: 54; 1958: 155), with only some differences in names and circumstances.

43. Zataevich was much given to such interpretations, with no apparent confirmation from native musicians or listeners.

44. Here again is Beliaev's equation of simple instruments with simple repertoire, which suits his evolutionary view of instruments and their music. As a counterweight, informants in Afghan Turkestan told me that fewer people play fiddles there than lutes because lutes are easier to play.

45. These "expressive traits" include great use of glissando, vibrato, harmonics, and legato phrasing which make kobiz music sound much like the music of the Mongol khur and Kirghiz kiak, neighboring horsehair fiddle-styles.

46. Zhanuzakov (1964: 228) gives Ixlas' last name as Dukenov, and says he came from the Chimkent area, near Tashkent in far southern Kazakhstan. Ixlas was among the first to use the kobiz as an independent "concert" instrument, removing it from its main role as accompaniment to shamanistic seances and epic recitals (*ibid.*).

47. The corresponding Kirghiz terms are *maktoo* and *tolgoo*.

48. This example of nineteenth-century Russian ethnographic reporting indicates that Beliaev's normal rhetoric is one which was standard as an approach to the cultures and musics of non-Western Russia before the revolution crystallized that rhetoric into Marxist terminology. Beliaev himself received his training in prerevolutionary times.

49. For an assessment of nineteenth-century Kazakh akins, *see* Winner (1958: Chapters 4 and 5), in which some of the songs introduced by Beliaev are discussed.

50. Jaiau-Musa's career is an interesting example of the type of musical acculturation which occurred as early as the mid-nineteenth century among the Kazakhs (and much earlier among the Tatars and the Volga peoples), but which did not reach the southern part of Central Asia until well into the twentieth century.

51. The distance from Omsk to Tobol'sk is nearly three hundred miles as the crow flies.

52. Dernova (1967) has written an interesting study of the difficulty of tracing the original melodies of Abay's songs, composed by the poet himself.

53. For a discussion of variants of Example 53, *see* Dernova (1967).

54. The English version given here does not attempt to duplicate either the Kazakh or Russian versions.

55. For discussion of variants of "Segĭz ayaq," *see* Dernova (1967).

56. "By 1887 the name of Pushkin and of his hero and heroine were known all over Kazakhstan through Abay's translations. They received wide distribution through the wandering *akins*. The most popular of these is probably his musical translation of Tat'iana's letter to Onegin" (Winner, 1958: 117). For a discussion of variants of Tat'iana's letter, *see* Dernova (1967).

57. As noted earlier, Eichhorn's work was published in 1963 in Beliaev's edition as *Muzykal'naia fol'kloristika v uzbekistane* (Tashkent: IZD-VO ANUzSSR)

58. In noting this vogue for the "ethnographic concert," one should keep in mind the strong inclination of Russian composers to incorporate "Eastern" tunes into their symphonic works, dating back to Glinka's "Persian March" in *Ruslan and Liudmilla*, which has become the standard of comparison for Soviet works incorporating "native" themes.

59. Erzakovich has written a small biography of Kenen Azerbayev (1961).

60. *See* the transcription dated 1948, in Erzakovich (1966: 78, Ex. 41).

61. Dina Nurpeisova, the great female dombrist, stands as another example of this trend. Song contests were apparently often conducted between men and women in traditional Kazakh society, and an informant of Winner (1958: 30) states that "the prize for the man was a night with his opponent."

62. Erzakovich (1966: 119, Ex. 64) gives Amre Kashanbayev as the source of this song, transcribed in 1932.

Composite Bibliography

In place of Beliaev's listings, a composite Kazakh bibliography follows, based on: 1) Beliaev's, 2) Zataevich's (from 1925), 3) the revised bibliography in the second edition of Zataevich, 1925 (edited by Dernova, 1967), and 4) some recent works.

In general, the bibliography on the Kazakhs is only rivalled by that on the Uzbeks, both of which are overwhelmingly more complete than the rare studies on the Turkmen, Kirghiz, and Tajiks.

For short accounts of the musics of some minority groups within Kazakhstan (the Tatars, Dungans, Germans, Cossacks), *see* a number of articles in Dernova (1967).

In the collection and study of Kazakh music, Zataevich's works continue to hold the paramount position nearly forty years after their publication. Evidence for this fact was provided by the sumptuous second edition of *1000 pesen kazakhskogo naroda* (Moscow: Muzgiz, 1962), which presents as complete an amplification and revision of a basic source as can be found in any ethnomusicological literature, East or West. Song texts, ignored by Zataevich, have been patiently tracked down, bibliography enlarged, notes annotated, and the like, and a special essay (by Dernova) has been included on the origins of the Zataevich volume. The centennial of Zataevich's birth was marked with commemorative events in Alma-Ata in 1969.

Among more recent works, Zhanuzakov (1964) is a valuable store house of instrumental music, subsuming items from no fewer than fifteen different archival sources. Erzakovich (1966), while including some useful examples, tends toward discursive style within the framework of a tight classification of song types. The anthology of essays edited by Dernova (1967) is a mixture of unique, useful, and run-of-the mill articles. I have unfortunately not seen Zhubanov's *Struni stoletii*, reputed to be the best account of dombra music. The most regrettable lacuna in the Kazakh bibliography is Beliaev's own *Muzyka kazakhov*, which has not been published; its existence is only alluded to in occasional notes.

Alekseev, A. "O kazakhskoi dombrovoi muzyke." *Sovetskaia Muzyka*, no. 3, 1947.

Akhan-sere. *Pesni*. Alma-Ata, 1959.

Altynsarin, I. *Izbrannye proizvedeniia*. Edited by B. S. Suleimanov. Alma-Ata, 1957.

Auezov, M. and Sobolev, L. "Epos i fol'klor kazakhskogo naroda." *Literaturnyi kritik*, nos. 11-12, 1939; no. 1, 1940.

Birjan Kozhagulov. *Pesni*. Alma-Ata, 1959.

Cheshikhin, V. "Sredneaziatskii muzykal'nyi etnograf 1870 g. *Russkaia Muzykal'naia gazeta* nos. 19-26, 29-32, 1917.

Chumbalova, G. "Pesni Abaia," In *Zhizn' i tvorchestvo Abaia*. Alma-Ata, 1954.

Dernova, V. "Kiuii v sbornike A. V. Zataevicha '1000 pesen kirgizskogo naroda'." *Izvestiia ANKazSSR*. seriia filologii i iskusstvovedeniia, vol. 2, 1960.

—— ed. *Narodnaia muzyka v kazakhstane*. Alma-Ata: Kazakhstan, 1967.

—— "Pesni Abaia." *Sovetskaia muzyka*, 1954.

Divaev, A. "Kirgizskie forumy." *Etnograficheskoe obozrenie*, no. 3, 1907.

Erzakovich, B. "Kazakhskiaia SSR." in *Muzykal'naia kul'tura soiuznykh respublik*. Moscow, 1957.

—— *Narodnye pesni Kazakhstana*. Alma-Ata, 1955.

—— *Pesennaia kul'tura kazakhskogo naroda*. Alma-Ata: Nauka, 1966.

—— "Russkie uchenye o kazakhskoi muzyke." *Vestnik ANKazSSR*, no. 9, 1954.

Gizatov, B. *Kazakhskii Gosudarstvennyi orkestr*. Alma-Ata, 1957.

Gotovitskii, M. V. "6 kharakternykh kirgizskikh (kazakhskikh) pesen." *Zapiski Turkestanskogo obshestva liubitelei estestvoznaniia, antropologii i etnografii*, vol. I (1).

Ivanovskii, A. "Kirgizskii poet Nogaibai." *Etnograficheskoe obozrenie*, no. 3, 1889.

Jaiau Musa. *Pesni i kiuii*. Alma-Ata, 1959.

"Jambul Jabaev" *Bol'shaia Sovetskaia Entsiklopediia*, vol. 14, 1952.

Karlson, I. "Narodnye pevtsy-kirgizy v Arkhivnoi komissii." *Orenburgskii krai*, no. 62, 1906.

"Kazakhskaia Sovetskaia Sotsialisticheskaia Respublika." *Bol'shaia Sovetskaia Entsiklopediia*, vol. 19, 1953.

Kazakhskie sovetskie narodnye pesni. Alma-Ata, 1959.

Klenovskii, N. S. *Etnograficheskii kontsert*. Moscow: Iurgenson, n. d.

Kunanbaev, A. *Polnoe sobranie sochinenii*. Alma-Ata, 1938.

Lane, G. "Pesni Altaia." *Muzykal'naia nov'*, no. 12, Moscow, 1924.

Levshin, A. *Opisanie Kirgiz-kazach'ikh ili kirgiz-kaisakskikh ord i stepei*. St. Petersburg, 1832.

Mironov, N. N. *Vostochnaia siuita "Turkestan"*. Moscow: Vostochnaia lira, n.d.

Mukhit. *Pesni*. Alma-Ata, 1960.

Muzykal'naia kul'tura Kazakhstana. Alma-Ata: 1955 (in Russian), 1957 (in Kazakh).

Muzykal'noe tvorchestvo Abaia. Edited by Erzakovich. Alma-Ata, 1954.

"Muzykal'noe tvorchestvo kirgizov." *Turkestanskii kur'er*, no. 16, 1909.

Narodnye pesni Kazakhstana, Edited by Erzakovich. Alma-Ata, 1955.

"O muzyke kirgizov." *Orenburgskii listok*, no. 19, 1897.

Orazbekov, N. "Zhizn' i tvorchestvo Jaiau-Musy." *Literatura i iskusstvo Kazakhstana*, no. 5, 1939.

Pesni Kenena Azerbaev, Edited by Erzakovich. Alma-Ata, 1955.

Pfennig, R. A. unnamed article in *Etnograficheskoe obozrenie*, III, 1889.

Rybakov, S. G. "Liubov' i zhenshchina po narodnym pesniiam inorodtsev." *Russkaia Muzykal'naia gazeta*, nos. 21-22, 1901.

Savichev, N. "Ot Kurmanovskogo forposta do Glininskogo." *Ural'skie voiskovye vedomosti*, 1868.

Shnitnikov, V. N. "Materialy po kirgizskoi i tatarskoi muzyke." *Zhivaia starina*, III-IV, 1913.

Tikhov, Sv. P. "O muzyke turkestanskikh kirgizov." *Muzyka i zhizn'*, nos. 3-4, 1910.

"Zataevich, A. V." Alma-Ata, 1958.

Zataevich, A. V. *1000 pesen kirgizskogo naroda*. Orenburg, 1925; 2nd ed., 1962.

——*500 kazakhskikh pesen i kiui'ev*. Alma-Ata, 1931.

—— "O kazakhskoi muzyke." *Literaturnyi Kazakhstan*, nos. 3-4, 1935.

Zhanuzakov *Kazakhskaia narodnaia instrumental'naia muzyka*. Alma-Ata: Nauka, 1964.

Zhubanov, A. *Kurmangazi*. Alma-Ata, 1960.

—— "K voprosu o vozniknovenii kazakhskogo muzykal'nogo zhanra kiui." *Kzyl-Orda*, 1936.

—— "O kazakhskikh narodnykh kiuiiakh i narodnykh muzykal'nykh instrumentakh." *Adebiet jäne iskusstvo*, no. 9, 1955.

—— Struny stoletii. Alma-Ata, 1958.

—— *Zhizn' i tvorchestvo kazakhskikh kompozitorov*. Alma-Ata, 1942

The above listing does not take into account individual articles in anthologies, or items in the Kazakh language.

The Music Culture of Turkmenia

The Development of Turkmen Music in the Pre-Soviet Period. In the pre-Soviet period Turkmen music developed through oral tradition, including both folk songs and professional vocal and instrumental artistry. Turkmen folk song shows traces of very ancient origin, based on conditions of pastoral nomadism, and is the foundation of all forms of professional music.

One of the characteristics of Turkmen professional vocal artistry is the introduction of complex poetic meters and strophic structures which belong to the realm of literate poetic styles. In this context the Turkmen are closer to the Uzbeks, Tajiks, Azerbaijanis, and Armenians, and are set off from the Kirghiz and Kazakhs, who do not use these types of verse forms . . . .[1]

THE BASES FOR THE DEVELOPMENT OF TURKMEN MUSIC CULTURE

Turkmen Folk Songs

The study of Turkmen folk music began only in the Soviet period. V. A. Uspenskii (1879-1949) undertook the large task of transcribing Turkmen musical monuments, the results of which were published in the work *Turkmenskaia muzyka* (Moscow, 1928), mostly dedicated to professional music.[2]

Genres of Turkmen Folk Song.[3] The available transcriptions of Turkmen folk songs are mostly in the area of women's and children's songs.[4] The former fall into the genres of work, ceremonial, daily-life, and lyric songs, while the latter are play songs. Their basic content is closely connected to the daily life of the Turkmen people, with their pastoral and agricultural pursuits.

129

The work songs reflect the varied jobs of the Turkmen woman. Thus, for example, the song "Xörle, düyäm, xörle!" ("Stand, Camel, Stand") is sung to quiet camels during milking (Ex. 1).

Ex. 1. "Xorle, düyëm, xorle!" (Transc. V. Uspenskii).   Moderately.

Xör - le, düy - ëm, xör - le, Xör - le - me - seng, boz - la!

Xörle, düyëm, xörle,	Stand quietly, my camel,
Xörlemeseng, bozla!	And if you don't want to stand, roar!
Ayrïl, xeley, bu yana:	Stand aside, woman,
Özüm sagayïn düyäni.	I will milk the camel myself.
Örküzhine ël etmez,	The hand doesn't reach to her hump,
Baxasïna pul etmez,	There's not enough money to buy her
Takïrja erde tagtam bar,	I have a couch in a flat place in the desert:
Alaja yüpden nogtam bar.	I have a rope of many-colored cotton.

"Xöküdik" is a song sung while working with a hand mill. The onomatopoetic word "xöküdik" recurs to the rhythm of the millstone (Ex. 2).

Ex. 2. "Xöküdik" (Transc. V. Uspenskii).   Moderately.

Xö - kü - dik, xö - kü - dik, gök - da - šï.

Xöküdik, xöküdik gök dašï,	"Xöküdik, xöküdik" knock
Degirmening ak dašï.	The grey and white millstones.
Mäzer gïsïng kürtesi,	Miazer's daughter has a colorful robe.
Özi geyip yïrtasï.	She'll wear it out herself
Gatï čörek dövülmez,	A stale loaf doesn't break,
Odun yüpi üzülmez.	A rope for carrying firewood doesn't tear.

The song "Tara gošgusï" ("Song of the Weaver") is more developed in comparison to the songs above. Weaving, especially carpet weaving, attained the status of a major art in Turkmenia long ago, and demands great expenditure of painstaking labor on the part of the craftsman. This song treats the theme of family oppression in the old Turkmen way of life, specifically the bride's dependence on the mother-in-law, as well as lyric motives (Ex. 3).[5]

Ex. 3. "Tara gŏsgusï" (Transc. V. Uspenskii).   Moderately.

Iki tara garšima-garši yupekdir, dönem!
Ol gelin saralar sarï sapakdïr, dönem!
Gaynï sakïrdayan garrï köpekdir, dönem!
Men-ä yandïm šu taranïng ičinde, dönem!

Two looms on which silk is woven, friend!
The bride winds the yellow threads.
Her mother-in-law grumbles ceaselessly;
I am wasting away at the loom.
Two looms on which one weaves
The young men are breathless at seeing us
If a young girl goes for water,
The young men wash their horses.
Measure by measure the cloth is woven
Sweat drips from my brow.
Tell me, Oraz-jan's daughter,
Did my lover forget me?

Among Turkmen ceremonial songs, "Yar-yar" can be introduced, a wedding song taking its name from the refrain, meaning "my beloved" (masculine or feminine). Similar wedding songs with this refrain and the same verse structure are widespread among the Uzbeks and Kazakhs. They are basically honorary and sometimes humorous, as we see in the following example (Ex. 4):

131

Ex. 4. "Yar-yar!" (Transc. V. Uspenskii). Fairly quickly.

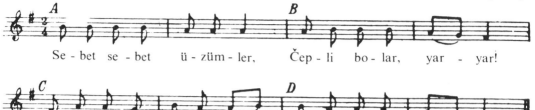

Se - bet se - bet ü - züm - ler, Čep - li bo - lar, yar - yar!

Biz - den si - ze gïz git - se, Sep - li bo - lar, yar - yar!

There are many baskets of grapes
That haven't been sorted out, yar-yar!
From us to you
Goes a girl with a dowry, yar-yar!

Two chests side by side
Have locks with scrolls, yar-yar!
From us to you
Goes a girl with curly locks, yar-yar!

I lost my needle.
For this my mother beat me, yar-yar!
I am going far away
So that she will calm down, yar-yar!

Cauldrons are full of dumplings
Called *katlak*, yar-yar!
Among three sisters
One is called Altyn (=gold), yar-yar!

Lyric themes of love and family predominate in Turkmen songs of daily life. Lullabies (*xüvdi*), an early type of lyric song, are the most important form. One of these lullabies is very simple (Ex. 5).

Ex. 5. "Xüvdi" (Transc. V. Uspenskii). Slowly.

Xüv - di xüv - di xüv - len - sin!

Suv - da ba - lïk köv - len - sin.

Xüvdi-xüvdi xüvlensin!
Suvda balïk kövlensin.
Balïk dïyip tutanïm
Yïlan bolup tovlansïn.

Rock-a-bye, sleep!
Let a fish flash in the water.
Let the fish that I catch
Roll up in a ring, like a snake.

132

Other lullabies are more developed melodically and can be performed to the accompaniment of the *dutar* [a two-stringed fretted lute—M. S.]. such as "Allalar balam!" ("Rock-a-bye, My Boy!; Ex. 6).[6]

Ex. 6. "Allalar balam!" (Transc. V. Uspenskii *Turkmenskaia muzyka* #40).   Moderately.

Rock-a-bye my little boy.
I'll wrap you in velvet,
And when you grow up,
I'll find you the most beautiful bride!

Rock-a-bye my warrior,
What luxuriant hair you have.
You are dear to my heart like fresh cream,
You are like a bouquet of fresh scarlet flowers.

Girls' songs, generally called *lale*, have love themes. For example, here is "Gülyar aydïmï," the drift of which can be translated as "my love is like a flower" (Ex. 7):

Ex. 7. "Gülyar aydïmï" (Transc. V. Uspenskii).   Moderately.

Mun - dan   bar - dïm   ya - tïp   siz,   *In - di   me - ni   yar*

134

öl - dür - se, yar, öl - dür - sin! Gül yas - dïg - na ba - tïb siz,

In - di me - ni yar öl - dür - se, yar öl - dür - sin!

I went by and looked; you are sleeping.
If my beloved wants to kill me, let him kill me!
You are lying on a pillow of flowers.
I wanted to lift that pillow
Since you, lying, are fresher than the flowers.
I gave my kerchief to be washed;
I ordered it to be hung on the black willow-bush.

While the preceding song is purely lyrical, another girls' song, "Lële," (while basically lyric), combines the work theme with that of the family. In musical terms this song is very typical in the melismatic make-up of its melody (Ex. 8).

Ex. 8. "Lële" (Transc. V. Uspenskii). Moderately.

Yo - la, yo - la ba - kar men Sa - rï ga - vun ë - ker

men Ey la - le Vay, la le!

Yola, yola bakar men,	Looking at the road
Sarï gavun ëker men.	I will sow yellow melons.
Sarï gavun bišipmi?	Did my melons ripen,
Sapagïndan düšüpmi?	Did they separate from the patch?

Menin zhoram Ay-Gïzlar.   My friend Ai-Gizlar
Yat illere düšüpdir,   Was given to a strange tribe.
Yat illere yaman il.   A strange tribe, a bad tribe
Oturtmadï tagtïmda,   There they will not put her in the seat of honor,
Daramadi vagtïnda.   And they will not comb her hair when necessary.

135

The *čüval-kïz* genre occupied a large place among prerevolutionary women's song, and was characteristic of the Turkmen way of life. This is the song of "the girl put into a sack," *i. e.*, already given into marriage, but sent back to her parents until the final payment of the bride price. The following song, which contains the deep expression of a young woman's grief, can serve as an artistic document of the existence of such a barbarous custom (Ex. 9).[7]

Ex. 9. "Čüval-kïz aydïmï" (Transc. V. Uspenskii).   Moderately.

Kararïm yokdïr oturmaga, turmaga,	I do not have the strength to sit or stand.
Gözel yarïm gözley-gözley barmaga.	I am ready to search for my beloved.
Muštak boldum yarïng yuzun görmäge,	I would very much like to see my dear one,
Iller goymaz yarım bilen gezmage.	But people do not let me go walking with him.
Alga yarïm, manga gamgïn bolandïr.	Cry, my dear one, I am very sad.

Turkmen children's songs, as mentioned earlier, are mostly for play; however, some of them contain ancient imagery. Thus "Yagiš yagara geldi" ("A Song for the Spring Rain") is a ceremonial song, an incantation or call for rain. In its structure it is close to the recitative work songs (Exs. 1, 2) and at the same time it represents the most ancient type of folk art (Ex. 10).

Ex. 10. "Yagiš yagara geldi" (Transc. V. Uspenskii).   Fairly quickly.

Gïz - lar oy - na - ra gel - di, Og - lan gac - dï, gïz kov - dï.

Ös, sa - čïm, ös, Ös - me - seng - kes!

It is time for the rain to come.
It is time to milk the sheep.
It is time for girls to play.
A fellow ran away, driven away by a girl.
Blow in the wind, my hair, blow;
And if you won't blow—cut it!

Among the repertoire of children's songs there are also spring congratulatory carols, sung by groups of carolers. The songs of shepherds and camel drivers have practical work significance. When they have to round up the scattered sheep, shepherds use the cry "Hurrai!" (Ex. 11).

Ex. 11. Moderately.

Gurr - ray, gurr - ray! gur - gur - gur - gur - gur - gur, gurr - ray!

The cry "Geč aylan'" is used to bring kids back to the herd (Ex. 12).

Ex. 12. Fairly quickly.

Geč ay - lan! Ge - ca!

If it is camels that are to be rounded up, then the shepherd cries "Ey! Xau aylan!" (Ex. 13).

Ex. 13. Fairly quickly.

Ey! Xa- u ay - lan!

Camels are driven to water with the cry "Xorop, xorop!" (Ex. 14).

Ex. 14.   Moderately.

Xo - rop, xo - rop, xo - rop!   xo - ro, xo - ro, xo - ro, xo - ro xo - ro!

Finally, the odd command "Kh! kh!," with special guttural noises, is given to make camels kneel for loading (Ex. 15).

Ex. 15.   Fairly quickly.

X!   x!   Čäk,   čäk!   čäk - čäk!

Melodies of Turkmen Folk Song. The melodies of Turkmen folk songs have a rapid fire recitative structure within the bounds of an unusually limited range. More often they are based on a descending contour from the highest tone to the lowest. The structure and melody of folk songs are marked by great simplicity, which is immediately connected to their early historical origin.

Example 1 (the song for milking camels), Example 10 (the children's song to the spring rain), and Example 2 (the song for working on a hand mill) are instances of Turkmen folk song melodies of the recitative type. The range of the first two is a major second, and the third song spans a perfect fourth.

"Lele" (Ex. 8) is a typical example of the more melodic type of Turkmen folk song. It begins with a descending leap of a fourth, which defines its basic range; this is characteristic of many similar melodies. It has a descending motion slowed down by oscillating turns of phrase which delay the appearance of the tonic until the final cadence. This creates the impression of tightening in the unfolding of the melodic line, and is typical of many Turkmen tunes. Sometimes melodies end with an added exclamation and a leap of a fourth to the tonic, as can be seen in Example 5, a lullaby.

Turkmen melodies typically encompass a fourth or fifth. In two examples given above (Exs. 7, 9), the range is widened to that of a minor seventh. In both cases the sixth is lacking (Ex. 16).[8]

Ex. 16.

138

The use of the tonic only at final cadences is typical of all of the types and genres of Turkmen music, both vocal and instrumental.[9]

Scalar Basis of Turkmen Folk Song.[10] The scales of Turkmen folk song, like their melodies, are mostly narrow, rarely exceeding a fourth or fifth in range. They make up three varieties of diatonic structure: 1) major, 2) minor, and 3) minor of the Phrygian type (Ex. 17).[11] All this indicates that Turkmen folk songs represent one of the earliest historic stages of the establishment of scales.[12] We see the culmination of this process in the output of professional artists.

Ex. 17

Rhythm of Turkmen Folk Song.[13] Turning to the rhythmic basis of Turkmen folk song, it should be noted that seven-syllable trochaic tetrameter is the most widely used verse line. It is declaimed in equal durational values with lengthening of the final syllable (Ex. 18).

Ex. 18.

Ë - šel - li   ba - da, ba - da.

It may also form other melodic-rhythmic figures, such as the following: 1) prolonging of even-numbered syllables in triple time (Ex. 19):

Ex. 19.

Xüv - di,   xüv - di,   xüv - len   sin.

2) prolonging the syllables of even-numbered feet (Ex. 20):

Ex. 20.

Ya - gïš ya - ra - di, ya

and 3) prolonging of the first syllable of even-numbered feet, which leads to quintuple meter (Ex. 21).

Ex. 21

Čar - xï bet me - xrin ë - lin - den.

The augmentation of syllables facilitates a wider melodic line and, in conjunction with this, greater development of the melody of songs. We have already seen an instance of this in Example 8 ("Lele," a girls' song). The following excerpt from a girls' song can serve as an example of the use of an eleven-syllable trochaic line with prolongation of the last three syllables (Ex. 22):

Ex. 22.

Kö - če - den ge - čen - dir a - ta - sïz ya - rïm.

All of these types of folk declamation form the basis for the development of melody and rhythm of professional Turkmen vocal and instrumental compositions to be discussed below.

Poetic Verse in Turkmen Folk Song. The basic verse form of Turkmen folk song texts is the quatrain. Several varieties of quatrain have no rhymes. Sometimes there are rhymed couplets, or perhaps all four lines rhyme. But for the Turkmen, as for many other peoples of the East, the basic rhyme scheme is *aaba* with the use of textual parallelism, as can be seen in the following example:

> Near the water is a row of cherry trees.
> Berries look into the water.
> Dear Ay-qizlar,
> Give me your bright glance!

Forms of Turkmen Folk Song. The forms of Turkmen folk song are as simple as its melodic, rhythmic, and scalar basis, and consist of the simplest varieties of strophic structure. These are mostly one-part or two-part half-strophe forms. One rarely finds a two-part whole-strophe form as the musical expression of the four line verse of the song text. All of these forms are sometimes augmented by the addition of short refrains.

Among the examples given earlier we find samples of the aforementioned forms. Thus the form of Example 1 and Example 2 are one part (A) with manifold repetition of a tune in duple meter. In Example 10 this form is applied in the following way, with the complication of an added refrain: AAAA+aa. Songs 5, 8, and 9 are composed in a two-part half-strophe form of the AB type. Their refrains are sung not after every stanza, but only after the conclusion of the whole song, *i. e.*, after the final strophe. In Example 7, this form is complicated by the introduction of refrains after every part of the strophe (AaBb), which approximates the two-part whole-strophe form ABCD.

Another way of complicating the AB form can be found in the lullaby "Allalar balam" (Ex. 6). Here an independent refrain is introduced after the repetition of the basic strophe: ABAB+abc. In Example 3 an AAAB form occurs, the simplest and also the rarest type of whole-strophe form. The ABCD structure, as in Example 4, is usually typical of this form.

Turkmen Epic Art

The Turkmen Epic. The *ozan* or *uzan* was an early representative of Turkmen epic tradition. These were epic storytellers who accompanied their tales with a fiddle, the *kobuz*.[14] They were replaced by the *baxši*, professional singers who performed their repertoire to the accompaniment of the dutar, a plucked lute.[15] A Turkmen proverb characterizes the significance of ozans and baxšis in folk life: "In good times, baxšis and ozans come to the people, and in bad times, the khans with their dust," . . . . The Turkmen term ozan or uzan for epic singers is analogous to the Armenian *gusan* and Georgian *mgosani* for storytellers.[16]

Early Turkmen epic narratives, like the *Oguz-nama* ("Tale of the Oguz" [an early Turkic confederation—M. S.] concerning the mythical ancestors of the Oguz and Turkmen, were cast as recitative narratives and were not preserved. However, they survived up to modern times in the form of *destan*s, or epic-novelistic stories. Monologues and dialogues of the characters are cast in song form, as in analogous types of tales among the Kirghiz, Kazakhs, and Uzbeks. The most popular of these narratives is the heroic destan Köroğlu [Turkmen variant of the widespread Turkic Köroğlu epic tale—M. S.] named for its hero.[17] This tale originated in the sixteenth to seventeenth centuries. The figure of Köroğlu is popular not only among the Turkmen, but also among the Azerbaijanis, Uzbeks, and other peoples of Central Asia and the Caucasus.[18] Each of these peoples has its own particular variant.

The content of the Turkmen destan about Köroğli is the following story: A son named Rowšan ("bright") is born posthumously to the warrior Adi-bek. Since his mother dies at his birth, the child is named Koroglu, or "son of the grave."[19] Khan Khunkar murders Köroğli's uncle, Momin, and blinds his grandfather, Jigali-bek, Köroğlu is brought up by his grandfather and aunt, Gulandam, the widow of the murdered Momin. Arab-Reikhan, an officer of Khan Khunkar, abducts Gulandam. Köroğlu, having matured, begins to revenge himself on the fierce Khan Khunkar. He leads forty warriors and makes raids, mounted on his legendary horse Girat. He threatens the horde of Khunkar, Arab-Reikhan, and others, and is helped in this by all the Turkmen tribes. He marries the fairy Ağayunus and, not having children, adopts his favorite warrior Awaz. The Köroğlu tale reflects the striving of the Turkmen people toward union and defense of their independence. Friendship, faithfulness to one's word, bravery, honesty, and straightforwardness of character are celebrated.

Destans were highly developed among the Turkmen. There is a whole series of destans of epic-novelistic and lyric-dramatic content. The themes of these destans are often shared by other peoples of the Near East and Central Asia, or may be local. Turkmen tales with a general Oriental subject matter are *Šasenem and Ğarif, Asli and Kerem* among others.[20] Among those on local themes are *Xürlukga and Xemra* and *Saiatli Xemra*. Basically folk in origin, these tales have been elaborated by Turkmen poets. The tales enriched literature with folk subjects and enriched music with texts created for them.[21]

Turkmen Professional Vocal Art

Turkmen professional vocal art developed with close connections to professional poetry. The great achievements of Turkmen culture during the period of Merv's flourishing [the ancient cultural center of the present-day Turkmen area —M. S.] in the twelfth and thirteenth centuries formed the basis for this development. The heirs to this culture were the Turkmen poets of later times, many of whom were also composers and singers (*baxši*s).

Professional poetry developed in two directions: 1) the elaboration of poetic episodes in the destans, and 2) creation of independent heroic, lyric, and historical works among others, reflecting the poet's position on current events . . . . Poetic forms of great complexity which had been elaborated by the peoples of Central Asia and the Near East were in use.[22]

Turkmen Prosody. In their work (mostly written), Turkmen poets used fixed and rigid verse forms which involve multisyllabic verse lines of up to fifteen or more syllables per verse. These are the *murabba, ghazal* and *muxammas.* This type of prosody is called *aruz, i. e.,* "learned versification," as opposed to the folk *barmak,* or "finger versification," the lines and syllables of which are counted on the fingers.[23]

All types of verse forms have the same basic rhyme scheme, which depends on an identical word repeated after each line (A). It stems from the folk quatrain with *aaba* rhyme scheme. The ghazal strophe consists of couplets with only one rhyme for the entire poem. Both lines of the first couplet use this rhyme, and only the second line of succeeding couplets keeps it: AA, bA, cA, and so forth. The rhyme scheme of the first two couplets is the same as that of the folk *aaba* quatrain.

The murabba is a quatrain. All four lines of the first strophe have the same rhyme. The first three lines of the next verse have a new rhyme, followed by the standard rhyme of the whole poem again: *aaaA, bbbA, cccA,* and so forth. Turkmen also use another type of quatrain: *bAbA, cccA, dddA,* and so forth. The muxammas is a five-line stanza in which the rhyme scheme is the same as in the murabba, with the addition of an extra line: *aaaaA, bbbbA, ccccA,* and so forth.

Inasmuch as Turkmen poets, like other Eastern poets, disseminated their work through the oral tradition, they put their name in the last line of verse so as to become well known.[24] The development of poetry facilitated the creation of new genres and forms in Turkmen professional vocal art and the enrichment of the means of musical expression.

The Means of Musical Expression in Professional Turkmen Vocal Compositions. The melody of Turkmen professional vocal compositions became so developed and rich in terms of line and scale that it became necessary to provide the dutar with a whole chromatic octave plus an upper major second for the purposes of accompaniment, as shown in the following example (Ex. 23):[25]

Ex. 23.

Two basic melody types arose within this range: 1) a measured declamatory style, usually narrow-ranging, in a lower tessitura, and 2) a wider recitative style of melody with descending contour and a broad range beginning with the highest tones of the scale (octave or ninth) and concluding on the lower tonic.

The broadening of melodic range in Turkmen professional songs, (as opposed to folk songs), led to great enrichment of their scalar basis. In the former we see all types of diatonic scales and several varieties of chromatically altered scales, such as scales with an augmented second.

One of the characteristics of text declamation is free rhythmic treatment of lines, with copious introductions of emotional exclamations such as *ax!*, *au!*, *yar, aman, aman!* ("spare me!"), among others. Also noteworthy is the development of the strophic form in these compositions, which attain great dimensions at times due to broadening of the basic text of the strophe, and especially to the addition of refrains, which often have a quite complex vocalise style.

The following two professional compositions can serve as typical examples of structure. The first, the lyric song "Sen-sen" ("Only You"), belongs to the declamatory type, and is an excerpt from the destan *Zohra and Tahir* (Ex. 24).

Ex. 24. "Sen-sen" (Transc. E. Dimentman, 20 *Turkmenskikh narodnykh pesen*, p. 45).

Fairly quickly (♪= 144).

sün - bül - den.   Ar - zu - vï vï - sal ëy - läp,   vas - pïng, ya - za - ram til - den,

Xoš - gä - xi kö - ngül - ler - ning xem šov - xï zï - ban sen - sen.

Why do you grieve? The most beautiful one is only you.
You are a newly-blossomed flower in the garden, stately as a cypress, only you.
You are more radiant than sunshine, you, a precious gem, only you.
Your honeyed speech captured my heart, contemporary of Seiad, only you
Because of you I lost my mind, enchantress of my soul, only you.

Dreams of you encircle me like the whirlwinds of the steppe.
Everyone who sees your beauty will be stricken.
The nightingale always thinks of the rose and longs for her.
At one thought of separation he burns as in a fire.
The rose, deprived of the nightingale's strength—only you.

This song is based on the muxammas, or five-liner, with constant rhyme. According to this structure, the strophe is five-part. The form of the first stanza is ABABB. In the second strophe, melodic changes are introduced, leading to a change of the original structure, which becomes CBABB. All of the melodic phrases of this song have descending contour, thus linking them with Turkmen folk melodies. However, the general range of the melodies reaches the interval of a seventh (Ex. 25).

Ex. 25.

I couplet   II couplet

The scale of the song is Phrygian, complicated by lowering of the fourth scale degree in melismatic sequential passages, which can be seen here also as raising of the third degree. In this case the melisma is based on alternation of minor and major thirds. The verse line consists of fourteen syllables. It is divided by a caesura into two hemistiches of seven plus seven syllables. The acceleration of the third and fourth syllables of each hemistich leads to an interesting rhythmic figure, which is maintained throughout the song (Ex. 26).[26] The instrumental accompaniment to the piece is based on free use of parallel fourths.[27]

Ex. 26

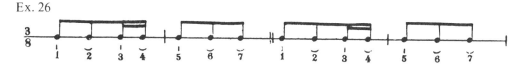

"Atčapar" ("The Horseman") is a typical example of the melodic recitative manner of the professional vocal style (Ex. 27).[28]

Ex. 27. "Atčapar" (Transc. V. Uspenskii, *Turkmenskaia muzyka*, # 54).   Moderately.

147

gü,   gü.

Ax!   Ma - nga

bir mü - zir at - lï diy - ip,   ay,   vay,   vay,   vay,

vay,   vay,   vay,   vay,   ag - la

- rïn

Pe - lek, ay - vay!

151

Pïragïng oduna günde yanar men, Xïsrav aydar günüm ax bilen gečer,
Čarxï pelek deiyn yüz müng dönermen, Bir gün ajal gelip, kepenim bičer,
Perimden ayrïlan garïp bende men, Özum ölenim-song čiragïm öčer,
Manga bir müzir-atlï gül diyp aglarïn. Manga ogul-atlï gül diyip aglarïn.

My life burns in the fire of separation.
The vault of heaven encircled me a thousand times since this separation began
I am unfortunate, separated from my fairy
I weep for the flower taken away from me.

I, Khusrau, say "My day is passed in sights.
My hour of death will come and I will be wrapped in a shroud.
I await the time when the flame of my line will expire.
And I weep that I don't have a son to prolong it."

The title of the song does not correspond to its lyrical content. This is explained by the fact that the melody was formerly known with a different text, by the poet Khusrau, from which it has received its name. Sometimes poetic excerpts from the tale *Xürlukga and Xemra* are sung to this tune.

"Atčapar" is one of the outstanding compositions of Turkmen professional art both in musical content and in form. The piece begins with a dutar introduction (I) in which the basic tonality of the stanza (up to the refrain) is given: C-major and e-minor. The second strophe (II), basically the same, has a wide and free melodic contour. The text of the verse is a quatrain (murabba) with an eleven-syllable line. This verse is musically expressed in a two-part form with ABCD structure, and has free melodic structure of the recitative type with insertions of added syllables into the line, introductory cries (*aa* and *BB*) and internal refrains (*a* and *B*) for the first two lines of text. The preservation in both halves of the stanza of the tonal sequence C-major-e-minor creates a quite complex structure for the whole stanza:

form: (aa + A + a) + (B + b) + (bb + C) + D
rhythmic structure: (4 + 5 + 5) + (8 + 8) + (4 + 3) + 5
scalar alternation: C-major-e-minor-C-major-e-minor

The melody of the stanza displays descending contour in the Phrygian scale, with an altered second step (Ex. 28).

Ex. 28.

The last beat of the strophe begins a well elaborated refrain, which can be divided on tonal grounds into three divisions (III, IV, and V). The first of these (III) is built on rising-falling sequences of a vocalise nature which begin in e-minor and end in C-major. This section broadens the scalar basis of the opening of the song by two lower tones (Ex. 29).

Ex. 29.

In the second section of the refrain (IV) the basic tonality of the piece (Phrygian a-minor) is confirmed with new melodic material; this is also the tonality of the third section of the refrain, its coda (V, Ex. 30).

Ex. 30.

Thus the tonal plan of this song is based on modulation from an incomplete e-minor Phrygian to an incomplete a-minor Phrygian a fifth lower through intermediary incomplete Ionian (Mixolydian?) C-major, as can be seen in this scheme (Ex. 31):[29]

Ex. 31.

Vocal compositions of the professional type, called *aydim*s (literally, "narratives"; the verb with the general meaning of "to speak" is also used in the sense of "to sing" among many peoples), are marked by great emotional rises and expression. Holds and cries on high tones sound intensely expressive. The refrains, with their own characteristic elaboration of sounds and timbres, are no less expressive. There are two types of these refrains, distinguished by their manner of performance: refrains on the syllable "gü" and those on the syllables "i-ki-ki." The first has a softer shading, while the second approaches a convulsive staccato. These manners of refrain performance testify to the preservation of very ancient artistic types of voice production in the work of Turkmen baxšis, who carry on a rich musical tradition.[30]

Turkmen Poetry and Music in the Eighteenth Century. The age-old union of Turkmen professional poetry and music received fresh stimulus in the eighteenth century. This was connected with the growth of patriotic feelings brought out by the struggle with the bloodthirsty invasions of Nadir Shah (1736-1747) . . . .

Maxtum-quli (1730-1782). Maxtum-quli, the father of modern Turkmen literature, was the outstanding representative of this movement and had great influence on the art of the baxšis. He was the son of Azadi, a major poet. He was educated in a medrese in Khiva. He was a peasant and also an artisan (harnessmaker and silversmith). His travels through the Near East are documented . . . .

The work of Maxtum-quli, rich in poetic genres, served as the basis for the creation of innumerable professional vocal compositions and as an important stage in the development of Turkmen music culture. "Jenan yarïm" ("My Wonderful Friend") can be introduced as an example of the musical embodiment of Maxtum-quli's poetry. The poem was written during the Persian attack on Sangu Dag, often visited by the poet, which he had to leave for a while. The poem's tone of warm love for native haunts, expressed in striking folk verse, led to the creation of an expressive, wide ranging melody. It is particularly original in its alternation between the Phrygian scale and a similar scale with augmented second step (Ex. 32).

The eighteenth century was a time of great development in Turkmen poetry. In this period other great poets also appeared who influenced music.

Ex. 32. "Jenan yarïm!" (Transc. V. Uspenskii). Moderately (♩.-96)

155

Ay sevdigim Songngi-dagï	O my beloved Sangu Dag!
Dagdanlïdïr bilen sening!	*Dagdan* grass grows on your crest.
Dušman görse döv dier,	If the enemy sees it, he will be frightened,
Yomut, gökleng iling sening.	For here live the Yomud and Goklen tribes.
Kesgin, kesgin yolïn gečer,	Your roads are quite steep.
Kïzïl biyir gövün ačar,	Your red slopes gladden the heart.
Sovük češme suvïn ičer,	You give the traveler water from your cold springs.
Dürli-dümen malïng sening,	Innumerable flocks graze upon you.
Dürli-dümen otïng biter	Various grasses grow on you,
Xer dergäng bir ile eter.	Tribes take shelter in each of your valleys.
Xatarlanšïp, kerven öter,	Caravans move across you, stretched out like a ribbon.
Naybadaydïr yoling sening.	Let Naibaday come to you across the mountain pass.
Öylükde yaylanï gürsak,	When we go to the *yeilāq* for summer pastures,
At čapdïrïp, bayrak bersek,	When we win prizes at the races,
Töreyitde xarman gursak,	When we build haystacks in the Toreit valley
Nan dekme xïyalïng sening.	Then we know you have only one thought: to give us as much bread as possible.
Magdïmgulï set ačandïr,	Maxtum-kuli stands on the road to the grave, ,
Bu dövran senden gečendir,	Having passed his whole life on you.
Üstünden iling gečendir,	His tribe wanders across you
Ničik gečer xalïng sening?	So, how are you yourself?

Turkmen Instrumental Music

Turkmen Musical Instruments.[31]   The Turkmen instrumentarium is similar to that of the other Central Asian nomadic peoples, though it has its own distinguishing features. It consists basically of stringed instruments (*ğičak* and *dutar*), wind instruments (*tüiduk* and *dili-tüiduk*), and an idiophone, the *gopiz*.

The *ğičak* is a fiddle with a round body.[32] It has three strings tuned in fourths and the following possible scale (Ex. 33):[33]

Ex. 33

156

The ğičak is used by the Turkmen both in monophonic and two-voiced music (based on parallel fourths). The dutar is a two-stringed, plucked lute with a tuning in fourths, frets, and the aforementioned chromatic scale with an upper major second on each string (Ex. 34).[34]

Ex. 34.

The dutar is the most frequently used instrument of Turkmenia. It is widely used in the performance of solo pieces and for accompanying songs.

The tüidük is an end-blown flute related to the Kirghiz čoor, the Kazakh sibizgi, and similar instruments of many other peoples. It is distinguished by a more complex scale, which includes chromatic steps. The six fingerholes of the tüidük, plus overblowing, give the following scale, which can also be extended above (though this is not practical, Ex. 35):

Ex. 35.

basic register

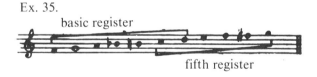

fifth register

Tüidüks are made in pairs with the same tuning, since works for this instrument are usually performed by two musicians in unison both for solo play or for accompanying songs.

The *dili-tüidük* is a reed pipe of the clarinet type which is close in construction to the Russian *zhaleika* and related instruments.[35] It usually has three or four fingerholes, but its range can be stretched to an octave by performers. The gopiz is a jew's-harp. It is used by Turkmen women and children. A comparison of the scales of the ğičak, dutar, and tüidük shows that they have the same basis (Ex. 36).[36]

Ex. 36.

Turkmen Instrumental Music. Turkmen musicians created a professional instrumental style parallel to and no less interesting than the related vocal style. Three basic steps can be distinguished in its development: 1) the repertoire of the dili-tüidük and ǧičak, which is close to the melody and structure of folk songs; 2) pieces for tüidük, which formed an instrumental analogy to professional vocal compositions, with broad descending melodic contours; and 3) works for dutar, characterized by a new type of three-part rondo composition which belongs to the largest and most highly developed repertoire of Turkmen music.

Melodies for Dili-tüidük. The dili-tüidük was originally a pastoral instrument, and it is mostly pastoral tunes and folk songs that are performed on it. Sometimes melodies for this instrument approach the style of professional vocal music, but in a more laconic form. The melody "Durnalar" ("Cranes") is of this type (Ex. 37).[37]

Ex. 37. "Durnalar" (Transc. V. Uspenskii. *Turkmenskaia muzyka* # 34.). Moderately (♩.₁₄₄).

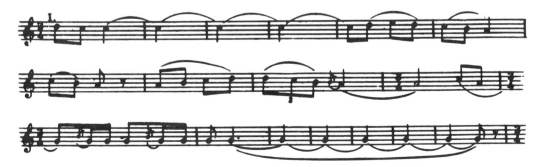

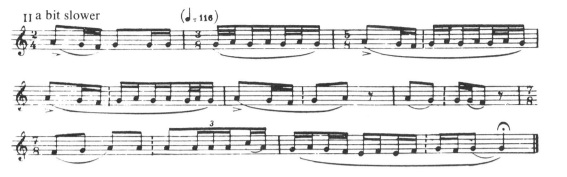

This piece is cast in the typical two-part structure of professional vocal compositions and has a wide descending melody. It is connected to the poetic image of the crane, a free and beautiful bird to whom the hero of Turkmen tales, separated from his loved ones, turns, asking the bird to carry a message about his fate.[38]

Pieces for Ğičak. Pieces for the Turkmen fiddle, the ğičak, are more legato than those for dutar, with the latter's abbreviated sounds. They approach folk songs in melodic make-up. A special technique on this instrument is the use of grace notes, which gives ğičak melodies a distinctive character. Ğičak pieces are programmatic. Both in theme and general content they are similar to other types of Turkmen instrumental music.[39] Polyphony is sporadically used, basically involving parallel fourths. "Garïplïk" ("Need") can serve as an example of ğičak pieces with simple song structure and social-daily-life content (Ex. 38).

Ex. 38. "Garïplïk" (Transc. V. Uspenskii, *Turkmenskaia muzyka* #105).   Moderately ($\bullet$=120).

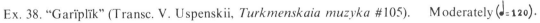

159

Pieces for Tüidük. Tüidük pieces are built like professional vocal compositions, with descending melodic contours. They are often instrumental versions of these songs, and preserve all the detail of the songs. In original form the melodies given here are performed in unison by two tüidüks. The piece is preceded by a lower-register introduction common to several different pieces. Tüidük pieces are named for the original songs, and have the same structure and mood. Broad descending melodies, beginning in the upper register, are often cast in a recitative vein and end with refrain-like turns of phrase. "Badï saba" ("Morning Breeze") is a typical example of tüidük pieces (Ex. 39).

Ex. 39. "Badï saba" (Transc. V. Uspenskii, *Turkmenskaia muzyka* #25).   Moderately ♩_80 .

161

Example 39 presents a lyric episode from the tale *Xürlukga and Xemra* in which Xemra, separated from Xürlukga, turns to the morning breeze with the request of carrying regards to his beloved:

> O morning breeze, carry my greetings to dear Xürlukga, carry my lament to the ears of my beloved!
>
> My beloved plunged me into sadness. I, like a nightingale in a cage, cannot fly to my friend. Tell her this. I would like to be a ray of light for my beloved, whose mouth is like a pistachio and whose lips are like sugar.
>
> My name is Xemra. No one hears my sighs. Maybe you, morning breeze, will take them to my dear Xürlukga.

The song consists of an introduction with fivefold presentation of a basic strophe with variants. It is in the Mixolydian scale, with a final cadence on the third scale degree.[40]

Pieces for Dutar. Compositions for dutar are an important and interesting subdivision of Turkmen music. They are rich in content, artistic significance, imagery, and mastery of developed forms. The basic structure of dutar pieces is a three part recapitulation form with the following divisions: 1) exposition of the main theme in the lower register; 2) middle section in the register a fifth higher; and 3) recapitulation in the original register. The tonal relations of parts of the piece arising from this form are the same as those in professional vocal works, but with a different type of alternation of scalar levels: in vocal works they descend, while in instrumental works they ascend and descend. A striking (and at the same time laconic) example of the typical structure of dutar works is "Bäri gel" ("Come to Me"), which has a programmatic-lyrical character (Ex. 40).[41]

163

The form of this piece consists of three parts. It begins with an exposition (I) of the main theme with descending contour in folk song style. This theme is cast in an incomplete Phrygian scale (a-minor), which is basic to the whole piece (Ex. 41).

Ex. 41

The theme is accompanied by quartal harmony, with free use of parallel fourths. After the exposition comes the middle part (II). The theme is sounded above a drone of the lower open string of the dutar, which is the tonic of the predominant tonality (e-minor). "Bäri gel'" features the rare use of the main theme for the middle section. Equally rare is the changing of the scalar basis of the theme, specifically its treatment in the Aeolian, rather than in the Phrygian, scale (Ex. 42).

Ex. 42.

After a full presentation of the theme in the middle section, a sequential transition in triple time leads to the recapitulation (III), consisting of full repetition of the exposition. The overall tonal plan of "Bäri gel'" is the following (Ex. 43):

Ex. 43.

It is made up of two narrow scale structures with different intervals; the tonics are separated by a fifth.

The example given above as typical of Turkmen dutar pieces is extremely concise in thematic material, and this is why it was chosen.[42] More often, both the exposition and middle section of these pieces undergo significantly greater development. Nevertheless, it must be said that "Bäri gel'," despite the laconicism of its musical expression, is characterized by exceptional unity and belongs to the best productions of Turkmen folk music. "Kïrklar" ("Forty") can serve as an example of the developed form for dutar. Its content derives from one of the episodes of the tale *Šasenem and Garib*. Each of the divisions of this impulsive and exciting piece undergoes significant internal growth (Ex. 44).[43]

The exposition of the piece (I) contains three themes in a-minor with augmented second above the lowered second step (A, B, C). In the middle section (II) two themes are given (D, E) in the predominant tonality, e-minor, after which a return to the original tonality appears (beginning with the episode marked F). The recapitulation of the whole piece (III) itself has a complex three part structure; after a short appearance of one of the main themes (A), an episode in the mediant tonality (c-minor) is introduced (G), followed by final presentation of the exposition (ACB).[44]

Ex. 44. "Kïrklar" (Transc. V. Uspenskii, *Turkmenskaia muzyka* #45).   Quickly ($\stackrel{}{}$=138)

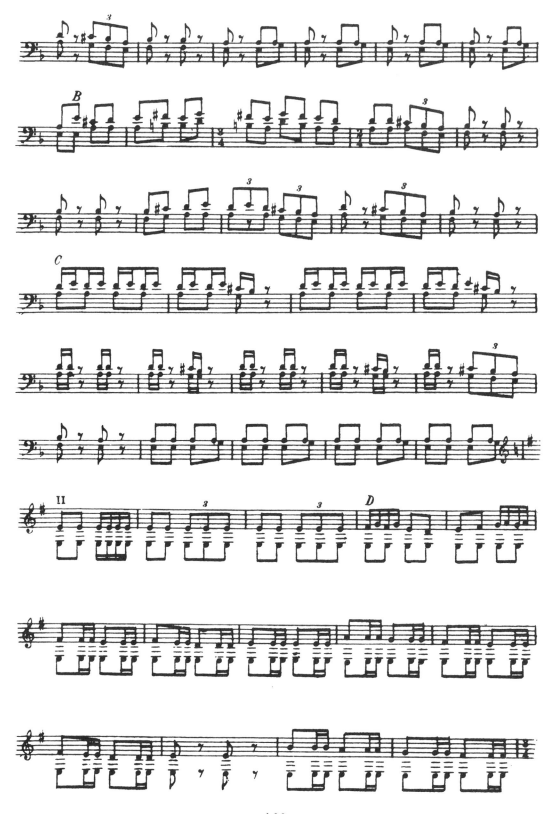

166

167

168

169

In all other types of Turkmen music the high point comes at the beginning, and the whole development of musical thought is connected to the gradual release of emotional tension toward the end; in dutar music the culmination shifts to the center, which strengthens the dynamic tension.

As a rule pieces for dutar are programmatic and strongly reflect the feelings and experience, way of life, and history of the Turkmen people, as well as literary subjects. In musical terms they are examples of great compositional and performing mastery. The two-voiced element of dutar pieces represents a significant step in the development of national polyphony . . . .[45]

Notes to Chapter III

1. This illustrates the fact of Kirghiz-Kazakh isolation from Near Eastern influence and underscores the intermediate position of the Turkmen, who belong on the one hand to the world of Central Asian pastoral nomadism and on the other to the Near East. They are the only one of the peoples described in the present book to live in the Soviet Union, Iran, and Afghanistan today; comparative Turkmen musical studies are just barely beginning.

As for Beliaev's view of Near Eastern influence on Turkmen music, it is clearly expressed in his 1928 book (with Uspenskii), in which he devoted Chapter 6 to the question of outside influence on Turkmen music. Such views were later disparaged in Soviet ethnomusicology (cf. Kon, 1961: 135).

2. Beliaev here modestly discounts his own considerable role in the publication of *Turkmenskaia muzyka*, of which he was coauthor. Uspenskii provided the basic transcriptions and travel notes, while Beliaev wrote the entire commentary on the music. *Turkmenskaia muzyka* is still the landmark, indeed the only, study of the music culture of the Turkmen of the USSR.

3. Beliaev (1928: 36) formulated the following six basic genres of Turkmen music: religious, disappointed love, military (including bandit and hunting), love, healing ("not without a shamanistic tinge"), and historical. This division by theme has been replaced by the functional classification current in Soviet ethnomusicology.

4. The examples which follow (Exs. 1-15, except Ex. 6) are quite valuable in that they were done by Uspenskii in the 1920s, and they represent types of songs not included in *Turkmenskaia muzyka* or other Soviet publications.

5. Silk weaving, mentioned in Example 3, is an important cottage industry in traditional Turkmen society. For information on Turkmen handicrafts (as practiced in Afghanistan today), see Dupaigne (1968).

6. This song is from the area of Merv, once a great capital along the Silk Route, which flourished until the Mongol conquest (1220). According to Uspenskii (see Uspenskii and Beliaev, 1928: 120) the song was performed by a professional musician who learned it from his mother, and it consists of two lullabies combined.

7. This interesting Turkmen custom of wife-avoidance is thoroughly described in William Iron's (1969) valuable study of the Yomut Turkmen of Iran. The period between marriage and the establishment of a joint household may last up to four years until the wife finally leaves her father's tent for her husband's.

8. This is a rather odd passage, in that Example 7 does not extend beyond a fifth, and Example 9 does include the sixth scale degree (*d-sharp"*).

9. Here Beliaev apparently means final cadences of large phrases, not of whole songs or pieces, as a return to tonic at the end of segments of a work is strongly characteristic of dutar music, and serves as a major formal marker.

10. In *Turkmenskaia muzyka* (*see* Uspenskii and Beliaev, 1928: Chapter 10) Beliaev cites data from Uspenskii's informants which indicate a strong Near Eastern influence in Turkmen music, including at least the rudiments of theoretical modal structures (not clearly defined) with such terms as *maqām, parde,* and others being used; none of this is mentioned in the present volume.

11. In the music of the Turkmen of Afghanistan, the "Phrygian" scale (that with a half step between first and second pitches) is by far more common than either major or minor scales. For a more thorough discussion of Turkmen scales, including nondiatonic varieties, *see Ibid.*: Chapter 11.

12. This is a clear statement of Beliaev's evolutionary theory of scale development, supported by such scholars as Sachs (1962), but not by the present editor.

13. The following discussion of the meters and verse forms of Turkmen folk poetry is among the most valuable sections of Beliaev's presentation, as it is virtually unparalleled and probably reflects Beliaev's first-hand experience with Turkmen materials.

14. This is a rare citation of the use of the kobuz, a basic Central Asian nomadic fiddle-type (*see* Chapter 2) by the Turkmen, who later took up the Arabic-Persian spike fiddle of the *rebab-kemancǎ* type under the name *ǧičak* (a term probably of Persian origin). The term *kobuz* (or kobiz) is still used by the Kazakhs for their horsehair fiddle, and is still in limited use in Afghanistan among urban Uzbeks and Tajiks as a shaman fiddle, but for the most part it has gone out of use among the sedentary Central Asian peoples.

15. The term *baxši* has a fascinating history. Apparently originating from the Chinese (Poppe, 1965), it has had varied use among Turkic peoples, finally settling down to mean professional musicians among the Turkmen and shamans among the Kazakhs and Kirghiz (as well as urban Uzbeks and Tajiks in Afghan Turkestan); whether Turkmen baxšis were originally also shamans is a moot point, awaiting further evidence. *Baxši* is also used to mean an epic singer among Turkmen and Uzbeks.

16. It is possible that these various terms all stem from quite old minstrel traditions, *e. g.*, the Parthian *gosan.*

17. For the most thorough recent study of the Köroğlu epic, including all its variants among Turkic peoples, *see* Karryev (1968).

18. "The Turkmen version [of the Köroğlu—M. S.] is an intermediate link between the Azerbaijan and Uzbek versions" (Zhirmunsky in Chadwick and Zhirmunsky, 1969: 303). Here we find a literary reflection of the role of the Turkmen as a trans-Caspian bridge, linking the Turkic Azerbaijanis (and through them the Ottoman Turks) to the Central Asian Turkic peoples, particularly the Uzbeks. It is possible that the Near Eastern imprint on Turkmen music also traveled *via* this route.

19. "The original name was 'Köroğlu,' meaning 'son of a blind man.' Later on this name was endowed with a fabulous folk etymology which is characteristic of all Central Asian versions: Goroghli is the 'son of the grave' *(gur-),* born in the grave of a dead mother" (Zhrimunsky in Chadwick and Zhirmunsky, 1969:302).

20. Zhirmunsky (*see* Chadwick and Zhirmunsky, 1969: 336) considers *Asli and Kerem* one of a series of "more modern romances, traceable to literary sources," which is what Beliaev means by "epic-novelistic" works.

21. The interplay between folk and literary plots and style is a fascinating but little studied area of Near Eastern and Central Asian literature.

22. Here Beliaev is referring to the classic Arabic-Persian scheme of verse meters and structures known as *aruz.*

23. On the question of Turkic adoption of the Arabic-Persian aruz system of versification, Meredith-Owens (1939: 677) has the following relevant observations:

> The adoption by the Turks of the Perso-Arabic metrical system was facilitated, not only by a genuine admiration for Persian *belle-lettres*, but also by the resemblance which the ancient Turkish method of versification [*parmak hisabi* equals Beliaev's "barmak" — M. S.] bore to the Arud meters. Both the original and the Arud systems enjoyed a parallel existence until the former was ousted by the latter during the XVth century. The main difference between the two forms is that in the parmak hisabi the verses were based not on quantity but on the number and beat of the syllables. The old system survived only in the folk-poetry of Anatolia.

Perhaps the old system also survived in the folk songs of the Turkic peoples of Central Asia; at least Beliaev's (and other Soviet) analyses indicate that syllable number predominates over quantity in Turkic folk poetry of Central Asia. This folk disinterest in quantitative verse can also be seen in the disparity between folk and literary prosody in Tajik verse (*see* Chapter 4).

24. It seems more likely that the Turkmen simply adopted the feature of *taxalos* ("use of pen name in the last line") directly from Persian versification.

25. This is a quite common Turkmen rhythmic figure.

26. Here Beliaev's belief in the primacy of vocal music is well illustrated, as part of his evolutionary theory of music cultures.

27. Like the majority of Soviet transcriptions of Turkmen music, Example 24 presents an unusually short and straight forward piece.

28. Uspenskii (*see* Uspenskii and Beliaev, 1928: 128) translated the title of this song as "The Horse Gallops." The song was performed by the twenty-eight-year-old Nobat Aman Sexet baxši of Taxtabazar in an area of the Sariq Turkmen.

29. My own analysis of the piece would differ somewhat from Beliaev's. The song, as noted in connection with the previous example, seems somewhat short, in that there is usually considerably more melodic development, change of registers, infix of dutar interludes, and the like in fully developed Turkmen songs. Notwithstanding, it would seem to me that Example 27 can be looked at in terms of larger structural units than Beliaev's. Basically there are two divisions: 1) the projection of text, and 2) what Beliaev calls the refrain, *i. e.*, the section based on vocalise starting from his III. His section V is a kind of coda which repeats the last line of text. In this scheme, the "refrain" consists tonally merely of a long involuted sequence (typically Turkmen) down the fifth from *e'-a*, with the "coda" (V) affirming the basic motion and lower end of the melodic range twice. The first section (Beliaev's I and II) plays with the upper range (*b'* down to *e'*) with considerable stress on *g'*, the third scale degree. The overall pattern just described for Example 27 seems a bit anomalous for Turkmen songs, which more often rely on continual departures from and returns to the lowest pitch, which can be taken as tonic. As for Beliaev's e-minor and C-major, such designations for individual pentachords or tetrachords seem unnecessary.

30. Turkmen vocal style is unique and extraordinary in the range of sounds employed. All of the various guttural sounds produced are considered as *gul* ("ornament"), at least by Afghan Turkmen, and there is a fair amount of indigenous typology for nonlanguage sounds. For more on this subject, *see* Uspenskii in Uspenskii and Beliaev (1928: 83-88), Rejepov (1966: 18) or, in English, Spector (1967: 448). None of these, however, offers more than brief glimpses into the complex world of Turkmen voice production.

31. For further information on Turkmen instruments, *see* the *Atlas* (1963: 115-17, Plates 551-66) and for instruments of the Turkmen of Afghanistan, *see* Slobin (1969b).

32. This ğičak, like that of the sedentary Uzbeks and Tajiks of Soviet Central Asia, is a variant of the Persian kamancha, as noted above; however, the same term is also used for a different type of fiddle used by mountain Tajiks of the USSR and Afghanistan and urban Uzbeks and Tajiks of Af-

ghanistan. The term may derive from Persian *ǧič* ("squeak") + *ak*, a diminutive suffix; in some areas the term is pronounced "*čiǧak*." To complicate the picture the term "*ǧičak*" is also mixed in usage with *sarinda* or *saranda* in the Herat area and among some Baluchi and Paštun speakers of Afghanistan. The vexing *ǧičak* question is only one of many complex examples of floating terms for musical instruments in the Afghanistan-southern Central Asia area.

33.   Again, Beliaev feels that a fretless fiddle can have a "possible scale."

34.   "Most Afghan Turkmen dutars have a completely chromatic scale without the whole-step placement of the top fret mentioned in the *Atlas*. Some Turkmen lutes of Afghanistan feature a different fretting, namely that of the Uzbek dutar, with whole steps between the fourth and fifth and eighth and ninth scale degrees." (Slobin, 1969b: 111).

35.   The closest relative of the dili-tüidük is the Uzbek *sibizik*, a reed pipe of similar dimension and description. The dili-tüidük, sibizik, and zhaleika are rather rare in being one pipe, single-reed aerophones, as most of the wind instruments of this type found across the Near East and the Balkans are paired.

36.   Such comparisons of scales are common in Beliaev's work, but seem to be at best highly theoretical constructs inasmuch as 1) the *ǧičak* is fretless, 2) the dutar has moveable frets, and 3) performers on the tüidük can hit almost any pitch they like through various techniques. Beliaev's interest in showing uniformity of scale construction is part of his general theory of scale derivation and historical development, presented in English in Beliaev (1935).

37.   Uspenskii (*see* Uspenskii and Beliaev, 1928: 114) states that "Durnalar" is adapted from a song in the tale *Saiatli xemra*. It was performed by Khoja Nazar Berdi Mamedov, a shepherd and amateur musician (*ibid.*, 111), in Merv.

38.   The long descending line and division into two rhythmically contrasting sections of Example 37 match the characteristics of some dili-tüidük pieces of northern Afghanistan.

39.   The *ǧičak* has practically disappeared among the Turkmen of Afghanistan. The suggestion of programmatic pieces for *ǧičak* is a hint of a link between Turkmen fiddle styles and those of the Kazakhs and Kirghiz, but it is not clear what Beliaev means by "programmatic" here.

40.   It strikes me that the tonal material consists of the fifth b'-f', in which b' is an undisputed tonic, rather than third-step "stand-in" for a supposed g' tonic. The "Phrygian" pentachord b'-f' is quite common in Turkmen music.

41.   "Bäri gel'" was transcribed from Bek Murat, a professional musician of Merv who told Uspenskii (*see* Uspenskii and Beliaev, 1928: 108) that the song from which the dutar version was taken had text by Navai. Uspenskii called the piece a "masterpiece" (*ibid.*).

42.   I chose "Bäri gel'" as an example of Turkmen dutar style (Slobin, 1969a) for the same reason of conciseness; however, it almost appears that "Bäri gel'" is an abridged verion of a piece Uspenskii (who notated by ear) heard, and its structure is surprisingly simple. Compare, for example, the length and complexity of "Bäri gel'" with the next example, "Kïrklar" (Ex. 44). The most salient feature of "Bäri gel'" is perhaps its wavering rhythm, typical of many dutar pieces.

43.   Uspenskii's notes for this piece (*see* Uspenskii and Beliaev, 1928: 127) are of particular interest. He feels it may display Azerbaijani characteristics, which ties in with the trans-Caspian connections alluded to earlier (note 18). Another interesting point raised by Uspenskii in connection with "Kïrklar" is that the name of the piece ("Forty") is thought to represent the number of its variants among the Turkmen tribes. Soviet Turkmen, however, feel that today such variations have vanished. Nevertheless, an Ersari Turkmen musician in Afghanistan told me that he did not like the music played over Soviet Turkmen radio because it was predominantly music of tribes other than his own (mainly Teke). Unfortunately, no thoroughgoing study of tribal differences in music was made when such variation in taste held for the majority of Turkmen.

173

44. Example 44 is a fine specimen of virtuoso dutar characteristics: 1) high speed of performance; 2) sudden, precise changes in rhythmic figuration; 3) long, involuted passages in the higher register which delay return to the tonic (lowest) level for maximum effect; and 4) alternation of drone and parallel fourths, with intermediate, almost contrapuntal, passages also present. This, of course, is only one side of the many-faceted world of the Turkmen dutar.

45. Across Central Asia, the presence of instrumental polyphony has been a boon to Soviet musicians seeking to create and disseminate Western-style polyphonic music as part of musical modernization. Thus, for example, a polyphonic choral piece might be based on the drone and parallel-interval playing of the dutar as a starting point for vocal polyphony, hitherto lacking in Central Asia.

Beliaev's Bibliography

Antologiia turkmenskoi poezii. Moscow, 1949.

Lobachev, Gr. *Turkmenskie pesni dlia golos s f-p*. Moscow, 1937.

Makhtum-quli. *Izbrannye stikhi*. Moscow, 1948.

Saryev, P. (transcribed by E. Dimentman). *20 Turkmenskikh narodnykh pesen* (in Turkmen) Baku, 1946.

Siniaver, L. *Turkmenskaia SSR. Seriia Muzykal'naia kul'tura soiuznykh respublik*. Moscow, 1955.

Uspenskii, V. and Beliaev, V. *Turkmenskaia muzyka*. Moscow, 1928.

It would be useful to add to this bibliography, but to the best of my knowledge Beliaev's listing represents the complete available body of works related to traditional (*i.e.*, pre-Soviet) Turkmen music in the USSR with the exception of one brief biographical pamphlet about a Turkmen musician (*Sakhi Jepbarov*, by S. Rejepov. Moscow: Muzyka, 1966), and the possible existence of works in Turkmen of which I am not aware. For music of Afghan Turkmens, *see* Slobin (1975).

The Music Culture of Tajikistan

The Development of Tajik Music in the Pre-Soviet Period. The music of the Tajiks in the pre-Soviet period, as of the other Central Asian peoples, developed as an unwritten art. However, whereas the music of the nomadic peoples (Kirghiz, Kazakhs, Turkmen) was almost undocumented, there is ample evidence for the music of the Tajiks, an old settled people. The data relate mostly to professional Tajik music, which arose quite early and attained a high level of development under conditions of urban life. Treatises on the theory and history of music occupy an important place in literary sources.

Various types of peasant songs and instrumental music served as the basis for Tajik professional music. Three local styles were defined: 1) that of Northern Tajikistan (Leninabad region), aligned with Bukhara, 2) that of the Pamirs, and 3) that of the western mountain regions (Garm, Kulab, Hissar). The last two, due to their location in inaccessible mountain regions of Tajikstan, preserved a number of quite ancient traits. The abundance of old strata and the simultaneous rich development of art music created the basis for the Tajik music culture, with its great variety of styles and genres. The birth and growth of Tajik music was linked to the historical conditions of the formation of the Tajik people. . . .

The process of formation of the Uzbek people, who speak a Turkic language, paralleled the development of the Tajiks on adjacent, and sometimes common, territory. As a result of these historical conditions a significant segment of both the Tajik and Uzbek populations spoke in two languages (Tajik and Uzbek) and the two peoples created their culture in close contact. From this stems the great similarity between these two cultures as a whole, and in the areas of poetry and music in particular.

175

THE BASES FOR THE DEVELOPMENT OF TAJIK MUSIC CULTURE

Tajik Folk Songs

Genres of Tajik Folk Song. Tajik folk art is based on work songs such as songs for plowing, reaping, and threshing, strongly linked to aspects of the agricultural way of life. Parallel to this arose artisans' songs, the songs of potters, blacksmiths, and representatives of other crafts. The connection between agriculture and metal-working is strikingly expressed in the text of the following song:

Oh you sickle, sickle!
Uncle sickle, sickle!
Ringing and jagged
Old iron sickle.

My father brought it
As a new stone
From Kastut, from Xostau
From Yagid-kulband.

My father threw the stone
Into the heart of a hot oven.
Mother brought brushwood.
Oh you sickle, sickle.

The stone blazed all night
And blossomed like a tulip.
The whole night the stone trickled
To the bottom of the smelting furnace.

Oh you sickle, sickle!
Uncle sickle, sickle!

Father collected the iron
From the bottom of the smelting furnace
The stone became malleable
Flat, bare, and black

Then it was beaten and flattened.
Oh you iron sickle!
Bent, wrapped, and sharpened.
Oh you sickle, sickle!

Bright as the moon
He runs along the wheat fields.
A man stumbles;
He runs along the wheat fields.

"Who are you, little man?"
"I am the iron sickle."
"Who are you, little man?"
"Old uncle sickle."

"Az kosagaron" ("From the Potters") can serve as an example of a humorous craft song with a cumulative, rapid-fire refrain (Ex. 1).

Ex. 1. "Az Kosagaron" (*Muzyka tajikov*, p. 107). Quickly.

176

The potters have a cup.
The pitcher-makers have a pitcher.
    Refrain: The cup and pitcher are in my hands
          Yalalum, grandfather, yalallah!

The carpenters have a saw.
The sheep-sellers have a sheep.
    Refrain: Cup, pitcher, saw and sheep are in my hands
          Yalala, etc.

The barbers have a razor.
The weavers have a shuttle.
    Refrain: Cup, pitcher, etc.

177

The wine-grape merchants have wine grapes.
The blacksmiths have a chain.
                  Refrain: Cup, pitcher, etc.

Other types of work songs include pastoral and domestic songs, the latter mostly about women's work. Many Tajik work songs develop the theme of social protest, as well as lyricism, satire, and other themes. In the women's song "Ašulai bofandagi" ("Weaving Song"), the position of Tajik women in prerevolutionary times is depicted in deeply expressive images (Ex. 2).

Ex. 2. "Ašulai bofandagi." (From materials in the Republic House of folk arts of the Tajik SSR.)   Fairly quickly ($\downarrow$ = 126).

Az sa-har to - šom po - čak me - za-nam - dar čah - ča-haq, Qo - ma-tam no - tob šud az rūz - ǧo - ri zin - da-gī. Zin - da-go - ni dar ja hon xor as - tu ḏar po sū - zan ast, Di - la-kam ǧam - gin šud az in ba-ho - ri zin - da - gī, Di - la-kam ǧam - gin šud az in ba-ho - ri zin - da - gī.

My heart's blood curdles from the sound of the loom.
My eyes are full of tears from broken threads.
From dawn to dawn I push my foot into the hole on which the loom stands
I live as if walking on thistles and needles.
My heart is sad in the spring of my life.

179

Tajik ceremonial songs can be divided into 1) practical and 2) family songs. Practical songs include songs of ceremonies of the agricultural routine, usually holiday songs, and incantations to the forces of nature, e. g., calls for rain during drought, purification by fire (jumping over bonfires), or water (bathing), and healing ceremonies. Most commonly the Tajiks celebrated the ceremony of calling in spring ([*gulgardani*; "flower-gazing"—M. S.]) and New Year's (*nowruz*), also marked during spring.[1]

The ceremony of calling in the spring included the following: groups of youths with huge bouquets of various flowers (snowdrops, irises, tulips) surrounded the houses of the village and sang congratulatory carol-like songs to the accompaniment of the dutar and tambourine. On this holiday the day concluded with a *bazm*, an evening with refreshments and the appearance of singers, musicians, dancers, and *masxarabāz* (folk comedians and wits).[2]

The celebration of nowruz took place on the day of the vernal equinox and followed the ceremony of calling in the spring. It consisted of a large folk promenade ([*sail*; "show"—M. S.]) organized in the outskirts of the village. During this promenade refreshments were organized, for which provisions had been gathered from every home selected by respectable "masters of ceremonies." After the appearance of the singers, dancers, and musicians various folk games and entertainments took place, such as wrestling, walking on stilts, riding, and cracking of eggs[3] as well as fortunetelling by various methods.

Characteristics of ancient spring rituals were preserved until recent times in the "tulip holiday" (*lola*) described by E. Peshcherova ("Prazdnik tiul'panov [lola] v selenii Isfar, Kokandskii uezd" in *Iubileinyi sbornik V. V. Bartol'du*, Tashkent, 1927). On the first day of this festival the large promenade (*sail*) was organized around huge trees, the branches of which were hung with bunches of tulips. Choral and dance pieces were performed to the accompaniment of musical instruments, and torchlit parades were organized. "Sarnaqš" songs (with male leader and chorus) played a large role in these. The most important of the ceremonial songs, "Naqši kalon" ("Great Naqš," or "melody") is a severe hymn (its text is in Uzbek; Ex. 3).

Ex. 3. "Naqši Kalon" (Transc. V. Uspenskii.)   Moderately.

Sarnaqš (leader);   Chorus

En - di   na   qi - lay,   En - di

na - qi - lay!   Ki   ǧam - xū   -   rim

180

yūk - dur, Kung - lim ti - la - gan

ya - go - na yo - rim yūk - dur.

Kūng - lim ti - la - gan ya - go - na

yo - rim būl - sa, E - gam qo - ši -

ga ūz - ga ro - zim yūk

dur. *A,* *tov* - *ba,* *yo* - *rim!*

How shall I be
Without a friend
Without the desired, loved one
When I will be with the loved one
I will have no more wishes of my Maker.
O I am a sinner, my friend!

Along with the ceremonial songs wedding songs were also sung, such as "Naqši Xurd" ("Small Naqš," Ex. 4).

Ex. 4. "Naqši Xurd." (Transc. V. Uspenskii).   Fairly quickly.

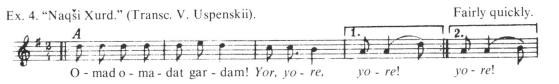

O - mad o - ma - dat gar - dam! *Yor, yo - re,*   *yo - re!*   *yo - re!*

181

Kad - du qo - ma - tat gar - dam! Yor yo - re,   yo - re!   yo - re!

Tu   bo in qad - du rux _ sor, Yor yo - re, yo - re!   yo - re!

Šo - xi an - ju - man bo - šī   Yor yo - re,   yo - re!   yo - re!

I will dance around you when you come.
I will dance around your figure.
With your figure and face
You will be the ruler of the gathering.

The second day of the holiday was dedicated to ceremonies in memory of the dead, which took place at *mazar*s ("cemeteries") with the participation of dancers and instrumentalists; purification rituals, connected to bathing in the river, were also featured.

Arising in the dim past, all of the ceremonies described were heavily influenced by Islam after its spread among the Tajiks. However this did not obscure their basic significance and connection to the [pre-Islamic —M. S.] way of life.

Family ceremonial songs principally include wedding songs, then birth songs and funeral laments. The wedding *tui* ("celebration," "feast") was prolonged for several days. Other family holidays were similarly organized, especially the celebration for the birth of a son. Ceremonies were more modest among the poor, though they involved heavy expenditures for the family. At the weddings of the rich, dancers, singers, musicians, comedians, and epic singers of the *Gur-oğli* tales (to be discussed) were invited. These entertainments were offered to guests in the evening, while the day was occupied with sporting contests and games, such as the goat catching race [*see* note 3 M. S.], wrestling, and tug-of-war and tightrope-walking contests. Weddings were usually held in the autumn after the completion of agricultural work.

"Šo faromod xonae" ("The Bridegroom Came into the House"), sung to the groom, is an example of the ancient melodic style of wedding song (Ex. 5).

Ex. 5. "Šo faromond xonae." (From materials in the Republic House of folk arts of the Tajik SSR.)

Moderately. (♩=78).

Šo far - o - mad   xo - na - e,   Čaš - mo - ni šo   ma - sto - na - e,

Ey,   čas-mo - ni xud bo - lo   ni - gor,

Ey,   šo ju - ra-ša me-do - na - e.

Mo-nan-di zo-ğo-i sar ba sar, Šo ay ba-ri jo-no-na-e.

The bridegroom came into the house
With eyes drunk with love.
Raising his eyes,
He recognized his beloved
And, like a raven,
He circled above her.

Another wedding song for the groom is "Naqš," with characteristic melody and rhythm (Ex. 6).

Ex. 6. "Naqš." (Transc. Z. Shakhidi.)   Con moto.

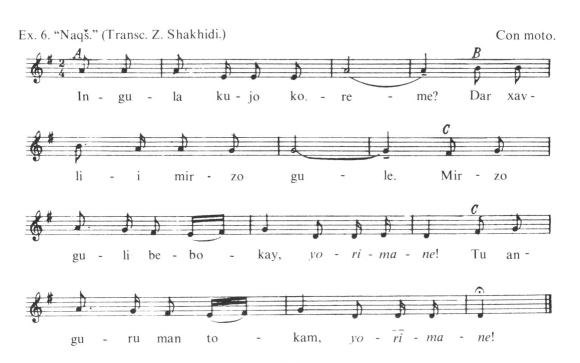

In - gu - la ku - jo ko. - re - me? Dar xav-

li - i mir - zo gu - le.   Mir - zo

gu - li be - bo - kay, *yo - ri - ma - ne!* Tu an-

gu - ru man to - kam, *yo - ri - ma - ne!*

Where shall we put this rose (bride)?
In the court of the prince (groom), who is himself like a rose.
Our groom is a beauty.
The bride is a bunch of grapes, and the groom a grapevine.

Both work and ceremonial songs belong to earlier types of folk music. In musical-stylistic terms all later and more developed forms stem from them.

The group of daily-life songs, including the broad and rich genre of lyric songs, is well represented among the Tajiks. The melodiousness of the latter is closely connected to the meter of song texts (which is highly developed) and exactly mirrors it. Three examples of lyric songs given below are constructed on different metric bases and with step-wise melodies. They are all love songs: "Ey, šūxi pari" ("O, Mischievous Fairy," Ex. 7), "Xay yor-i jon" ("O, My Darling," Ex. 8) and "Xokistari dil" ("The Ashen Heart," Ex. 9); an analysis of their structure will be given later.[4]

Ex. 7. "Ey, šūxi pari." (*Melodii Pamira*, p. 102.) Moderately.

Ey, šūxi parivaš az kujoī,
Andar nazaram či xušnamoī.

Monandi tu nozanin nadidam,
Na dar Xūtanu, na dar Xitoī.

Ošufta du zulfi sunouli tu,
Šamšodqadiu dilraboī.

Dandon ču durast, dahon ču pista,
Širin qadi tu, zi sar to poī.

O mischievous fairy, where are you from?
How beautiful you are.

I haven't seen such beauty
Either in Khotan or China.

Your two locks are charming,
Your figure is as attractive as a poplar.

Your teeth are pearls, your lips—pistachio's.
You are sweet from head to foot.

Aybe ba tu, ey sanam nadidam,
Aybi tu hamin ki bevafoī.

I see no flaw in you, dear.
You have only one flaw—inconstancy.

Mexond Zuxuri in ğazalro,
Bo jam'i rafiqu ošnoī.

Zukhur composed this *ghazal* (poem-M. S.)
You please all of his friends.

Ex. 8. "Xay, yori jon." (*Melodii Pamira*, p. 68.)   Moderately.

My supple darling came walking in the garden
Early in the morning, in a quiet time, with a quiet smile.

Ex. 9. "Xokistari dil" (*Melodii Pamira*, p. 72.)   Moderately.

185

Či nak - hat? Nak - hat - ti an - bar.

Či an - bar? An - ba - ri so - ro.

I fell in love with a beauty who tortures me.
What a beauty! What a sweetheart!

She has a hundred charms. Look at her locks.
What looks! What an aroma of beauty!

The content of the song texts is permeated with the typical similes and epithets of prerevolutionary Tajik poetry. Some of these images became standard, carried over from one work to another unchanged, such as "locks," "birthmarks," "waist," "flowerbed," "tulip," "rose," "nightingale," "moth encircling a flame," among others.[5] They are also used in professional poetry.

It is interesting to note that in Tajikstan, as in the Caucasus, the tune used by Glinka for the "Persian Chorus" in his opera *Ruslan and Liudmilla* is widespread.[6] One of its variants is the melody of the Tajik love song "Meravi ay nazaram" ("You Hid From My Eyes," Ex. 10).

Ex. 10. "Meravi ay nazaram." (*Muzyka tajikov*, p. 40.)   Fairly quickly.

Me - ra - vī ay na - za - ram yo

du ku - nam, yo na - ku - nam?

In di li ǧam - za - da - ro šo -

186

du   ku - nam   yo   na - ku - nam?

She hid from my eyes; should I remember?
Should I gladden my sorrowful heart or not?

Other variants of this tune were transcribed in the 1880s by Eichhorn (to be discussed in Chapter 5).

Dialogue songs between two persons, usually a boy and girl, called *lapar*, are especially widespread. They are marked by frank feelings and lively imagery, although one sometimes finds bookish similes and phrases in their texts, as in the following lapar, where the youth calls his sweetheart "queen" and himself her "slave," using, in this instance, images preserved from the feudal epoch (Ex. 11).

Ex. 11. "Šoh duxtar." (*Muzyka tajikov*, p. 28.)   Lively. (♩ = 100).

Boy:	Šoh duxtar, šakar duxtar,	Boy:	Queen maiden, sugar girl,
	Šohi duxtarone!		Queen of girls!
	Čašmakat ba man binmo,		Show me your eyes
	Man ba tu ǧulome!		And I will be your slave.

Girl:	Čašmakam či mebinī,	Girl:	Why should you gaze at my eyes,
	Yori bad gumone!		Treacherous friend!
	Dar bozor surma nadidī?		Have you seen mascara at the bazaar?
	In ham misli hamone!		They are like that.
Boy:	Šoh duxtar, šakar duxtar,	Boy:	Queen maiden, sugar girl,
	Šohi duxtarone!		Queen of girls!
	Dandunta ba man binmo,		Show me your teeth
	Man ba tu ğulome!		And I will be your slave.
Girl:	Dandunma či mebinī,	Girl:	Why do you want to gaze at my teeth
	Yori bad gumone!		Treacherous friend!
	Dar kapon birinj nadidī?		Have you seen rice at the bazaar?
	In ham misli hamone!		They are like that.
Boy:	Šoh duxtar, šakar duxtar,	Boy:	Queen maiden, sugar girl,
	Šohi duxtarone!		Queen of girls!
	Gardanta ba man binmo,		Show me your neck
	Man ba tu ğulome!		And I will be your slave.
Girl:	Gardanma či mebinī,	Girl:	Why do you want to gaze at my neck,
	Yori bad gumone!		Treacherous friend!
	Har jo karčuğay nadidī?		Have you seen a falcon's neck?
	In ham misli hamone!		It is like that.

Tajik lapars consist of simple folk poetry and short lines. Their text is often improvised.[7] Besides love lapars, there are also humorous lapars, satiric to the point of sharp abuse, indicating the close ties between this genre and folk life. They are often accompanied by dance movements.

Dance is highly developed among the Tajiks.[8] Women's dances have a strong practical (depiction of work processes) or ceremonial character, while men's dances are more virtuoso, humorous, or military (dances with swords). Dances are accompanied by rhythmic hand-clapping, solo playing on the *doira* (tambourine), choral performance by the spectators of dance songs, or by an ensemble of folk instruments.

Tajik dance tunes usually consist of manifold repetitions of a short motive, first in duple, then in triple time, as can be seen in the following mountain tunes[9] (Exs. 12, 13):

Ex. 12. Dance tune. (Transc. L. Knipper.)   Moderately

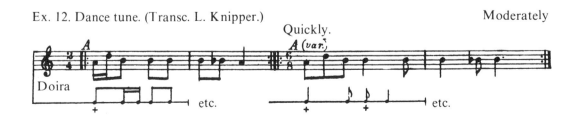

variants

dutar.

Ex. 13. Dance tune. (Transc. L. Knipper.)   Moderately

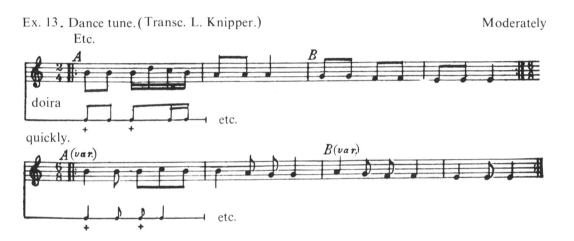

The changes of rhythm in Tajik dance melodies (to triple from duple time) has great significance for the development of musical rhythm among many Eastern peoples, including the peoples of the Caucasus, especially the Azerbaijanis and Armenians.

Ğāribi, or "transients' songs," are especially widespread among Tajik songs of social protest. They are songs of poor people and transient workers, compelled by necessity to leave their homes and look for work.[10] The poetic motive of "strange lands" is interlaced with the content of the lyric song "Guli lola" ("Tulip Blossom"), named for its refrain (Ex. 14).

Ex. 14. "Guli lola." (*Muzyka tajikov*, p. 60.)   Lively.

Ma - ro   on - jo   bu - bar   ki   so - ya   bo - šad,   lo - la,

lo - la,   gu - li   lo - la!   Da - rax - ti   zan - ja

- bil   šo - xaš ha - li - li,   Lo - la,   lo - la,   gu - li   lo - la!

Maro onjo bubar ki soya bošad.	Lead me to a place with shadows
Daraxti zanjabil toza bošad.	Where there is a young ginger tree.
Daraxti zanjabil šoxaš xalili,	The ginger tree with dark red branches;
Xama dar vatanu man dar ǧaribī.	Everyone is at home, and I am alone in strange lands.
Iloxī biškanad šoxi halili.	I wish to God that the dark red branch was broken.
Iloxī gum šavad xomi ǧaribī.	I wish to God that the word "strange lands" disappeared.

Melodies of Tajik Song. There are two types of melodic motion in Tajik songs: 1) descending, usually after a leap outlining the range of the melody, and 2) rising-falling motion. In both cases the basic melodic motion is step-wise and rocking. Both types of melody are found independently, in simple songs, and in conjunction, in songs of more complex structure.

Example 14 ("Guli lola"), Example 10 ("Meravi ay nazaram"), and others display descending melody. "Dance Tune" (Ex. 12) has descending motion with an opening leap outlining the basic melodic range.

The following mountain dance tune is simple, though typical, consisting of a rise and subsequent fall (Ex. 15).

Ex. 15. (Transc. L. Knipper).   Moderately.

190

The conjunction of both types of melodic motion occurs in the following way: the first half of the song is cast in an ascending-descending motion, and the second, usually starting with a higher pitch, reached in the first half of the song (usually the fifth scale degree), uses descending motion. The melodic line arising from the mixture can be expressed in this scheme (Ex. 16).

Ex. 16.

Examples of the Tajik melodic structure can be seen in Example 8 ("Xay yori jon") and in the lyric dialogue between a boy and girl "Šoh duxtar" (Ex. 11).

It is interesting to note that the same principle of melodic mixture is clearly evident in Example 5, the wedding song "So faromod xonae," with its narrow range of a third.

By means of the melodic structure outlined above, the melodic climax occurs at the beginning of the second half of a two-part verse form, usually of the ABCB type, *i. e.*, in section C, designated by a special term among the Tajiks, *auj*, or "rise." The lyric song "Lola" ["Tulip"—M. S.], marked by regularity of melodic and formal structure, can serve as a typical example of the auj (Ex. 17).[12]

Ex. 17. "Lola." (*Muzyka tajikov*, p. 96).   Moderately.

191

dux - ta - ri kin - ǧo - la! O yu, in dux-

ta - ri kin - ǧo - la ba mo dil doš - tast!

Oy, du čaš - mi si - yah za - bo - ni bul - bul doš - tast!

Oy, gandum lola, miyoni gandum lolae!
Oy, ošuq šudayam ba duxtari kinǧola!
Oyu, in duxtari kinǧola ba mo dil doštast!
Oy, du čašmi siyah zaboni bulbul doštast!

Oy, in kūtali rū ba rū baroem xolī!
Oyu, sesad ǧazalu bayta bigūem xolī!
Oyu, mardum gūyand ika čuva menolī!
Oyu, yorum raftai kanorum monday holi!

Oy, in čormaǧzi čor gūšai la'li gardum!
Oyu, ey čuraī jon xoli labota gardum!
Oy, aybi padarum naboša šarmi mardum!
Oyu, medonistum girdi sarut megaštum!

O red tulip among the wheat.
O I am in love with a beautiful girl.
O this girl favors me.
O she has black eyes and a nightingale's tongue.

O we go into the mountains together, gazing at one another.
O we read three hundred ghazals and baits (couplets).
O people say, "why do you cry?"
O my girl friend left, my embraces are orphaned.

O this four-sided nut growing in the wheat!
O how I am enchanted, dear, by the mole on your lips.
O if not for fear of your father and shame before people
O I would sacrifice myself for you.

Scalar Basis of Tajik Folk Song. Tajik folk music is based on a system of diatonic scales common to many peoples. It includes major-like scales (Mixolydian, Ionian) and minor scales (Aeolian, Dorian, Phrygian). Along with the diatonic

192

scales chromatic scales are well developed, with altered steps above a single tonic. This type of chromaticism affects the second, third, sixth, and seventh scale degrees. The process of chromaticism in Pamir melodies leads to the creation of a scale with an augmented second on the second step, as in Example 45 ("Dar dilam").

We see the complex picture of scales with augmented seconds on steps two and six alternating with the major hexachord in the remarkable melody "Pamir Dance," transcribed by L. K. Knipper (Ex. 18).[13]

Ex. 18. Pamir dance. (Transc. L. Knipper).   Moderately.

The following successions of pitches are found in this dance (Ex. 19):

Ex. 19.

Together, they give an almost complete chromatic scale (missing the augmented fourth and minor third, Ex. 20).[14]

Ex. 20.

Example 9 ("Xākistari dil") represents an intersting type of scale structure, as can be seen in the following scheme (Ex. 21): Here the resultant scale involves the upper range of the full octave in the following complex intervalic structure (with an augmented second on the second step, Ex. 22).

194

Ex. 21.

Ex. 22.

The scalar basis of the humorous craft song "Az kosagaron" (Ex. 1) can be variously dissected: as Dorian d-minor with cadences on steps 1 and 6, as Aeolian a-minor with cadences on 4 and 2, or as Mixolydian C-major with cadences on the dominant and third.[15] The last is the most likely explanation if one considers that in Tajik music a cadence on the third can be used as a final cadence. The following example gives three melodic cross-sections of this scale, with final cadences (Ex. 23):

Ex. 23.

Wide ranging scales are created in Tajik songs by uniting quartal and quintal registers (tetrachords and pentachords with the same or differing interval content) with important pitches at the fourth and octave, as can be seen in the following examples (Exs. 24 or 25):

195

Ex. 24.

Ex. 25.

In "Naqši xalon" (Ex. 3), the Dorian scale is maintained throughout, relating to the second of the types just described (Ex. 26).

Ex. 26.

As for the scale of the lyric song "Lola" (Ex. 17), it belongs to the first type of wide-ranging scale, created by tetrachordal conjunction. At the same time it is an example of scalar modulation from Aeolian e-minor to Aeolian a-minor, which leads to chromaticization of the common basis of these scales (abundance of f-sharps and f-naturals). In Aeolian e-minor it is a chromaticized scale and contains a lowered second step in its tonic cadences (Ex. 27). One also finds examples of pentatonicism in Tajik music. All of this testifies to the rich complexity of Tajik scalar systems developed through the long existence of the Tajiks' music culture.[16]

Ex. 27.

Rhythm of Tajik Folk Song. The rhythmic side of Tajik song, arising from the great development of prosody, is no less rich than its scalar side. Tajik song rhythm is based on a two-syllable trochaic foot. This rhythmic cell is called *zarb-i qadim*, or "ancient rhythm" in Tajik music (Ex. 28)[17]

Ex. 28.

The most common rhythms in Tajik songs are 1) the eight syllable trochaic tetrameter (Ex. 29), and its truncated form, the seven syllable line (Ex. 30), and 2) the prolongation of the eight syllable line to an eleven syllable hexameter (Ex. 31).

Ex. 29.

Ex. 30.

Ex. 31.

The eight-and seven-syllable trochaic lines are usually declaimed in duple time (Ex. 32). But they may well be expressed in triple time (Ex. 33).

Ex. 32.

Čaš - ma - kat či me - bi - nī

Ex. 33.

Yor o - ma - du yor o - mad.

Examples were cited above (Exs. 12, 13) of the appearance of triple rhythm after duple in Tajik mountain dance tunes. Eight and seven syllable trochaic verse lines often alternate. There are also other alternating lines, such as, for example, seven and six syllable lines in the following rhythm (Ex. 34).

Ex. 34.

Šoh dux-tar, ša - kar dux-tar, Šo - hi dux-ta - ro - ne.

The eleven-syllable trochaic verse line is often used in Tajik songs, giving rise to various melodic-rhythmic structures. These are based on even declamation (sometimes complicated by dotted rhythms) of the syllables of this line with a pro-longed final syllable (Ex. 35).

Ex. 35.

Ko - li si - yoh do - na - do - na kam za - nad.

Rhythmic modification of this type of declamation leads to a doubling of the value of either each even numbered foot (Ex. 36) or each odd-numbered foot (Ex. 37).

Ex. 36.

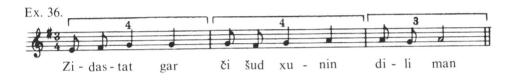

Zi - das - tat gar či šud xu - nin di - li man

Ex. 37.

Ey, al - ma a - nor bi - yo ba bo - li - nam

The prolongation of one syllable in each pair of trochaic feet gives rise to quintuple meter (Ex. 38). Especially typical of Tajik rhythm is a seven beat meter of the following structure (Ex. 39):[18]

Ex. 38.

Ey, bi - ro - dar, bo tu gu - yam qis - sa - ro.

199

Ex. 39.

Di - la - kam zar - dob šud az

As mentioned earlier, the types of verse lines and rhythmic structures of Tajik folk songs cited above are the basic ones. However they by no means exhaust the wealth of Tajik poetic and musical rhythm. The incursion of literary texts into folk music led first of all to the appearance of multisyllabic feet in folk practice (four or five syllables) and also to the formation of verse lines made up of varying syllabic structure, usually consisting of a great number of syllables (up to fifteen, sixteen, or more).

Here are some examples of such verse lines. First, an instance of an eight syllable line of two four syllable feet with the strong beat on the fourth syllable (Ex. 40):

Ex. 40.

Šu - dam bar su - ra - te o - šiq.

Example 41 gives a fifteen syllable line of three five syllable feet with the strong beat on the fifth syllable of every foot. Example 42 displays an eleven syllable line made up of three groups of three plus four plus four syllables, and, finally, Example 43 is a thirteen syllable line with four syllabic groups of three plus four plus three plus three syllables.

Ex. 41.

Yo - ri si - hi - qad az - mi ča - man kard, ay, yo - ri jo - nam.

200

Ex. 42.

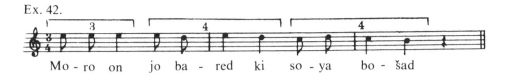

Mo - ro on jo ba - red ki so - ya bo - šad

Ex. 43.

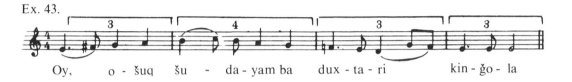

Oy, o - šuq šu - da - yam ba dux - ta - ri kin - ǧo - la

As is evident from the examples given, the rhythmic structure of verse is regularly reflected in the rhythm of the melodic line of the song. The great complexity of Tajik melodic rhythm leads to frequent use of syncopation, which is particularly characteristic of professional compositions.

Strophic Structure of Tajik Folk Song. The basic strophes in Tajik folk song are two types of quatrain: 1) the *rubāi* or *čārbait* with an *aaba* rhyme scheme, and 2) the *tarāna*, with a single rhyme for all lines: *aaaa*. Both types of quatrains are usually made up of eight, seven, and eleven syllable trochaic verse lines.

Ex. 44. "Az dur menamoī." (*Melodii Pamira*, p. 110).   Quickly. ($\quarternote$ = 116)

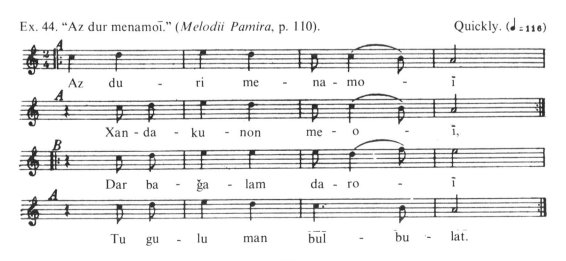

Az du - ri me - na - mo - ī

Xan - da - ku - non me - o - ī,

Dar ba - ǧa - lam da - ro - ī

Tu gu - lu man bul - bu - lat.

201

You appeared from afar.
You walk with a smile.

Come to my arms;
You are the rose, and I the nightingale.

Ex. 45. "Dar dilam." (*Melodii Pamira*, p. 120). Quickly.

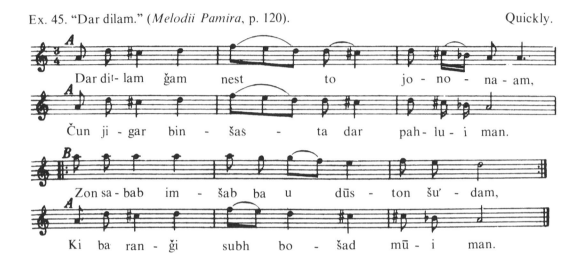

Neither I nor my love are sad.
She sits alongside, dear and near.
I became her friend this evening,
For life, until our hair is gray.

Ex. 46. "Zarra-Gul." (N. Mironov, *Tajikskie pesni*). Fairly quickly.

Didam ba mulki Hisor
Duxtaraki gul uzor.
Zarra-Gul!
Ba ruxaš az du taraf
Zulfi siyoh tobidor.
Zarra-Gul!

Refrain:
I was among the cliffs of Hissar
And saw a rose-maiden, Zara-gul!
The black lock by her temple
Caressed the dark skin.

203

Komati ziboi ū,	Her figure and curls were mountain roses
Zulfi sumansoi ū,	I haven't forgotten them till today.
Nargizi šahloi ū,	Her glance is a sly thief.
Burda zi dilho qaror.	It stole my tranquility (Refrain).

Didam . . .

Bo labi širin zi qand,	Sweet honey flowed from her mouth
Bo šakarin nūšxand,	All blossoming with smiles.
Došt ba dastaš kàland,	She had a hoe on her shoulder;
Bud ba ijroi kor.	Her work awaited her in the valley.
	(Refrain).

Didam . . .

Uzv ba kolxoz bud,	In the early morning
Uzvaki dil sūz bud,	She went with one thought:
Har šabu xar ruz bud,	That her own kolkhoz
Dar šiddati koru bor.	Should blossom with luxuriant gardens.
	(Refrain).

Didam . . .

Xusnaš az in rū čunin	Because of that since then
Gašta maro dilnišin.	I love the rose from the mountains.
Husni ba mehnat karin	Beauty, the child of work,
Pahlavonu zarbdor.	Is joy and sorrow for the heart.
	(Refrain).

Didam . . .

The following quatrain exemplifies the typical make-up of the rubāi, which has the same rhyme for first, second, and fourth lines and an unrhymed third line (from Ex. 46):

Didam ba mulki Hissor
Duxtaraki gul uzor
Ba ruxaš az du taraf
Zulfi siyoh tobidor.

Or, in translation:[19]

I was among the cliffs of Hissar
And saw a rose-maiden
The black locks by her temple
Caressed the dark skin.

This and other types of quatrain, with different rhyme schemes, express complete thoughts and form a basis for strophic structure.

Forms of Tajik Folk Song. The following forms predominate in Tajik folk song:
1) half strophe two part forms of the type AB, connected with the singing of two lines of text (Exs. 8, 10), and 2) the whole-strophe two-part form of the type ABCB of Examples 4, 7, and 11. There are also some other types of forms, such as ABCC in "Naqš" (Ex. 6) and AABA, which is an exact reproduction of the *aaba* structure of the rubāi. Let us look at "Az dur menamoī" ("She Appeared from Afar") and "Dar dilam" ("In My Heart") as examples of this form (Exs. 44, 45).

In some cases these forms are complicated by the introduction of refrains, broadening the structure, which can be seen in Examples 6 and 14 among others. In the comic craft song "Az kosagaron" (Ex. 1), the refrain is closely tied to the basic content, which continually expands.

The chain three-part form is a special type of Tajik verse form, also found among the Uzbeks. It starts with a refrain, which is then repeated after every verse. Its overall structure can be shown by the following diagram: ABABA, in which each three-part link consists of a refrain (A), verse (B) and repeat of the refrain (A), which becomes the first part of the next link. The refrain is usually composed in the lower (tonic) register and the verse in the register a fifth higher, appearing as an auj. The popular Tajik lyric song "Zarra gul"can serve as a beautiful example of this form; it is named for the recurring refrain, the name of a Tajik girl. The song is now popular with its new Soviet text (Ex. 46).

All the forms of folk song described above are widely used in Tajik professional songs as well. They grew into more complex structures through musical embodiment of the texts of elaborate poetic subjects.

Tajik Instrumental Music

Tajik Musical Instruments.[20] The Tajik instrumentarium developed during the course of the long growth of national music and is very rich. It can be divided into two groups: instruments of the mountain Tajiks and those of the people of the river valleys and cities.

The mountain Tajiks have relatively few instruments and these are of simple structure. They include: wind instruments (*tutik* and *košnai*); string instruments (*ğičak, dumbrak*, and Pamir *rubab*); and percussion instruments (*doira* and *tavlak*).[21]

The tutik is a type of pastoral whistle flute with a small number (two or three) of fingerholes. The košnai, or *juftnai,*[22] is a pair of reed pipes with a single reed and an equal number of fingerholes. The ğičak is a fiddle with three or four strings,[23] usually tuned to a fourth. In the mountains its body is usually made of gunpowder tins.[24] The dumbrak is a two-stringed fretless lute tuned to a fourth. It is used both as a solo instrument and as accompaniment to epic recitation. The Pamir rubab is a fretless lute played with plectrum. Its three melody strings, of which the upper two are doubled, are tuned to a fourth. The doira is a tambourine with a group of metal rings on the inside of the frame. The *tavlak* is a type of single headed drum with a pot shaped body, over most of which a skin is stretched.

The second group of Tajik musical instruments is used in the valleys of Tajikstan, mostly among the urban population. It is quite diverse. The instruments are marked by careful external detail and sometimes by delicate bone inlay ornament. In this group the wind instruments are *nai, surnai,* and *karnai;* the string instruments, besides the ǧičak, are the *dutār, tanbur, rubāb,* and *čang;* and the percussion instruments, besides the doira, are the *qairāq* and *naǧara.* The nai (literally "reed") is a transverse flute with full diatonic scale. The surnai is a large oboe with a full diatonic scale. The karnai is a large bass brass horn of which the following typical fanfares can be played (Ex. 47):

Ex. 47.

The dutar is in widespread use for solo play and for accompanying songs. It is a two-stringed fretted lute with silk strings tuned to a fourth or fifth. Its scale is the following (Ex. 48):

Ex. 48.

The *tanbur* is a three stringed fretted lute using a plectrum and metal strings; it is used both as a solo instrument and as an accompanying instrument for professional singers. The tuning of the tanbur depends on the scale of the piece performed (Ex. 49).

Ex. 49.

The scale of the upper (melodic) string of the tanbur, with adjustment of its sixth fret to a minor, neutral, or major seventh will yield the following (Ex. 50):

Ex. 50.

The tanbur has very high frets made of thick gut. This allows the player to apply variable pressure near the fret to produce a vibrato. A tanbur with one or more doubled strings is called a *čartār* ("four–stringed"), *panjtār* ("five–stringed") or *šaštār* ("six-stringed" lute).[25]

The rubāb is a three–stringed fretted instrument played with plectrum; the two upper (gut) strings are doubled, the strings are tuned to a fourth and give the following scale (Ex. 51).

Ex. 51.

In its lower octave the rubāb has a number of metal resonating strings in a diatonic sequence tuned according to the piece being performed.[26]

The čang is a cymbalum-like instrument with a range in three registers of a minor seventh each (Ex. 52).[27] The qairāq is a type of castanet of two bone or stone plates held between the fingers. The naḡara is a small clay kettle drum.

Ex. 52.

All of the instruments listed above (with the exception of the surnai, karnai and nagara, which belong to the military orchestra) belong to the Tajik national orchestra, and are used for performances of both vocal and instrumental works.

Tajik folk musical instruments, like those of other peoples, do not have tempered scale structures.[28] The scales of the stringed instruments approach the Pythagorean tuning. In the scales of the wind instruments one finds neutral intervals, such as the neutral third, which is connected to the placement of finger-holes at approximately equal distances.[29] As already indicated, the tanbur's scale contains neutral intervals. Aside from the neutral third, all of the other intervals of Tajik music instruments are close to those of the tempered system.

Archaeological excavations have unearthed ancient terracotta statues which depict musicians playing on the obsolete musical instruments of the Tajiks' ancestors. Among them are: open end-blown flutes, panpipes, various shapes of drums, lute-like instruments, and harps called *čangs*. One also finds depictions of animals (monkeys and others) playing musical instruments. Of special interest is the frieze found near Termez [the Airtam frieze—M. S.] on the Amu-Darya, dating to the first to second centuries A.D., depicting musicians. They hold barrel- and hour-glass-shaped drums, cymbals, a paired flute, harp, and rubāb. The latter is identical in structure to the modern Tajik rubāb, which testifies to the high development of musical art among the Bactrians, among the forerunners of the modern Tajiks.[30]

Tajik Instrumental Music. The instrumental music of the Tajiks, like their vocal music, is quite rich in various types of compositions, in both folk and art styles. Among folk pieces there are some practical pieces and melodies, usually pastoral, as well as those of daily-life and ceremonial significance. As an example of semi-improvised melody, here is a Pamir "pastoral tune," performed on the tutik (Ex. 53):[31]

Ex. 53.

The dutār repertoire usually consists of song tunes, performed in a two voiced manner with parallel fourths and fifths or a drone on the lower open string. Examples of two-voiced dutar style can be seen in the accompaniments of Tajik songs given above (Exs. 10, 11).

Musical instruments with legato sounds (ǧičak, košnai, nai, and surnai) are used to perform daily-life, ceremonial (*e. g.*, wedding), and other melodies, and are especially used to accompany dance. Let us look at "Larzon gul" ("Trembling flower"), a dance tune, in a version for surnai. This song, in many variants, is widespread in both Tajikistan and Uzbekistan. Its first transcriptions belong to the last quarter of the nineteenth century (Ex. 54).

Ex. 54. "Larzon gul." (N. Mironov, *Muzyka tajikov*, p.64).   slowly

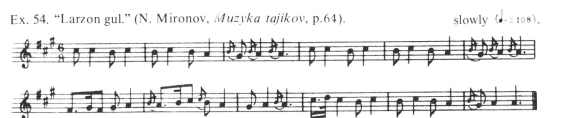

All the varieties of Tajik music, both vocal and instrumental, are accompanied by percussion instruments (doira or naḡara). Their rhythms, often quite long and complex, are called *usul*.[32] They are made up of alternating bass and treble tones. The lower strokes are indicated in the present work by crosses attached to the notes. Special mnemonic syllables are used by the Tajiks for both verse meters and usuls, from which various rhythmic structures are made, as in the following (Ex. 55):[33]

Ex. 55.

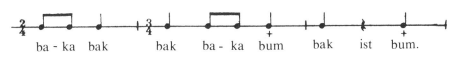

ba - ka bak   bak ba - ka bum   bak   ist   bum.

Historical Ties between Tajik and Uzbek Music. The centuries of shared experiences of the Tajiks and Uzbeks, who have been living on common ground in northern Tajikistan and southern Uzbekistan, their bilingualism, and long collaboration in science and the arts have all led to the closeness of their music cultures.

The folk songs of these peoples developed on the basis of similar melodic, scalar, and rhythmic foundations and similar formal principles. Accordingly, the same melodies may have both a Tajik and Uzbek text. The musical instruments spread in the valleys of Tajikstan are also Uzbek instruments. Finally, the styles and forms of Tajik art music also crystallized under conditions of shared creativity with Uzbek musicians (vocalists and instrumentalists).

THE EARLY PERIOD OF DEVELOPMENT OF TAJIK MUSIC (TO THE TENTH CENTURY)

Tajik Epic Art

Tajik Epic. Tajik epic art springs from sources deep in the past. The cycle of heroic-mythological tales incorporated into the early sections of Firdausi's (934-1020) *Shāhnāme* were created by the ancestors of the Tajiks and belong to an early type of epic. B. G. Gafurov writes:

> Among the most striking creations in the culture of the ancestors of the Tajiks were their epics and mythology, for example the tale of the eternal struggle of light against darkness, of good spirits against evil demons, of fire against the dragon Aji-daxak ("Azhdahau" in Tajik folklore and "Zahak" in Firdausi). In this struggle man stands on the side of light and the good spirits. The blacksmith Kova (whose figure is undoubtedly connected with the beginnings of ironworking) conquers the dragon Aji-daxak. This poeticization of historical development gave birth to cycles of legends about heroes (*Istoriia tajikskogo naroda* 2nd ed., Moscow, 1952, pp. 26-27).

The hero and warrior Rustam is the most popular figure in these legends. Until recently, his image was carried during carnival parades in the shape of a gigantic puppet.

The prototype of the tales about Zarina, the "golden beauty," which still circulate in Tajikistan, is the Saka tale about Zarina the "golden-haired," the warrior-heroine, described as early as the first century B.C. by the Greek historian Diomedes of Sicily.

The cycle *Dastān-i Gur-oğli Sultān* is a basic type of epic tale among the Tajiks even today. The central figure has the same name as the hero of the Turkmen and Azerbaijani *Koroğli or Guroğli* epic.[34] As in the other cycles which arose or developed in the feudal epoch, the Tajik *Gur-oğli* epic, in various variants of individual episodes, exists in both a popular-democratic and feudal-aristocratic version. In the folk version, Gur-oğli is characterized as a "peasant ruler," coming from the *dehqān* ("peasant") masses.

In his declining years the Sultan remembered
To break open the state treasury;
They started to give money to the peasants
The peasants chose themselves a king.
A simple peasant began to rule them,
Giving joy to the unfortunate.

In these legends the singer Saqi plays an important role as the closest, wise counselor of Gur-oǧli; Saqi stands for the creative genius of the people.

Structure of Tajik Epic Tales. We cannot say whether the tales of Rustam and Zarina were originally performed with instrumental accompaniment or only as solo recitative. But it is certainly true that the early form of proto-Tajik epic tales was performed without accompaniment. Today the *Gur-oǧli* epic is transmitted by storytellers called *gur-oǧli-gu*, accompanied by the dumbrak, a variant of the dutar.[35] Before each episode the storyteller gives a small melodic prelude, then goes on to measured recitative declamation of the verse lines of the narration, which is completed by a slow coda.

The rhythm of Tajik epic verse is rich and varied. The most common verse line is a three–syllable dactylic foot used to construct dactylic hexameter, well known from the ancient Greek epic tales, the *Iliad* and *Odyssey*. Here is an example of Tajik hexameter (Ex. 56):

Ex. 56.

Ay ǧa - mi iš qi tu sar ba ku - yi ga - brun me - ni - xum

The following are examples of tunes on which the declamation of *Gur-oǧli* is based (Ex. 57):

Ex. 57. Transc. L. Knipper.   Slowly.

Con moto.

211

molto rit.

The instrumental accompaniment of Tajik epic tales is usually of the following variety (Ex. 58):

Ex. 58.   Con moto.

Epic-novelistic Works. Epic-novelistic works arose alongside the heroic epic in Tajikistan. They are partly prose and partly verse tales, with faithful love as the predominating theme, *e. g.*, "Leili and Majnun" and "Taxhir and Zuxra" among others. The subjects of some of these tales are widespread among many peoples of the Near East, Central Asia, and the Caucasus. Some mountain Tajik tales are quite early in origin, content, and musical setting. One of these has been published by E. E. Romanovskaia and A. A. Semenov ("Tāsh-bek i Gul-Qurbān," *Sovetskaia muzyka* No. 7, 1937).

Growth of Musical Professionalism

Music in the Cities of the Proto-Tajiks. The growth of urban life on the territory of Soghdia and Bactria facilitated the birth and growth of musical professionalism. This is borne out by archaeological and literary monuments. There is evidence of the existence of various musical and artistic professions in Bactrian cities of the second century B.C. As noted above, the Airtam frieze, dating from the early centuries A.D., contains depictions of musical instruments and the figures of professional musicians of that epoch. Finally, the *Shāhnāme* of Firdausi paints a poetic protrait of Barbat, the famous, semilegendary singer of the late sixth to early seventh centuries A.D. Barbat served the Near Eastern poets of succeeding generations as the image of the ideal professional musician with outstanding voice, great mastery of performance, and a huge and varied repertoire. Professional musical art also lent glamor and splendor to court life.

The blow dealt to the Central Asian peoples by the Arab conquest of the seventh to nineth centuries, including destruction of cities, plunder of cultural and artistic monuments, and annihilation of libraries, checked the development of Tajik music culture until the last quarter of the ninth century.

TAJIK MUSIC FROM THE TENTH TO THE FIFTEENTH CENTURIES

Tajik Professional Musical Art

. . . *Professional Vocal Art.* The age-old development of Tajik culture created the basis for the formation of written poetry and the closely related vocal art music. The vocation of poet, especially at the beginning of the development of poetic and musical professionalism, was inseparable from that of musician (singer), performer of poetic works, and composer of melodies for new poetic texts. The term *hāfiz* ("master singer") was also given to poets. For example, the great poet of the fourteenth century, Shamsuddin Muhammad Shirazi, took the literary pseudonym of Hāfez.

Having created new verse forms to express poetic content, the Tajik hāfezes also developed musical forms. They went from simple strophic songs to complex structures of vocal compositions, giving full expression to not just one strophe of poetic text, but to a whole poem consisting of several strophes.[36]

213

Tajik Professional Prosody. The basic verse forms of Tajik literature to receive high artistic elaboration were the ghazal, murabba, and muxammas, discussed earlier. The meters of professional prosody differ from folk verse: 1) in the introduction of multisyllabic feet (four and five syllables), along with simpler feet; 2) in the evolution of multisyllabic lines; (up to twenty syllables) and 3) in the formation of verse lines of feet of different syllabic and rhythmic structures. Some examples of such lines were given above.

The great development of prosody in Tajik professional poetry was crystallized in the cultivated theory of metrics called *aruz*, the theory of learned prosody. Tajik [*i. e.,* Persian—M. S.] prosody is quantitative, *i. e.,* based on long and short syllables. Special mnemonic devices signifying types of feet are used for the practical working-out of the aruz, from which the formula of rhythmic structure of a given foot can be established. Thus, for example, the metric structure of the trimeter introduced in Example 34 and called *ramal* ("running verse") is indicated by the following formula (Ex. 59):

Ex. 59.

fa - i - lya - tun,   fa - i - lya - tun,   fa - i - lyun.

Each type of verse line has its own name. In addition to ramal, the following might be mentioned: *sari* ("quick"), *xafif* ("light"), *saqil* ("heavy," or "slow"). The emotional character of each meter can be clearly seen in its name.[37]

Inasmuch as the poems of Tajik poets were mainly spread orally, through sung performances, the author tried to gain recognition by putting his name in the final strophe instead of signing his verse, as do modern poets.[38]

The metric basis given above is the highly developed foundation for the creation of melodic lines in the Tajik art song.[39]

Means of Musical Expression in The Art Song. The means of musical expression in the art song consists of further elaboration of techniques developed in the folk song. This is mainly connected to the rise of new musical forms for art songs, growing to large dimensions and consisting of several divisions in strophic form equal to the stanzas of the poetic text. The segments are differentiated from one another both by melodic content and by tessitura. Such forms, in terms of their internal structure, can be called multistrophic. As an example, here is "Ghazal" (or "Ğazel") on a text of the Tajik poet Ğiāsi from the maqām (*see* below) *Buzruk* (Ex. 60):[40]

214

Moderately (♩ = 104)

daxr, yor, mušk bū bū.

You shot an arrow straight into my heart.
A fire of passion has seized me.

With uncovered head, barefoot, I moaned, remembering you
As I wandered through countries, cities and towns.

I am an instrument full of sounds, I am
The goblet of Jamshid, in which the whole world is reflected.
I am the clear mirror, reflecting the face of my beloved.

Ghiasi, you are threading the gems of another world;
You have filled the curls of the Universe with the redolent musk
    of your words.

The form of "Ǧhazal" is made up of four parts, as can be seen in the following diagram, where the internal structure of each verse is given in terms of registral change (Ex. 61):

Ex. 61

A   A   B   A   C   D   E   A   C   D   F   E   A   C   H   B   A

In Example 61 it is clear that in the first verse a rise of a fourth is made from the basic tonic register with a subsequent return at the end of the verse. The second and third strophes, beginning in the octave register and serving as an *auj* ("climax") of the whole piece, return through the register of a fourth to the basic tonic range. And, finally, in the fourth verse after a rise of a fifth the melody again makes its transition to the tonic cadence through the intermediate register of a fourth above tonic.

Thus the basic melodic structure of a gradual rise toward the middle of the verse to a higher register, found in Tajik folk songs, also typifies the forms of art music. In the latter case it is more developed and occupies a greater melodic range, but preserves the step-wise motion taken over from folk songs.

In the "Ghazal" examined, the basic Mixolydian scale is preserved in all the transitions from one register to another, while the lower register contains some elements of the pentatonic scale. In other vocal works changes in scale accompany registral transitions, which considerably enrich these works. This happens, for example, even in well developed Tajik folk songs such as "Lola" ("Tulip," Ex. 17).

It should be noted that the manner of vocal performance among Tajik art singers is marked by particular traits, of which the most important are emotional saturation (especially in the auj sections) and the marking-off of rhythmic pulsations through oscillating vibrato in prolonged notes.[41]

TAJIK POETRY FROM THE TENTH TO THE FIFTEENTH CENTURIES AND TAJIK PROFESSIONAL VOCAL ART

We have already noted that the Tajik art song developed in close conjunction with professional poetry. The father of both can be considered Rudaki (d. 941), a blind poet, singer, and musician, whose works are used even today as song texts by Tajik singers. He was born into a peasant family, was "the first among his contemporaries in the area of versification," and was kept at the court of one of the Samanid emirs. At the end of his life he was driven from court and died a pauper in his native village of Panjurdak. Rudaki's popularity was exceptionally great among succeeding generations of Tajik poets and singers. In the quatrain of one of the poets living during the time of the Mongol upheaval Rudaki is compared to the semilegendary Barbat, and the work of both is treated as the greatest cultural achievement of the Tajik people of those times.

Of all the treasures collected by the Sassanians and Samanids
Nothing has reached our times, beyond the songs of Barbat
Nothing has remained, besides the sweet verses of Rudaki.

The twelfth-century Tajik litterateur Nizami Aruzi-as Samarqandi comments on a famous poem of Rudaki composed in the ramal meter, which begins with the following verses:

Bui jui Mulion oyad xame
Edi yari mexrubon oyad
Regi Omy doruštixoy u
Zeri po čun parnion oyad xame.

I remember the babbling of Muliana's stream (in Bukhara—V. B.)
I remember tender meetings with my beloved.
The broad Amu-darya, with silk-rustling sand;
I remember the damp sparkling of the pebbles.

Nizami remarks on the fact that it was performed to a melody in the *ušāq* mode ("Mixolydian"). This testifies to a significant development by the tenth century of Tajik professional vocal style in its rhythmic, scalar, and, consequently, melodic basis.

Later, the poetic works of Abu-ali ibn Sinā, known in Europe as Avicenna (*ca.* 980-1037), were widely used in Tajik art songs. Also used were the works of Nasir-i Khusrau, (1003-1088), who travelled to many lands in his lifetime, and of the classic authors of Eastern poetry, such as the world famous Omar Khayyam (1040-1123), Sa'adi (1184-1291), and Hāfez (d. 1389).

Turning to the spiritual content of his own works in contrast to the vapid poems of many of his contemporaries, Khusrau says: "Respect poetry like a bride, and music like her jewels and fine clothing." In Hāfez' works, protest against the existing order coincides with thoughts of a bright future . . . . The works of other great Tajik poets are also used in vocal art: Kamal Xojand, a contemporary of Hāfez (d. 1390 or 1405) and the famous Abdurrahman Jami (1414-1492) . . . .[42]

Professional Instrumental Art. Solo and ensemble music received further development in Tajik professional instrumental music, and acquired virtuoso features. The styles of art music are the following: 1) *contrafacta* of folk songs, taking on instrumental characteristics; 2) dance melodies with typical change from duple to triple meter; 3) holiday pieces in forms similar to strophic structure; and 4) large rondo-like structures.

The origins of rondo-like forms are connected with the desire of Tajik composers to create large instrumental compositions which would unify thematic material in a way similar to that found in large forms of vocal music. We can see the beginnings of the rondo forms in the structure of the three-part strophic chain forms. The principle of rondo design is clearly enough expressed in a song-like melody of surnai, "Kušroni," ("The Path of the *Omač*," a Tajik wooden plow), connected with agricultural work (Ex. 62).

Ex. 62. "Kušroni." (N. Mironov, *Muzyka tajikov*, p. 79).   Con moto (♩.₌₁₀₄)

219

Ensemble music is especially well developed. This relates primarily to holiday music, accompanying folk outdoor fetes, such as the sails, carnival parades, presentations by tightrope walkers, puppet theater performances, wrestling matches, and other entertainments. Mixed wind-string orchestras or wind bands performed. The melody "Nay rez" ("The Rapture of Flute Sounds")[43] can serve as an example of holiday pieces. It is marked by heightened character and march-like rhythm, alternating with lively dance movement through rhythmic modifications of the basic melody. (Ex. 63).

Ex. 63. "Nay rez." (N. Mironov, *Muzyka uzbekov*, p. 58).   In march time (♩=144).

The Tajik military wind band was an indispensible accessory of court life and was housed in a special open pavilion, built over the gates of the city citadel, the residence of the feudal ruler. In telling the hours of the day the orchestra played specific works.[44] The pavilion was called the *naǧāra xāna* ("kettledrum balcony"), and the leader of the orchestra was the *naǧārači* or kettledrum player, who had the court title of *mexter*, or master. In addition to these basic functions, the military orchestra also took part in campaigns, parades, and military exercises of the *sarbāz*, the Khan's soldiers. Here is a transcription of a Bukharan military march of the 1880s (Ex. 64):

Ex. 64. Bukharan march. (Transc. A. Eichhorn). In march time.

Suite Forms of Tajik Professional Music

The Maqām and its Structure. The great development of various types of Tajik art music led to the origin of suite forms called *maqāms*.[45] In Tajikistan, this term also has the connotation of "melody" at times. In the old literature it was often used as the title of a collection of tales. The Tajik maqām is a multipart suite, consisting of two large divisions: 1) instrumental, and 2) vocal with instrumental accompaniment. The former is called *muškilot* (literally, "difficulty"), and the latter *nasr* (literally, "prose," a composition with text).

222

The muškilot contains five basic parts, performed by a mixed string and wind orchestra, in which the tanbur plays the leading part: 1) *tasnif*[46] ("melody," sometimes also called "maqām"); 2) *tarje* (literally, "repetition," a piece with the rhythm of the preceding part); 3) *gardun* (literally, "firmament"); 4) *muxammas;* and 5) *saqil* (a section in slow tempo). Each of the parts of the first section of the maqām, with the exception of the gardun, have a rondo form and consist of various melodic sections called *xona, i. e.*, episodes [literally, "house, room"— M. S.], concluded by a repetition of the *bozguy* [literally, "said again"—M. S.], the unchanging basic theme.

The tasnif is composed in a unique rondo called *pešrav*[47] which means "companion" or "fellow traveller" [literally, "forerunner" or "introduction"—M. S.]. This form consists of a descending sequence of short motives, each time beginning a step up and concluding with the bozguy, as can be seen in the following example of a tasnif from the maqām *Buzruk* (Ex. 65):

Ex. 65. Tasnif from Maqām Buzruk. (*Šašmaqam* vol. I, p. 29).   Fairly quickly (♩ = 92).

225

Both the episodes (*xona*) and the basic rondo theme (bozguy) are marked by specific dimensions. In the muxammas this equals sixteen beats of 2/4 time, and in the saqil twenty-four beats of the same meter. The length of the complex rhythm of the usul corresponds to the melodic structure of the muxammas and saqil. As an example of muxhammas structure, here is "Muxammas Nasrulloy"" from the same maqām, *Buzruk*, consisting of three sections (Ex. 66):

Ex. 66. "Muxammas Nasrulloy," From Maqām Buzruk. (*Šašmaqām*, vol. I, p. 40). Moderately. (♩=74).

227

Bozguy.

As for the form of the tarje, it is less strict, sometimes approaching the form of the tasnif and other times that of the muxammas. The gardun has an usul of disproportionate beats and does not feature rondo structure. It consists of a series of musical phrases of similar rhythmic structure, as can be seen in the example from *Buzruk* (Ex. 67).

Ex. 67. Gardun from Maqām Buzruk. (Šašmaqām, vol. I, p. 35).   Fairly quickly (♩=116).

1 xona.

2 xona.

3 xona.

In various sections of the first part of the maqām we find the typical Tajik technique of a melodic rise to the high register for emotional climax, followed by a return to the basic lower register, where the music becomes calm.

As a whole the first section of the maqām serves as a kind of broad multi-part instrumental introduction to the vocal section,[48] consisting of four large solo parts: 1) *saraxbār*, an introduction; 2) *talqin*, a type of vocal melody; 3) *nasr*, another type of vocal melody; and 4) *ufār*, a conclusion in dance rhythm.

The text of these sections consists of great lyric poems, usually in the ğhazal or muxammas forms. Between these large sections of the second part of the maqām occur shorter parts, called *tarāna*, performed by a group of instrumentalists.

The tarānas contrast with the large solo vocal movements of the maqām and link them, preparing the scalar or rhythmic appearance of the new sections. The number of tarānas performed in interludes between solo sections varies from two to six or more. The song "Ghazal" by Ğiāsi from *Buzruk* (Ex. 60), is an example of a tarāna.

Ex. 68. Saraxbār from Maqām Buzruk. (*Šašmaqām* vol. I, p. 50.).   Moderately(♩ = 84).

The saraxbār of *Buzruk* begins the second section of that maqām and is an example of a large solo section from the vocal half of the maqām (Ex. 68).

The text of this saraxbār is a lyric ğazal of the Tajik poet Anvari (d. *c.* 1191).[49]

The sun is enraptured with the perfection of your beauty.
Your locks are the dark of night fringing your face, the sun.
Where your locks are, the dark of night reigns;
Where your face is, the sun shines.
Your face is a garden, wherein grow the fruits which are
    your eyes, the stars.
Your figure is a cypress, wreathed with the fruit of your
    face, the sun.
Your moon-like face is ringed by the musk of your plaits.
Bliss hides in the tulips of your lips.
Aromatic plaits encircle your face, the sun.
Your face is the sun, and your kiss, sugar.
The sugar of your lips is worthy of your face, the sun.
By decree of fate your face is decorated with a birthmark.
Even the sun could not refuse to have it on his face.
If, O Anvari, you wrote these lines
With a golden tassel on cosmic pages, the sun too would
    be astonished!

239

The seven couplets of this ǧazal form the seven verses of the saraxbār. The scale of the first three verses is Dorian d-minor, with a rise to the register a fourth above tonic. The climax (*auj*) occurs in the fourth and fifth verses, in which a rise to the octave register is made. The basic scale of these verses can be considered Mixolydian D-major with a hold on the third degree of the scale in the fifth verse. In the sixth verse, beginning with the scale of the auj, a transition is made to the dominant of the basic scale, after which in the seventh, final verse the Dorian d-minor and basic register of the saraxbār return. The change of registers and scales in the melodic structure can be delineated by the following diagram (Ex. 69):[50]

Ex. 69.

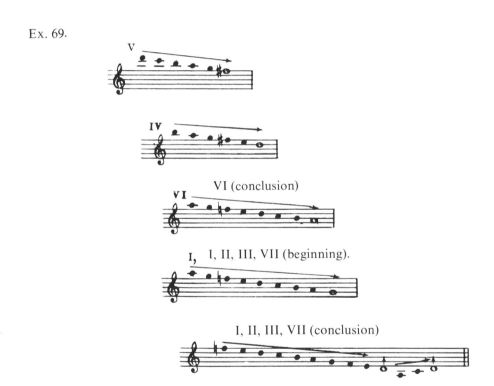

In its large overall internal structural complexity the saraxbār is a whole in melody and theme. A broad lyrical development of feelings is given, with gradual rise in tension to the auj and subsequent calming down toward the end of the piece.

240

The maqām combines a variety of musical forms and a wealth of poetic imagery and styles in its texts; thus, it unites the highest achievements of national culture of the feudal period. However, the maqām as a musical work is marked by internal contradictions: its form and musical content (as is the case with other types of folk production) remain truly unchanged works, while the texts of individual sections can change as long as the meter of the verse is preserved. This allowed the maqāms to be used by court singers to propagate the ideology of the rulers of feudal society and to express shameless flattery and low servility toward the rulers and their favorites.[51] The maqāms, like other types of Tajik art music, are a valuable historical heritage and have remained extremely popular to the present day.[52]

The "Šašmaqām". As a result of the long development of the suite form in Tajik professional music, a cycle of six maqāms was formed: 1) *Buzruk*, 2) *Rāst*, 3) *Navā*, 4) *Dugāh*, 5) *Segāh*, and 6) *Irāq*,[53] named for the scale in which they are composed. The term *Buzruk* (properly *bozorg*) means the "large" scale, close to the term "major" in meaning. *Rāst* means the "true" scale and *Navā* the "melodic" scale. *Dugāh* and *Segāh* are the second and third scales respectively.[54] Finally, *Irāq* means the Iraqi mode.

All these maqāms have the internal structure described above. The basic scalar system of the šašmaqām is quite complex, as individual sections of every maqām may have modulations to other scales.[55] These scales are called *šu'ba* ("branches") of the basic scales. There are twenty of these in the entire šašmaqām. They are based on the registral modulations discussed earlier.

Vocal Suites. There are smaller vocal suites with instrumental accompaniment, usually consisting of five sections with various *usul*s (metric schemes) which are parallel to the large suite forms of the maqām, with its instrumental and vocal-instrumental divisions. The parts of the small suites are: 1) *sowt*, 2) *talqinča*, 3) *Kašgarča* ("Kashgar style"), 4) *sāqināme* (with poetic text on the theme of the "cup-bearer's song"), and 5) *ufār* in dance rhythm.

The first part of such suites consists of a solo vocal piece with multistrophic form which serves as a kind of theme for the whole work. The remaining sections are rhythmic variants of the first part, in which its basic form and melodic outline are kept while different poetic texts (with different meters) are used. Example 70 gives a comparative chart of one of these suites in the scale *Sabā*; one can see at a glance how the melody of the first part of the suite is transformed in the following sections[56] (Ex. 70).

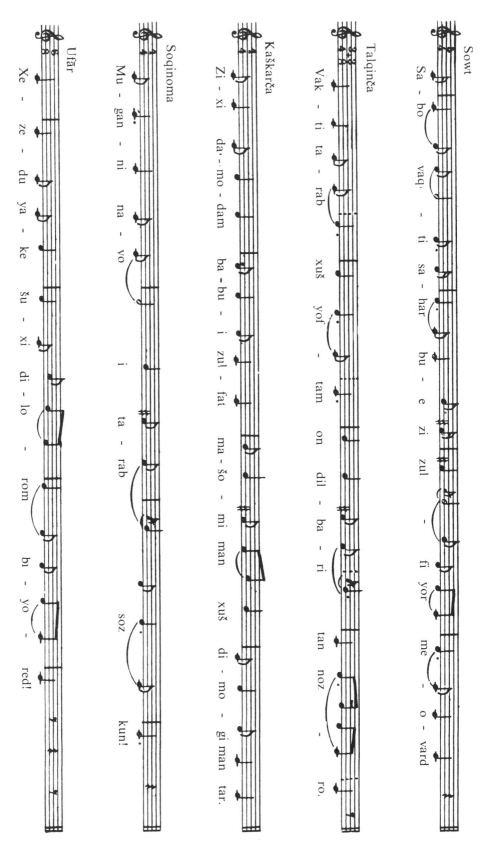

Ex. 70.

The basic melodic-rhythmic structure of parts of the suite consists of verse lines of the following syllabic and metric structure:

Sowt: 4+4+4+3 = 15 syllables
Talqinča: 7+7 = 14 syllables
Kašgarča: 5+5+5+5 = 20 syllables
Sāqināme: 5+5 = 10 syllables
Ufār: 5+5+3 = 13 syllables

Of special note are the originality of such a suite and the great mastery of Tajik professional musicians in the technique of varying melodic material.

Tajik Musicology

Theoretical Works. The rich development of professional music was reflected in the proliferation of theoretical musical thought. Works of great significance for their time appeared; they elaborated on the problems of the origin of musical art and its influence on man, and also researched questions of the scalar and rhythmic basis of art music.

Among these works the most outstanding are: the mathematical treatise of Abu-ali ibn Sinā (980-1037), called "Kitāb-aš-šifa" ("The Book of Numbers"), which has a special section on music; the "Risāle-i musiqi" ("Treatise on Music") of Abdurrahman Jami (1414-1492);[57] and excerpts of the work of Abdul Qadir (d. 1435), preserved in an anonymous treatise of the fifteenth century and especially valuable in that it gives a detailed description of the various types of music practice used in his time (*see* R. d'Erlanger, *La Musique arabe*, vol. I, IV, "Traité anonyme XVe s," Paris, 1930-1939).

Historical Works. In the same period historical and literary works were created, among them memoirs containing valuable data about musical life in the large Tajik cities. Among these works are: the *Babur-nāme*, the memoirs of Babur (1483-1530; the founder of the Mogul Dynasty); the memoirs of the poet Vasifi (first half of the sixteenth century); and the notes of Navāi (1441-1501). These and other sources acquaint us with scores of names of outstanding musical performers and composers, and authors of various compositions. In characterizing musicians' talents and artistic qualities, the writers of that time reach for such refined and hyperbolic expressions as "the phenomenon of his time," or "the rarity of the age," "the pride of musicians," "the captivator of the flowerbed of musical science," and others. As a special tribute to composers they speak of the unusual difficulties they surmounted in composing musical works.

All of this was connected with the spread of musical art among the urban Tajik population. Among the less wealthy and the students of the medrese there was a custom of men's weekly gatherings with poetry readings (usually of works composed by the participants themselves) and performances of musical works. In the meetings of the Tajik intelligentsia, and particularly among its best members, there was group discussion and criticism of various questions of litera-ture and art.[58] The conversation also touched on music; the performance of a new work was the topic of a lively exchange of opinions about its value, both in a general artistic sense and a theoretical musical context. Music also occupied an important place in court life. The sultans and emirs, seeking to gain a reputation as enlightened supporters of science and the arts, drew outstanding musicians to their courts.

Music was also widely used in urban festivals, the main participants of which were the craft guilds. During Tamerlane's entry into Samarqand in 1396 one such festival was organized (see AM. Belenitskii, "Iz istorii uchastiia remeslenikov v gorodskikh prazdnestvakh v Srednei Azii v XIV-XV vv." Gosudarstvenniy ermitazh, *Trudy vostoka* II, Leningrad, 1940). Jewelers, blacksmiths, leather workers, weavers, and masters of other crafts erected over a hundred superb pavillions in the streets and bazaars near which singers sang, musicians played, and dancers and tightrope walkers displayed their skills. The voices of the singers "put Venus into ecstasy." The dancers "swept tranquility out of hearts." And: "Golden-tongued singers and sweet-sounding musicians played and sang to motives in Persian style, to Arab melodies according to Turkish practice and with Mogul voices following Chinese laws of singing and Altai meters." This evidence depicts the multinational make-up of the performers collected by Tamerlane in Samarqand from all the lands he conquered.

TAJIK MUSIC FROM THE FIFTEENTH TO THE EARLY TWENTIETH CENTURIES

Tajik Music from the Sixteenth to the Nineteenth Centuries. The conquest of Central Asia by nomadic Uzbeks at the very beginning of the sixteenth century brought about great changes. Samarqand and Herat lost the significance they had had for the past two centuries as the greatest centers of Tajik culture and music. Uzbek feudal rules established new states, the most important of which were the emirate of Bukhara and the khanates of Khiva and Kokand. In this connection a drain of cultural and musical strength began from Herat to Bukhara, Samarqand, Tashkent, and other cities of Central Asia. Bukhara became the greatest center of Tajik culture during this period . . . .

During this time the song genres which characterized the difficult position of the workers became highly developed, such as songs of transients (ğaribi), those of seasonal workers, and those about women's lot. Also widespread were satirical songs, denouncing the ruling elite, their accomplices and stooges, and the mullahs, with their hypocrisy and sanctimoniousness, as well as songs of social protest and of popular uprisings.

During this period professional musicians performed works of the traditional repertoire and also composed new works in a more complex style. The works of classic poets (and accompanying music) resounded in the meetings of the literary-musical circles of the Tajik intelligentsia. Here new progressive poetic works were performed in their musical version as, for example, the poems of the great poet Said Nasafi (d. *ca.* 1707), who was a weaver by trade, and of Bedil (1644-1721), who lived in India but was very popular in Central Asia.[59]

They set themselves apart fcom court poets and developed civic and social motives in their work.

Various musicological works of historical and theoretical content also arose, such as those of Kaukabi and Dervish-ali. The work of Najmuddin Kaukabi (d. 1576), an outstanding Bukharan musician and theoretician of the sixteenth century, contains an exposition of the sequence of the vocal parts of the Šašmaqām, including the texts used at that time and indications of the scale structure. Kaukabi's work presents a version of the Šašmaqām which approaches that used today. It must be noted that a whole series of maqām texts in Kaukabi's version and the modern Šašmaqām coincide, thus showing how they were preserved in the practice of Tajik performers over the course of four centuries. The appearance of Kaukabi's work testifies to the fact that the Šašmaqām was already fully formed in the feudal period as the height of professional Tajik musical art.[60]

The work of Dervish-ali, *Risale-i musiqi* ("Treatise on Music" translated by A. A. Semenov, Tashkent, 1946), belongs to the first half of the seventeenth century. It is divided into two basic sections: theoretical and historical. The former is devoted to a review of the basic questions of the origin of music and its influence on man, as well as an exposition of scales, rhythms (*usul*), and a description of musical instruments. The second section is a collection of biographies of outstanding Tajik musicians (composers and performers of the fifteenth and sixteenth centuries). While the first section of Dervish-ali's work is not particularly novel and contains material borrowed from earlier well known works, the second section is highly valuable and interesting for the history of Tajik music in terms of the wealth of data presented. As in other medieval musical treatises, the work of Dervish-ali contains many legendary episodes and is not free of anachronisms.

Dervish-ali begins his musical "genaeology," including nine names, with Safi ud-din Abdulmumin (d. 1294), the famous theoretician of Baghdad. He also includes the famous Abdul Qadir (d. 1435), and then a number of Herati musicologists of the fifteenth century and Bukharans of the sixteenth century. In this "genaeology" Dervish-ali gives an historical portrait of the development of Tajik musicology, indicating the mutual exchange with the Western Iranians [*i.e.*, Persians—M. S.]. This is parallel to the literary exchange mentioned earlier in connection with the names of Hāfez and Sa'adi.

TAJIK MUSIC AFTER THE ANNEXATION OF CENTRAL ASIA TO RUSSIA (THE LATE NINETEENTH AND EARLY TWENTIETH CENTURIES)

Two great figures arose in Bukhara in this period: Akhmad Donesh (1827-1897), founder of enlightenment, who was a doctor, astronomer, artist, poet, and musician, and Sadriddin Aini (1878-1954), one of the greatest Tajik writers of the first half of the twentieth century. Meetings in Tajik cities between local migrant workers and Russian workers played an enormous revolutionary role and created the basis for the formation of a Tajik proletariat.

The main types of music in this period continued to be folk song and art music. Directly responding to events in the people's life, Tajik song reflected the growth of liberation movements. A striking example of this trend occurred in the songs of the 1885 uprising, led by the peasant Vose. At that time thousands of Tajik peasants, having lost patience with the infringements and violence of the emir's rule, defeated his army and seized the fortress of Baljuan, threatening the homes of the wealthy and the higher Muslim clergy. After the insurrection was quelled, Vose was hung.

The two songs below about Vose's uprising ("Šureši Vose") sharply reflect the great strength of the protest of the Tajik peasants against the yoke of the emirate. They are close in content and represent two parts of a single text. The first song paints a picture of the revolt and describes the military activity (Ex. 71).

Ex. 71. "Šuriši Vose'." [7] (From materials of the Republic House of folk arts of the Tajik SSR).

246

Vose' ğazost imrūz,
Jon mubtalost imrūz,
Ḡavğoi rūzi mahšar,
Dar fuqarost imrūz

Vose' hambad sangi mir,
Muqobili zulmi mir,
Boyad namudan tadbir.

Vose' ğazost . . .

Vose' sari sangonay
Poi aspuš langonay,
Xudaš mardi mardonay.

Vose' ğazost . . .

Vose' xambid sui Norak,
Kupruka karda porak
Mongito šud ovorak.

Vose' ğazost . . .

Refrain:
Vose rose up for a holy war.
Life is full of grief.
A cry as of the Last Judgement
Went up among the people.

Vose wanted to break the yoke of the emir.
One must find some defense
Against the emir's yoke.

(Refrain)

Vose on the stone wall.
His horse is crippled.
He is a valorous man.

(Refrain)

Vose went towards Nurek;
Broke down the bridge.
The Mangiti (=last Bukharan dynasty) were alarmed.

(Refrain).

The second song tells of the execution of Vose and his followers and of the cruel judgment against those who revolted (Ex. 72).

Ex. 72. "Šuriši Vose'." (From materials of the Republic House of folk arts of the Tajik SSR).
Moderately.

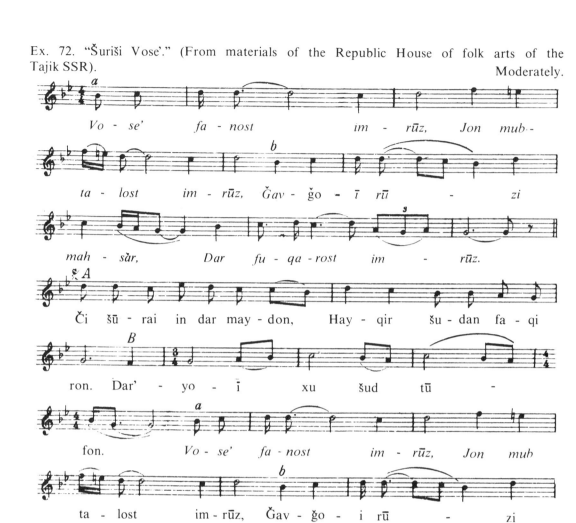

Vo - se'   fa - nost   im - rūz,   Jon mub -

ta - lost   im - rūz,   Ğav - ǧo - ī rū   -   zi

mah - săr,   Dar   fu - qa - rost   im - rūz.

Či šū - rai   in dar may - don,   Hay - qir   šu - dan   fa - qi

ron.   Dar' - yo - ī   xu   šud   tū   -

fon.   Vo - se'   fa - nost   im - rūz,   Jon   mub

ta - lost   im - rūz,   Ğav - ǧo - i   rū   -   zi

mah - šar,   Dar   fu - qa - rost   im - rūz.

Refrain:
Vose dies today
Life is full of grief
A cry as of the Last Judgement
Went up among the people.

What agitation on the square!
The poor people are perishing.
As in a storm, a river of blood arose
(Refrain)

Both songs are strongly expressive in melodic and emotional make-up. While the first song has a depth of feeling especially expressed by the choice of the Phrygian scale, with its concentrated character,[61] in the second the strength of feeling reaches an exceptional freedom of melodic development. Both songs feature artistic justification of the use of the three-part chain form with its constant repetition of the refrain carrying an emotional, semantic change.

In the 1880s an original system of notation called Khwarizm notation was devised which had great significance for the development of art music.[62] This notation was devised by the Khivan poet and musician Niāz Mirzābaši Kamil (d. 1889). The Khwarizm notation is a type of instrumental tablature. Its staff consists of eighteen lines corresponding to the frets of the tanbur, signifying the height of pitches. The length of notes is designated by dots placed on the lines, equal to an eighth-note or one stroke of the plectrum on the string of the tanbur. For notating a given composition its scale and usul are written out and the subdivisions of the piece into segments (*xona*) is also given. As an instrumental notation, Khwarizm notation was not suited to exact transcription of vocal works. Texts were written on the tanbur part, and the melodies were performed by the singer in alignment with this part.[63]

The whole Šašmaqām was transcribed into Khwarizm notation, as well as several separate works of both art and folk styles. Here is an example of this notation (Ex. 73), with a "translation" into modern notation (Ex. 73a):

Ex. 73

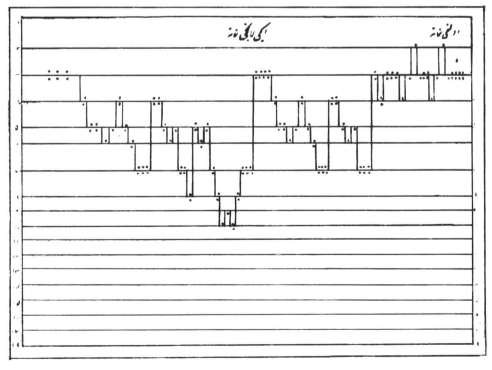

Ex. 73a

The invention of Khwarizm notation testifies to the high level of talent among Tajik musicians in the solution of complex theoretical questions . . . .

NOTES to Chapter IV

1. The term *nowruz* refers to the New Year of the Persian solar calendar, which falls at the vernal equinox. For full description of Tajik folk entertainments for festivals, *see* Nurjanov (1956).

2. The term *bazm* is still used with a similar connotation among mountain Tajiks of Afghanistan.

3. The egg cracking game is called *toxmjangi* ("egg fight"); players strike painted hard boiled eggs together, and the loser is the one whose egg cracks first, while the winner collects the eggs. The game is also played in northern Afghanistan and parts of the Near East. Also common to Tajikistan and northern Afghanistan are such sports as *buzkaši*, the famous horse-riding contest involving the capture of a stuffed goat (or calf), which must be deposited at a goal.

4. The use of the *ğazal* form ("couplets") rather than the folk *rubai* ("quatrain") indicates probable urban origin for Examples 5-6 and 7.

5. These are the standard images of classical Persian verse, frequently adopted by present-day folk song text writers in towns of Tajikistan and northern Afghanistan.

6. The nineteenth-century Russian Romantic composers' use of "exotic" themes in their works is a topic of frequent commentary in Soviet ethnomusicology. Later attempts at adapting "Eastern" tunes to Western harmonic principles are usually compared to Glinka (and to a lesser extent to Rimskii-Korsakov, Borodin, and others) as the standard of harmonication and setting. *See* Chapter 5 (p.   ) for some early harmonizations of Central Asian tunes.

7. The quatrain verse structure and partly or wholly improvised basis of these songs puts them clearly in the mainstream of Tajik folk tradition, as opposed to the literary ghazals given earlier (Exs. 7-9).

8. Soviet sources frequently comment on the lack of dance among the nomadic Central Asian peoples—the Kazakhs, Kirghiz, Turkmen—as opposed to the lively dance tradition of the sedentary Uzbeks and Tajiks; I know of no significant theoretical discussion of this question, beyond general statements such as "the nomadic conditions of life did not incline the Kazakh people to the dance" (Tkachenko, 1967: 203), which fit in with the overall Marxist evolutionary approach to the arts. Afghan Turkmen, however, do dance.

9. This duple-triple alternation is also very characteristic of Uzbek and Tajik dance music (vocal and instrumental) of northern Afghanistan.

10. Such songs and work patterns are still widespread in the mountain Tajik areas of northeastern Afghanistan.

11. The sentiment of this song provides a curious counterpart to that of Schubert's "Der Lindenbaum."

12. Section C seems merely a transposition up a fifth of section A, a feature shared by various Central Asian musics.

13. A and B sections of two-part tunes are frequently differentiated both by register and by raising or lowering of scale degrees in Uzbek-Tajik music in northern Afghanistan as well; Example 18 seems to have an unusual amount of such alteration.

14. The creation of such "resultant" scales in which all the pitches used are combined is interesting, but somewhat artificial.

15. This is a fine example of the problems one encounters in trying to accomodate octave-species "Greek" church modes to music based on tetrachordal and pentachordal structures.

16. Here is another theoretical axiom of Beliaev: an older music culture will have more "means of expression" in such items as scale structures than a younger music culture. This seems to run counter to a general Soviet approach to scalar development, which states that fewer, rather than more, scales will be used as a music culture advances, by analogy to the reduction of Western scales from twelve to two in the eighteenth century.

17. The contrast between Tajik folk and literary song texts can be rather sharp. Folk texts, as indicated by Beliaev, can be viewed syllabically, with the total number of syllables per line as the principle distinctive feature, whereas literary texts rely on the learned and complex aruz system (mentioned in earlier chapters of this volume) of prosody employed in classical Persian poetry, based on vowel length. In Examples 32-43 it is interesting to note how often the durational values of the notes contradict the long-short patterns of the vowels; in contrast, *cf.* Tsuge (1970); Tajikova (1968)

251

and Slobin (1971) for detailed discussion of the close correspondence between musical and poetic lengths in classical Persian and Tajik songs.

18. In Afghanistan this characteristic four plus three rhythm is more typical of mountain Tajiks (in the northeast) than of Tajiks or Uzbeks of the steppe country of Afghan Turkestan.

19. This is not a literal translation of the Tajik, but rather a Russian rhymed, metric version which the English translation does not pretend to duplicate.

20. For a complete description (with illustrations) of Tajik instruments on the Afghan side of the border, *see* Slobin (1969b).

21. For more detail on the instruments of mountain Tajiks, *see* Dansker (1965).

22. *Košnai* is the Uzbek term and *juftnai* the Tajik; in both cases the Persian *nai* ("reed") is used, while *koš* and *juft* are Uzbek and Tajik respectively for "paired."

23. The *Atlas* (1963: 128) speaks of two-stringed ğičaks of "fairly primitive construction"; to judge by scholars in Tajikistan and findings in northern Afghanistan, it seems that the two-stringed fiddle is more common in the mountain regions, with three-or four-stringed models belonging to the Uzbek-Tajik urban tradition.

24. Nizam Nurjanov of the Tajik Academy of Sciences told me that he and his colleagues have not yet determined what material mountain Tajiks used for fiddle bodies before tin cans, and the same problem is unsolved for the Afghans.

25. The naming of lutes by string number reaches *yazdāhtār* ("eleven–stringed") in Tajikistan (*Atlas*, 1963: 127).

26. This rubāb is directly related to the Afghan rubāb (and is sometimes so termed in Tajikistan), the same lute-type played today by the Paštuns of Afghanistan and which served as the model for the north Indian *sarode*.

27. The čang is related to, and probably derived from, the Persian santur. Tajiks in Afghanistan lack the čang (as dulcimer), but use the term for their jew's-harp, as do other Central Asians. In earlier times, čang also meant "harp" in Persia.

28. This point, clearly established by Beliaev in his excellent 1933 work on Uzbek instruments, was severely criticized at one time by other musicologists as being "reactionary," due to the need of establishing tempered scales for all instruments to perform Soviet music. For the harshest criticism, *see* Kon (1961).

29. Sachs has discussed this placement of fingerholes as well (1962: 99ff).

30. For more on early depictions of instruments in Central Asia, *see* Marcel-Dubois (1941) and Huth (1954) *inter alia*. As for the lute on the Airtam frieze, it is gently curved in guitar-style, rather than deeply cleft like the rubāb, and as the neck section has been lost, it is hard to determine the overall shape.

31. For transcription and discusssion of similar flute tunes from Tajikistan and northeastern Afghanistan, *see* Slobin (1969b).

32. *Usul* meaning "rule" comes from Arabic through Persian.

33. The use of mnemonics for drum patterns and the extensive role of drum accompaniment clearly show the urban, Near-Eastern-connected nature of much Tajik (and Uzbek) music, as opposed to the general absence of membranophones (outside the imported military drums) among the Turkmen, Kazakhs, and Kirghiz.

34. For discussion of the Tajik version of the *Kör-oğli* epic, *see* Braginskii (1956) and Karryev (1968).

35. Though both lute-types have two strings, they differ completely in such major features as presence or absence of frets (dutār and dumbrak respectively); the dumbrak is a variety of dutār only inasmuch as both are descended from an early type of Persian tanbur. However, Dansker's remark concerning mountain Tajiks' terming the dumbrak *dutār-i maida* ("small dutār") indicates folk support for Beliaev's statement (Dansker, 1965: 248).

36. Beliaev's criterion of complexity is that different settings be composed for the various strophes of a long poem; in other words, "through-composed" songs are by definition more advanced than strophic songs.

37. The preceding paragraph is a simplified presentation of the complex network of classic Arabic-Persian prosody.

38. *See* Chapter 3, note 24.

39. It seems apt to translate Beliaev's "professional vocal composition" as "art song," and "professional instrumental art" simply as "art music," since his terms do not take into account professional folk music. The folk-art distinction is clearer in Uzbek and Tajik music than in the music of the Kazakhs, Kirghiz and Turkmen.

40. To judge by recordings and live performances of the *Šašmaqām*, the transcription given here is skeletal, in that it does not reproduce either the untempered pitches or the high degree of melisma that must have characterized the original performance.

41. Both these features can be noted in classical Uzbek music as well, though definite differences in timbre distinguish the vocal style of the Tajiks from that of the Uzbeks.

42. The styling of Jami as a Tajik, rather than as a Persian, poet is typical of the Soviet approach. In the West Jami is generally regarded as the last great representative of classical Persian poetry.

43. The music of the nağara xona is interesting counterpart to the contemporaneous urban "clock" music of German cities, the *Turmsonaten*.

44. A piece with the same title is played by mountain Tajiks of northeastern Afghanistan for public entertainment.

45. The term *maqām* for a mode, or musical composition, clearly stems from the Arabic, and has the same meaning among Arabs even today. In Central Asia, maqām is used by Tajiks, Uzbeks, and Uighurs to mean fixed suites of instrumental and vocal music. The historical connection between the Arabic and Central Asian maqāms has not been well established. The fact that Beliaev describes the maqām in the chapter on Tajik, rather than Uzbek, music indicates that he viewed it primarily as being associated with Persian culture. I have suggested (Slobin, 1967) that the Uzbek-Tajik maqāms represent local variants of Persian art music, as crystallized in Central Asia after 1500, when the Safavids culturally isolated Transoxania from the Near East. Laurence Picken (private communication) feels that Uighur sources indicate a quite ancient origin for maqām suites in eastern Turkestan, perhaps dating back to the days of Central Asian cultural importance in T'ang Dynasty China (seventh-tenth centuries A.D.) It seems possible that these views might be reconciled by viewing the maqām as a Central Asian form under varying influence in its long history.
The maqām, as presently constituted among the Uzbeks and Tajiks (and, to a certain extent, the Uighurs, for whom evidence is scanty), is permeated with Persian terminology and Near Eastern

instruments, and approximations of Persian modes (*see* Spector, 1967). However, such key factors as manner of performance (voice quality, use of instruments, solo-ensemble alternation, among others) and musical structure are quite non-Persian and non-Arabic. Song texts are mixed; some stem from classic Persian and Čagatay poets and others from local Uzbek and Tajik writers. Also unresolved is the question of the Central Asian maqāms' relation to the musical composition of the same name played in Kashmir under Persian names—*Segāh, Rāst,* for example (I am grateful to Harold S. Powers for data on the Kashmiri maqām.) In summary, it is clear that a good deal of spadework remains before we can properly understand the background and connections of the Central Asian maqām.

46. *Tasnif* is still used in Persian music to mean a kind of urban song in classical modes. Beliaev (1964) published a little known collection of Teheran tasnifs of the early twentieth century which is a useful document for the study of Persian urban song and contains a valuable introductory essay on comparative metrics. Like many works of Soviet ethnomusicology, *Persidskie tesnify* came out in a tiny edition: one hundred ninety copies (the smallest I have yet seen).

47. *Pešrav* is one of the few terms in the Central Asian maqām's glossary to match terms still in use for the same function in Turkey and the Arabic world. Oddly enough, the word is Persian.

48. This parallels the function of instrumental interludes within songs, in which the ensemble (or solo instrument in the case of a single accompanist) prepares the tessitura for the singer. A similar technique can be found in Turkmen songs accompanied by dutar.

49. Again, the English text is a translation of the Russian version.

50. This change of registers and "scales" is part of the general Central Asian concept of differentiating segments of pieces, whether instrumental or vocal, with changes of various musical parameters, such as meters (*e. g.,* duple to triple), tempo, dynamics, register, and pitch content. The last two factors are the most frequently used to mark off structural divisions.

More specifically, in the maqām the introduction of varying pitch content, especially in the auj, is connected to a theoretical concept called *namud* (Persian, "appearance.") According to Karomatov and Rajabov (1969: 92), who know the maqām system intimately in both theory and practice, the namud is a kind of melodic trademark of a certain mode (*maqām*) or submode (*šub'a*) within a large *maqām* (*i.e.,* suite), and is named for that mode, *e. g., namud-i Nava.* The namuds are introduced in specific order at the appropriate points in the sections of the maqām. Thus, any given maqām presents a tightly knit network of modal references and cross references carefully worked out and presented in fixed, rather than improvised, form. The fullest discussion of the namud is in Karomatov (1966, in Russian and Uzbek).

51. Perhaps more neutral reasons for the fixed nature of the music *vs.* changeable texts is that music was traditionally considered the handmaiden of poetry in Persian culture and that only a few basic verse meters were used in the Uzbek-Tajik courts.

52. For a discussion of whether maqāms should be considered folk or "feudal" art and the effect upon modern compositional practice of the outcome of this debate, *see* Veksler (1965).

53. These are all clearly Persian terms, used to designate modes of art music in Iran. An interesting Central Asian feature is the changing of the Persian *bozorg* ("large") to *buzruk* in old Tajik dialect.

54. "Second" and "third" probably originally referred to the finger used on the fret of the lute-type taken as a standard basic scale.

55. This is a clear similarity to the Persian *dastgāh (avāz)* system, in which a given mode has specific subsidiary modes for modulation in the course of performance. Here Persian practice coincides with the Central Asian preference for registral and/or pitch changes cited earlier in connection with the *namud* concept (*see* note 45).

56. Example 70 is an extremely lucid presentation of the variational process used in the non-maqām suites. Whether this relates to the variational principle found in folk instrumental music is a moot point; in general, the facinating area of interplay between folk and "classical" music styles in Central Asia has been almost totally overlooked, save for polemics such as the debate on the "folksiness" of the maqāms mentioned earlier (*see* note 52).

57. Translated by A. A. Semenov, with extensive commentary by Beliaev, as *Abdurrakhman Jami: Traktat o Muzyke* (Tashkent, ANUzSSR, 1960). This valuable contribution to Islamic music theory includes a photocopy of the original treatise in Semenov's and Beliaev's edition.

58. Such meetings were also a feature of Uzbek life, and continued into recent years among prosperous Uzbek families of Afghanistan.

59. Bedil is held in exceptionally high regard in Afghanistan today among both the savants of the capital Kabul and the professional musicians of outlying regions.

60. Excerpts from Kaukabi's work have been published in Russian (translated by P. R. Rajabov) in *Muzykal'naia estetika stran vostoka*, Moscow: Muzyka, 1967, pp. 320-24.

61. Vissarion Belinskii and Nikolai Chernishevskii, prominent Russian literary critics and thinkers of the late nineteenth century.

62. This is an interesting carry-over of mediaeval European music theory into the assessment of Tajik music.

63. *See* Beliaev (1924) for an early report in the West of this notation. Curiously enough, the date for Khwarizm notation given there in the Islamic calendar (according to years of the Hegira) was thought by some to be Western dating, which has led to unfortunate confusion down to the present, as for example in Werner Bachmann's excellent book on the origins of bowing, where the author states that "Khwarizmic tablature dates from *ca.* 1200" (Bachmann, 1969: 47). Also curious is the fact that the West was perhaps first made aware of Khwarizm notation through Henri Moser, a non-musical Swiss traveller. In his memoirs (1885: 259), he describes a kind of tablature devised for a "three stringed guitar" by "a certain Palvan Divan," an official and enthusiastic musician at the court of Khiva. Note durations were indicated by signs of varying number along a line, according to Moser (*ibid*.), which confirms that the tablature he saw was the so-called Khwarizm notation.

64. This is a strong indication of instrumental predominance in the performance of maqāms.

Beliaev's Bibliography

Antologiia tajikskoi poezii. Moscow, 1951.

Gafurov, B. *Istoriia tajikskogo naroda,* vol. 1, Moscow: Gospolitizdat, 1952.

Lenskii, A. "Tajikskaia SSR." *Seriia Muzykal'naia kul'tura soiuznykh respublik*, Moscow, 1954.

Melodii pamira. Stalinabad-Tashkent, 1941.

Muzyka tajikov. Stalinabad-Tashkent, 1941.

Romanovskaia, E. and Semenov, A. "Toshbek i Gul-Qurban: Pamirskaia narodnaia skazka." *Sovetskaia muzyka,* no. 7, 1937.

Šašmaqām, vols. 1-4 (edited by Beliaev). Moscow: Gosizdat, 1950-1958.

As is the case with the bibliography of Turkmen music, there is little to add in Russian outside of the combined volumes 5-6 of the *Šašmaqām,* which apparently was published in Dushambe in 1969, and the few items which follow. There is more literature in Tajik, but it is not possible to give a comprehensive listing of such items at the present. Abbreviated citations are given, since the items added are listed at the end of this book: Beliaev (1924); Dansker (1965); Karomatov and Rajabov (1969); Tajikova (1968).

The Music Culture of Uzbekistan

The Development of Uzbek Music in the Pre-Soviet Period. The music of the Uzbeks, like that of the other Central Asian peoples, developed as an unwritten art through oral transmission and preservation of its monuments. The most important factor in the achievement of a high level of musical art among the Uzbeks, as among the Tajiks, was their sedentary, highly urbanized way of life, which allowed for the growth of musical professionalism. The Uzbeks and Tajiks lived on adjacent and partly shared territory, which caused the similarities in the music cultures of the two peoples, although the Uzbeks speak a Turkic language and the Tajiks an Iranian language. Where both peoples lived together, the population used both languages. . . .

THE BASES FOR THE DEVELOPMENT OF UZBEK MUSIC CULTURE

Uzbek Folk Song

Genres of Uzbek Folk Song. Over the years, an enormous wealth of song genres developed in Uzbek folk art, carried down to our own Soviet epoch. The songs strikingly reflect the life of the people and testify to the Uzbeks' outstanding musicality.

Work songs, sung during agricultural work, craft work, at home or in social situations, formed the basis of folk song. Uzbek work songs are quite varied in content and in poetic and musical make-up, starting from ancient and simple tunes and ending with later, more elaborate types. Social motives are sharply outlined among Uzbek work songs of the prerevolutionary period. This can be seen, for example, in "Padači" ("Shepherd's Song") where, describing the exhausting life of the itinerant shepherd, the performer curses the *bai* landlord (Ex. 1).

Ex. 1. "Padäči" (Transc. F. Karomatov). Fairly quickly.

Sä - rä - tan - dä   pa - dä   boq - dim,

Mo - lä - rim - ni   i - či - ni   yoq - dim,

Boy   a - tim - ğä   uč ming - ni   taq - di,

Pa - dä   baq - qän - lä - rim   qur - ğäy!

I herd the flock in July.
My sheep are exhausted from heat.
The *bai* assigned me a fine of three thousand.
Damn this kind of work!

The basic theme of the widespread women's work song "Čärx" ("Spinning Wheel") is angry protest against the inferior position of women under polygamy. Here are two specimens of this song (Exs. 2, 3):

Ex. 2. "Čärx" (Transc. V. Uspenskii). Moderately.

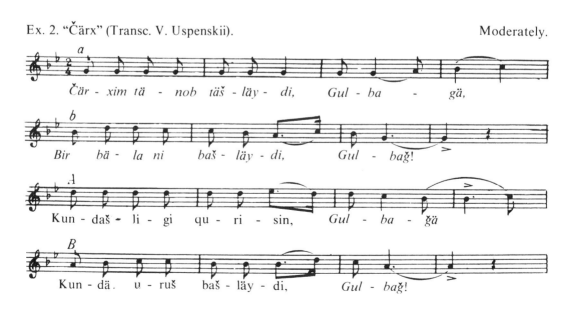

Čär - xim tä - nob täš - läy - di,   Gul - ba - gä,

Bir   bä - la ni   baš - läy - di,   Gul - bağ!

Kun - daš - li - gi   qu - ri - sin,   Gul - ba - gä

Kun - dä.   u - ruš   baš - läy - di,   Gul - bağ!

258

My spinning-wheel throws off the thread, flower-garden*
Foretelling some misfortune.
May polygamy be cursed,
With daily fights of rival wives.
My spinning-wheel throws off the thread,
Foretelling some misfortune.

*"flower-garden" is repeated after each line.

Ex. 3. "Čärx" (Transc. E. Romanovskaia). Moderately.

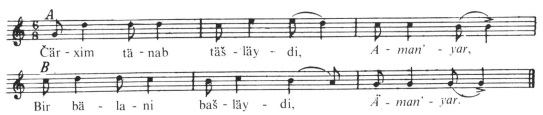

Along with such work songs of simple structure connected with work rhythms as "Čärx," the Uzbeks also have more developed songs. Songs of other genres are often sung during work to lighten the labor. The lyric song "Etim qiz" ("Orphan Girl") was popular among tanners in Andijan. It tells of the sorrow of a girl who has lost her father. The song has been transcribed with dutār accompaniment (Ex. 4).

Ex. 4. "Etim qiz" (Transc. V. Uspenskii). Moderately.

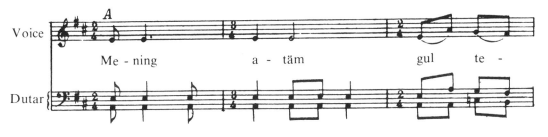

259

Mening atäm gul terädi,	My father gathered flowers
Qūli tūlmäy barädi;	But couldn't fill his hands.
Ūrtä būyli mening atäm,	My father wasn't tall
Dunyagä tūymäy barädi.	He left the world without being sated with life.
Dadxayim-sänäm, ey,	You felt sorry for me,
Aq saqal, alä saqal,	White-bearded, lion
Ärslanim aṭäm, ey!	My father.

There is also evidence of songs based on texts of popular Uzbek poets such as Muqimi and Furqat being sung during work.

Among ceremonial songs one finds domestic songs (primarily wedding songs and funeral laments). Wedding songs with a standard refrain are called *yār-yār* ("dear, dear," masculine or feminine). The content of individual strophes varies, being congratulatory, humorous, sorrowful (in the bride's lament upon leaving her home), and so forth. A typical wedding song is Example 5.

Uzbek yār-yār songs are similar to those of the Turkmen and Kazakhs in content, strophic and musical structure. This is an example of preservation among the Uzbeks of artistic ties to related Turkic nomadic peoples.

261

Ex. 5. "Yar-yar" (*Uzbekskie narodnye pesni*, Vol. I, p. 151).   Fairly quickly.

Häy-häy ūlän, jan ūlän,
Ūlän kūpdir, yar-yar!
Ūlän äytgän tilingdän
Mengä ūptir, yar-yar!

Hävadägi yulduzni
Säkkiz denglär, yar-yar!
Säkkiz qizning särdari
Keldi denglär, yar-yar!

Xävadägi yulduzni
Atgän atäm, yar-yar!
Ūz qizini tänimäy
Satgän atäm, yar-yar!

Ūz qizining uringä
Badam eksin, yar-yar!
Badam yaxši qäyrilsä,
Baläm desin, yar-yar!

Šäldir šuldur qämišgä
Sirgäm tušdi, yar-yar!
Sinämägän yigittä
Singlim tušdi, yar-yar!

O a song, a song
Greater than songs, yar-yar (yar-yar = refrain)
More than a song

O a song, a song
Greater than songs
Let me kiss your little tongue
That sings the song.

Count eight stars
In the sky.
Say which of eight girls (who came)
Is the most important.

My father gave away
A star in the sky.
Not recognizing his daughter,
My father sold her.

Instead of his daughter
Let him plant a pistachio tree.
If it grows up
Let him count it as a child
My earring fell
Among the noisy reeds
An untested youth
Got my sister

Some laments have a mournful improvisatory nature, such as "Yiği" ("Funeral Lament," Ex. 6).

Ex. 5. "Yiği" (Transc. F. Karomatov).   Moderately.

My dear mother, ai, ai! (Refrain)
When I asked her for bread, she gave me roast meat.
When I asked for water she gave me wine.
Don't grieve that you have no son;
I am a son and a daughter to you.
Always troubling about her only daughter.
Going to the bazaar and bringing me honey,
Bringing me a whole skirtful of delicacies!

Other types of lament belong to the repertoire of professional mourners and are cast in the developed forms of Uzbek folk song (Ex. 7).

Ex. 7. "Yiǧi" (Transc. V. Uspenskii).   Moderately.

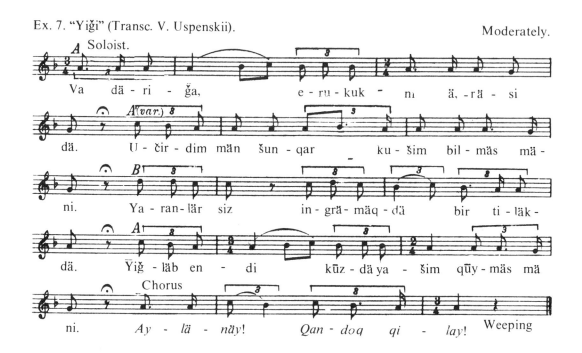

Soloist.
Va dä - ri - ǧa,   e - ru - kuk - nᵢ ä, -rä - si

dä.   U - čir - dim män šun - qar   ku - šim bil - mäs mä -

ni.   Ya - ran - lär siz in - grä - mäq - dä   bir ti - läk -

dä.   Yiǧ - läb en - di   kūz - dä ya - šim qūy - mäs mä

Chorus
ni.   *Ay - lä - näy!   Qan - doq qi - lay!* Weeping

A hawk took flight high above the earth; woe!
He flew from my hands to the sky like an arrow
I am left quite alone, I regret my friend.
Tears flow all day from my eyes like a river.
Woe unto us! How shall we live! (Chorus)
(Weeping)

The simplest type of daily-life songs are lullabies and childrens' songs, with their own typical content and means of expression. Here are two types of *alla* ("Lullaby"; Exs. 8, 9):

Ex. 8. "Alla" (*Uzbekskie narodnye pesni*, vol. I. p. 162).

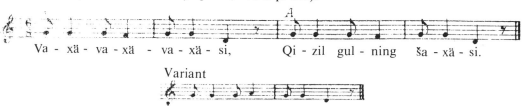

Va - xä - va - xä - va - xä - si,   Qi - zil gul - ning ša - xä - si.

Variant

Vaxä-vaxä-vaxäsi,	Rock-a-bye
Qizil gulning šaxäsi,	A branch of a red rose.
Qumdä salin äylänsin	The sandy steppes and your mother adore you.
Mamasi gelin äylänsin,	The sweets on a plate adore you
Täväqdä ijjan äylänsin,	And your aunt Nizjan.
Xaläsi Nizjan äylänsin.	
Ätäškir belčä äylänsin,	The coal tongs adore you
Sämar tunčä äylänsin,	And a boiling samovar.
Äylänib turgän učukdek,	Your aunt caresses you
Qazan yaläğän kučukdek,	Like a turning spindle,
Mirilläb yatgän pišikdek,	Like a puppy upsetting the pan,
Tūti xaläsi äylänsin.	Like a meowing cat.

Ex. 9. "Alla" (Transc. F. Karomatov).   Slowly.

265

Rock-a-bye, rock-a-bye my dear!
My dear little one
I will raise you to be big
Your braids are like gold; in the water fishes gambol.

The children's spring song "Bayčečäk" ("Snowdrop") preserves the character of a spring ceremonial carol, based on rhythmic recitation of a text which changes to simple speech (Ex. 10).

Ex. 10. "Bayčečäk" (Transc. E. Romanovskaia). Parlando.

Bay - če - čä - ğim bay - län - di,   Qa - zan tū - lä   äy - ran - di,

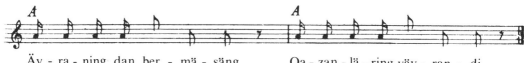

Äy - ra - ning dan ber - mä - säng,   Qa - zan - lä - ring väy - ran - di.

Bayčečäğim bayländï	My snowdrop bloomed.
Qazan tūlä äyrandi,	The cauldron is full of sour milk.
Äraningdän bermäsäng	If you don't give me sour milk
Qazanläring väyrandi.	Your cauldron will fall apart.
Qättiq erdän qozilib,	The snowdrop grew up
Čiqqän bayčečäk.	On hard soil.
Yumšaq erdän yugurib.	The snowdrop struggled up
Čiqqän bayčečäk.	Through loose soil.

Here is the text of another children's carol:

Rain, fall!
Serve, hostess! (repeated after each line).
Wheat, ripen!
Cow, eat up!

In the area of daily-life songs among the Uzbeks (as among other peoples), lyric songs are the richest in form and content. These are divided into love songs, songs of nature, contemplative songs, among others. "Uzganča"[1] ("Uzgenč Song" [a city in Khwarizm, on the lower Oxus River—M. S.]) and "Aidek tūlibdir" ("Full as the Moon") can serve as examples of love songs. They both belong to the best and most typical variety of such songs (Exs. 11, 12).

Ex. 11. "Uzgänča" (*Uzbekskie narodnye pesni* vol. I, p. 118).   Moderately.

Tağdä ärčä ming yil umr kūrurmi,
Šaxi sinsä, zärgär kumuš qilurmi?
Zärgärni qilğäni ärčä būlurmi,
Bilib bergän kūngul juda būlurmi?

Sen gūzälni izläb, čūllärni kezdim,
Ūšäl kezgän čūllär, būston ëmäsmi?
Sening janing mening janim ëmäsmi?
Mening janim sengä-ya, qurban ëmäsmi?

Sämärqänd soyidä qaldi uzugim,
Qäčan kelgäy mening-oxu kūzläri suzugim?
Ägär kelsä mening kūzläri suzugim,
Ulärdin äylänsin-ä tillä uzugim,

Seni undä, meni bundä yärätdi,
Arämizdä aqär därya yärätdi.
Aqär därya ëkän aqdiu ketdi,
Beväfa yar ëkän täslädi ketdi.

Bäländ tağ ustidä bir qizni kūrdim,
Uzi hur, läbläri qirmizni kūrdim.
Jädälläb bardimu bir sūz qatäy deb,
Kūzi uyqidä būlsä uyğätäy deb.

Qizil gul ačilib qildi nišanä,
Sening išqing meni qildi devanä,
Sening išqing mengä käydän yapišdi.
Tänämdin ūt čiqib bäğrim tutašdi.

Qizil gul qätmä-qät gul ärğuvani,
Qizil gullär erur ašiqning kani.
Qizil gul tägigä barsäm kūrärmän
Seni janu-dilim birlän sevärmän.

267

Is it true that the *archa* in the mountain lives
   a thousand years?
If you break off a branch, can the jeweler
   really weld silver to it?
Does the archa become what the jeweler makes of it?
Is it true that someone can abandon the one to whom
He has given his heart?

I scoured the desert in search of you, beauty
Isn't the steppe full of flowers?
Isn't your soul my soul?
Didn't I sacrifice my soul to you?

I left a ring in a valley near Samarqand.
When will my gazelle-eyed love come?
If my gazelle-eyed love comes
I will give her my golden ring.

You were born there and I here.
A large river is between us.
Her waters flowed and left.
A faithless friend abandons and leaves.

I saw a girl on a high mountain.
I saw a houri with scarlet lips.
I went to her to say a word.
To wake her, if sleep closed her eyes

The first full roses have opened up.
I am made for love of you
Whence comes this love?
Fire came from my body and burns my heart.

The red rose has many petals.
Red roses are lovers' blood.
I go to you as to a rose,
For I love you with my whole heart and soul.

Ex. 12. "Aydek tūlibdir" (Transc. V. Uspenskii).   With ardor.

268

Aydek tūlibdir janan yuzingiz
Vah janim alǧay fattan kūzingiz.

Xuban ëlining sultanidirsiz,
Kūzlärgä surmä bosgän izingiz!

Vah, jilvä birlän men xästä dilni
Äyläb giriftar ketgän ūzingiz

Neča širinlär širin ëmäsdir
Širin älärdin härbir sūzingiz!

My love has a face like the moon.
My love's eyebrows are like the dark night.

She is like a rose among other girls.
And her glances are like spring flowers.

But o! My friend is strict with me.
My meetings with her are forbidden.

My life's sweetness is taken from me.
How unhappy are those who love.

269

Ex. 13. "Čämändä gul" (Transc. V. Uspenskii).   Lively.

Čämändä gul ačilibti,
Čäkkänggä taq, čäkkänggä!

The field is covered with a carpet of flowers, ei!
Pick them, friends!

Kašingni qarä kilǧän,
Baǧdägi karä usmä.

That girl's glance disturbs me
Whose brows are decorated with mascara.

Čämändä . . .

Kūngilni šäyda kilǧän
Aldingä beli täsmä.

I am always sighing over her,
Whose waist is tied in by a band.

Čämändä . . .

Qašing äsli karädir
Ūsmä qūygäning yalǧan.

Don't lie and say you paint your eyebrows;
They are black without mascara.

Čämändä . . .

Sening učun men küygän,
Sening kuygäning yalǧan.

Don't lie and say you love me;
Save your lies for others!

Čämändä . . .

The songs "Čämändä gul" ("Flowers in the Field") Qäylärgä baräy?" ("Where Shall I go?"), and the Khwarizm song "Rūmalim" ("My Kerchief") are outstanding examples of lyric songs of a livelier nature (Exs. 13, 14, 15).

270

Qašingni qarä qilgän, janimä,
Taǧdägi bärrä usmä.
Äqlimdän jida kilgän, janimä,
Uydägi beli täsmä.

Qäylärgä baräy?
Qäylärdä turäy?
Ätläsläri·būlmäsä, janimä,
Märǧilan barä qaläy!

Tal ëkkänim yūq ëdi, janimä,
Toldirdi bilägimni.
Yar sevgänim yuq ëdi, janimä,
Yandirdi yurägimni.

Qäylärgä . . .

You blackened your eyebrows
My dear
With mountain *usma*
You have driven me mad
My dear
With your waist, narrow as a band.

Where can I go?
Where shall I stay?
If you don't have satin,
My dear,
I'll go to Marghelan for it.

I didn't plant a willow-bush
My dear
But my arms are tired.
I haven't loved before
My dear
But now my heart burns with anguish.

271

Ex. 15. "Rūmalim" (*Uzbekskie narodnye pesni* vol. II, p. 63). Lively.

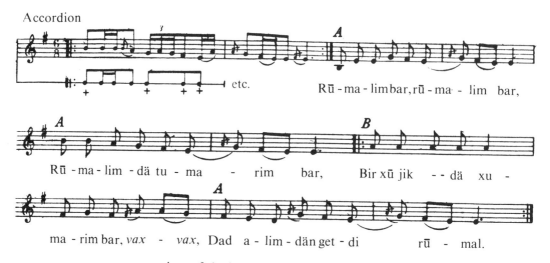

variant of the introduction for other verses:

Rūmalim bar, rūmalim bar,
Rūmalimdä tumarim bar,
Bir xujikdä xumarim bar,
Dad alimdän getdi rūmal.

Rūmal tušib getdi yapä
Yar ëšitsä būlur xäfä,
Yargä barib äytmäng, apä,
Dad alimdän getdi rūmal.

Rūmalimning uči šayi,
Ūrtäsidä bardir oyi,
Alib bering janim dayi,
Dad alimdän getdi rūmal.

Xup čiraylik ëdi rūmal,
Alimdän učirdi šämal,
Atäm-anäm häm kämbäğäl,
Dad alimdän getdi rūmal.

Rūmaldä ëdi-ya xäyalim,
Zäbun buldi hämmä ähvalim,
Häm tūšär yadimä yarim,
Dad alimdän getdi rūmal.

I have a kerchief;
On the kerchief is an amulet.
I love a certain fellow
The kerchief flew out of my hands

The kerchief fell off and flew away at once.
If my love finds out, he'll be angry.
Don't tell him about it, sister.
The kerchief flew out of my hands.

The fringes of my kerchief are silk.
It has half-moon decorations in the middle.
Get it for me;
My kerchief flew out of my hands.

The kerchief was very beautiful.
The wind took it from my hands.
My father and mother are poor.
The kerchief flew out of my hands.

I think about my kerchief all the time.
I feel bad.
I remember my darling.
The kerchief flew out of my hands.

272

The Uzbeks, like the Tajiks and some other peoples, have a widespread form of lyric dialogue song called *lapar*, which is a humorous declaration of love between a boy and a girl, often in the style of a competition in wit and resourcefulness. "Qarä sač" ("Black-haired One") is a fine example of a lapar with this type of content and a delicate melodic outline (Ex. 16).

Ex. 16. "Qarä sač" (*Uzbekskie narodnye pesni* vol. I, p. 160).   Jokingly.

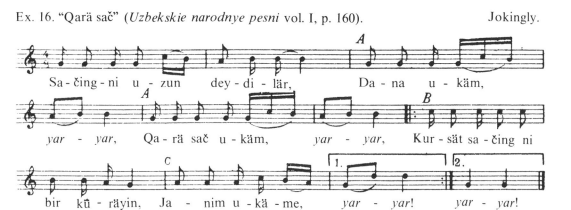

Sa-čing-ni u-zun dey-di-lär, Da-na u-käm, yar-yar, Qa-rä sač u-käm, yar-yar, Kur-sät sa-čing ni bir kū-räyin, Ja-nim u-kä-me, yar-yar! yar-yar!

*Sačingni uzun deydilär,	They say you have long hair
Dana ukäm, yar-yar,	My dear sister, yar-yar
Qarä sač ukäm, yar-yar,	Blackhaired sister!
Kūrsät sačingni bir kūräyin,	Show me your hair
Janim ukäme, yar-yar!	Let me see it just once.
Sačimni kūrib nimä qiläsiz,	Why do you want to see my hair
Siz äkäjanim, yar-yar,	Dear brother?
Jan äkäjanim, yar-yar,	Sweet brother?
Bazardägi sačpäpukni	There are wigs in the bazaar;
Kūrmäbmidingiz, yar-yar?	Haven't you seen them?
Qašingni qarä deydilar	They say you have black eyebrows
Dana ukäm, yar-yar,	My dear sister,
Qarä kaš ukäm, yar-yar,	Black-browed sister
Kursät kašingni bir kūräyin	Show me your eyebrows
Qunduz qaš ukäm, yar-yar!	Let me see them just once.
Qašimni kūrib nimä qiläsiz,	Why do you want to see my eyebrows
Siz äkäjanim, yar-yar,	Dear brother?
Jan äkäjanim, yar-yar,	Sweet brother
Qaldirǧačning qänätini	Haven't you seen
Kūrmäbmidingiz, yar-yar?	Swallows' wings?
Kūzingni qarä deydilär,	They say you have black eyes
Dana ukäm, yar-yar,	My dear sister
Qarä kūz ukäm, yar-yar,	Black-eyed sister
Kursät kuzingni men kūräyin	Show me your eyes
Kuräläy kuz ukäme, yar-yar!	Let me see them just once.

*verses alternate boy-girl.

273

Kūzimni kūrib nimä qiläsiz,	Why do you want to see my eyes
Siz äkäjanim, yar-yar,	Dear brother?
Jan äkäjanim, yar-yar,	Sweet brother?
Axūlärning kūzlärini	Haven't you seen
Kūrmäbmidingiz, yar-yar?	Doe's eyes?
Yuzingni qizil deydilär,	They say you have rosy cheeks
Dana ukäm, yar-yar,	My dear sister
Qizil yuz ukäm, yar-yar,	Rosy-cheeked sister,
Kursät yuzingni men küräyin	Show me your cheeks
Gul yuzli ukäm, yar-yar!	Let me see them just once.
Yuzimni kūrib nimä kiläsiz,	Why do you want to see my cheeks
Siz äkäjanim, yar-yar,	Dear brother?
Jan äkäjanim, yar-yar	Sweet brother?
Bazardägi širman nanni,	Haven't you seen
Kūrmäbmidingiz, yar-yar?	Rosy breads in the bazaar?

In this case both participants repeat the entire verse of the song; in another lapar, the girl sings the first half of the verse, and the boy the second (Ex. 17).

Ex. 17. "Läpär" (Uzbekskie narodnye pesni vol I, p. 158).   Allegro molto.

Dear, I'll say again	You've worn satin;
What I said before:	Wear satin again.
Buy me satin.	Your dress will rustle before me!

The lapar, as a dramatic song form, is used by the Uzbeks not only for lyric songs, but also for humorous and satiric songs, in the latter case for social criticism.

Lapar performance is usually accompanied by gestures, mime, and dance motions. This genre is close to Uzbek dance and play songs. "Päxtä terädi" ("Cotton Picking") is a fine example of a girls' game song, performed antiphonally by two unison choruses and accompanied by a depiction of the whole process of cotton planting, harvesting, weaving and sewing a girl's beautiful holiday dress. In the alternation of the two choral groups one can see a typical example of the "question and answer" form of melodic construction, especially apt here (Ex. 18).

Ex. 18. "Päxtä terädi" (Transc. E. Romanovskaia).   Giocoso.

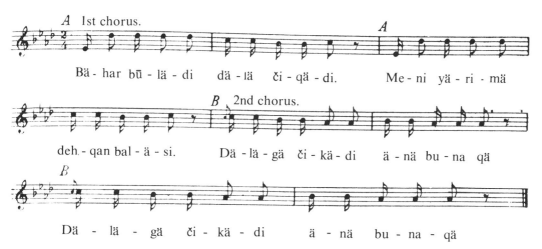

Bähar būlädi, dälä čiqädi,	Spring is here, the fields awake
Meni yarimä dehqan baläsi	The farmer's daughter, my dear,
Dälägä čiqädi änä bunaqä	Goes out to the field, like this.
Dälägä čiqib nimä qilädi	What will she do in the field?
Meni yarimä dehqan baläsi?	She will work with the hoe like this.
Ketmän čapädi änä bunaqä	

Ketman čapib nimä qilädi
Meni yarimä dehqan baläsi?
Märzälär qilädi änä bunaqä.

Having broken up the soil, what will she do?
She will make furrows, like this.

Märzälär qilib nimä qilädi
Meni yarimä dehqan baläsi?
Čigit ёkädi änä bunaqä.

Having made furrows, what will she do?
She will sow cotton seeds, like this.

Čigit ёkib nimä qilädi
Meni yarimä dehqan baläsi?
Päxtä terädi änä bunaqä.

When they grow, what will she do?
She'll pick cotton, like this.

Päxtä terib nimä qilädi
Meni yarimä dehqan baläsi?
Xirmän qilädi änä bunaqä.

Having picked the cotton, what will she do?
She'll ready the threshing-floor, like this.

Xirmän qilib nimä qilädi
Meni yarimä dehqan baläsi?
Čiqärib alädi änä bunaqä

Having cleaned the threshing floor, what will she do?
She'll clean the fibers, like this.

Čiqärib alib nimä qilädi
Meni yarimä dehqan baläsi?
Säväb alädi änä bunaqä.

Having cleaned the fibers, what will she do?
She'll beat the cotton with twigs, like this.

Säväb alib nimä qilädi
Meni yarimä dehqan baläsi?
Yigirib alädi änä bunaqä.

Having beaten the cotton, what will she do?
She'll spin the threads from the cotton, like this.

Yigirib alib nimä qilädi
Meni yarimä dehqan baläsi?
Tändä qūyädi änä bunaqä.

Having spun the threads from the cotton, what will she do?
She'll stretch it on a stand, like this.

Tändi qūyib nimä qilädi
Meni yarimä dehqan baläsi?
Dūkangä salädi änä bunaqä.

Having stretched it on a stand, what will she do?
She'll weave fabric on the stand, like this.

Dūkangä salib nimä qilädi
Meni yarimä dehqan baläsi?
Tūqib alädi änä bunaqä.

Having woven the fabric, what will she do?
She'll take it off the stand, like this.

Tūqib alib nimä qilädi
Meni yarimä dehqan baläsi?
Bičib alädi änä bunaqä.

Having taken it off the stand, what will she do?
She'll cut out a dress pattern, like this.

Bičib alib nimä qilädi
Meni yarimä dehqan baläsi?
Tikib alädi änä bunaqä.

Having cut the pattern, what will she do?
She'll sew a nice dress, like this.

Tikib alib nimä qilädi
Meni yarimä dehqan baläsi?
Kiyib alädi änä bunaqä.

Having sewn a nice dress, what will she do?
She'll put on the dress, like this.

Kiyib alib nimä qilädi
Meni yarimä dehqan baläsi?
Ūynäb kirädi änä bunaqä.

Having put on the dress, what will she do?
She'll walk like a peacock, like this.

It should be noted that Uzbek dances are sometimes accompanied by a single *doira* (tambourine), performed in virtuoso style. The solo scene "Pillä" ("Silk Spinning") depicts the process of preparing silk, and starts with the rhythmic figure below, (the figures numbered 3 and 6 indicate a transition to the next choreographic episode, Ex. 19):

Ex. 19. "Pillä" (Transc. I. Akbarov).   Con moto.

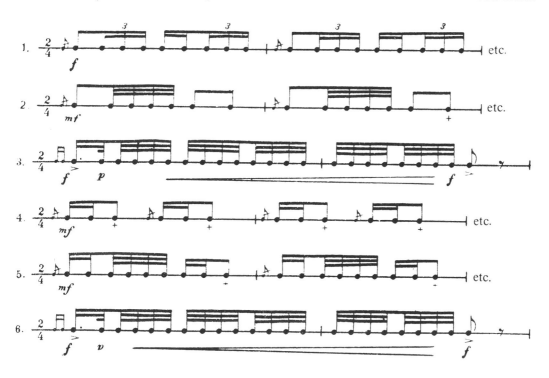

Simple songs are included in Uzbek puppet theater presentations to enliven them. Two songs called "Kuğirčak rubapläri" ("Puppeteer's Songs") belong to this type of song; both have the same quatrain (Ex. 20).[2]

Ex. 20. "Kuğirčak rubapläri" (Transc. V. Uspenskii).   Con moto.

Con moto.

If you were on that street!
If I was on this street!

If you were a rose in the garden,
Then I would be a shamrock near you.

Wai, wai wai! Wai, wai, wai!

Here is an example of an historical song, arising in response to the 1920 earthquake, when the city of Andijan was heavily damaged. "Andijan zilzilasi" ("The Andijan Earthquake") is cast in a developed form with hyperbolic images in the text (Ex. 21).

Ex. 21. "Ändijan zilziläsi" (Transc. V. Uspenskii).   Moderately.

Šuh - rä - ti   ə - läm - ni tut — di "Än - di - jan Rum būl - di" deb;

Key - ni - din   a - fät - gä uč - räb, ket - di däv - ran Än - di - jan.

They said everywhere that Andijan
was the second Byzantium
And now, after its tribulations,
the prime of Andijan is past.

Melodies of Uzbek Folk Song. Let us turn to a short description of the means of musical expression which especially typify Uzbek folk song. First of all, it should be noted that there are two basic types of melodic motion: 1) ascending-descending, and 2) descending; both types are used independently or in conjunction, as is also characteristic of Tajik music. The melody of "Čärx" (Ex. 3) is an example of the use of descending contour after an opening leap outlining the basic range. In the other version of "Čärx" (Ex. 2) and in "Padäči" (Ex. 1) one finds the ascending-descending contour in its simpler form.

The conjunction of both types of melodic motion is found in the majority of examples given, *e. g.*, Examples 12, 13, and others. The frequent use of syncopation is very typical of Uzbek folk song, especially in approaching the cadential tone. In the diagram below, A indicates the simplest type of declamation of the first line of text of Example 21 ("The Andijan Earthquake"), and B gives its elaboration through the use of syncopation (Ex. 22).

Ex. 22.

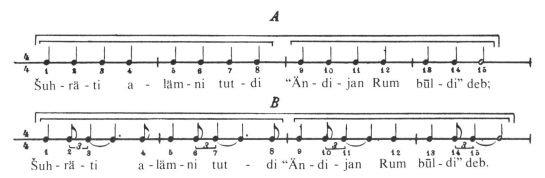

Scalar Basis of Uzbek Song. The scalar basis of Uzbek song, like that of Tajik song, is a system of diatonic scales, including major-like scales (Ionian, Mixolydian) and minor-like scales (Aeolian, Dorian, Phrygian). In rare cases, one also finds the Lydian scale at a cadence on the third degree of the Dorian scale (Ex. 23), and in a similar cadence in Mixolydian, the Hypophrygian results (Ex. 24).

Ex. 23.

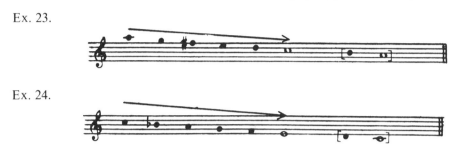

Ex. 24.

In a song the mixture of scales above a common tonic leads to scalar alteration and chromaticization of the basic scale, usually of its second, third, sixth, and seventh degrees. Thus, the replacement of the Dorian scale with the Aeolian scale yields an altered sixth, and a change of the Aeolian scale to Phrygian scale gives an altered second step.

Rhythm of Uzbek Song. Despite the differences in the structure of the Uzbek and Tajik languages, the basic metrics of song are the same among both peoples, both in terms of syllable and foot structure. The types of rhythmic-melodic declamation are also similar. Thus, we need not introduce examples of declamation of various types of verse lines, and can limit ourselves to introducing a table of the more frequent rhythmic figures used in singing eight-syllable trochaic lines (Ex. 25).

Ex. 25.

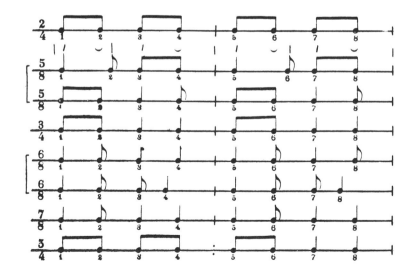

280

These rhythmic figures are further elaborated and complicated first by introducing various types of syncopation, and secondly by melodic extenstion of individual syllables of text. What has been said for eight-syllable lines holds true for
both smaller (five-to seven-syllable) and larger (nine-to sixteen-syllable or more)
lines used in Uzbek folk song. It should be noted that the metric basis of the
yār-yār songs rests on an alternation of seven and six-syllable lines of the following structure (Ex. 26):

Ex. 26.

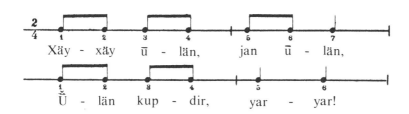

Uzbek prosody can be divided into two basic parts: 1) *barmak* and 2) *aruz*.[3]
The first type is used in lines with a small number of syllables, (from five to eight
and up to eleven). It is called barmak, or "finger," because its syllable and foot
formulas are counted on the fingers. This type of prosody is found in simpler
folk songs.

The second type, aruz, is connected with the use of complex verse lines and,
as was noted for Tajik music, is the "learned," or professional prosody. Its basic
traits have already been characterized. Poetry cast in the aruz style may be used in
more developed Uzbek folk songs.

Strophic Structure of Uzbek Folk Song. Different types of strophe arise depending on whether barmak, the simpler form of prosody, or aruz, the more complex
type, is used. Barmak texts are associated with folk quatrains (*rubāi*) with the
familiar *aaba* rhyme scheme. The number of syllables in rubāi lines is usually
seven, eight, or eleven, in trochaic meters. Aruz texts are linked to continuous
rhyme schemes such as the ǧazal, murabba (quatrain), and muxammas (five-liner),
which arose on the basis of the rubāi. All types of strophe listed above are used in
the development of form in Uzbek folk songs.

Forms of Uzbek Folk Song. The predominant form among all the widespread
types of song form are the half-stanza, two-part strophe forms. Various refrains
(as in Exs. 2, 4, 9, 12, 14) and opening calls (Ex. 6) play a large role in the development of these forms.

Some more complex strophic forms arise on the basis of longer stanzas, such
as five-and-six liners, and through the repetition of individual lines of quatrains,
using different melodies. This can be seen in the second "Puppeteer's Song"
(Ex. 20). The singing of two or more verses leads to the formation of complex

structures. The popular dance song "Qäri näva" ("Old Tune") can serve as an example of this process. It was used by Gliere and Sadykov in their opera *Gulsara*. It is cast in a broad three-part form with a large refrain for every section (Ex. 27).[4]

Ex. 27. "Qäri näva" (*Gul'sara*. Music transc. T. Sadikov, words Ya. Nugmanov, Allegro. Tashkent, 1941).

doira;

I *A*

Men a - čil - dim ën - di ūst - lär,

bir - gu - li rä'- na bū - läy,

B

Bu čä - män - ning

iš - qi - dä bir bul - bu - li šäy - da bū - läy,

bul - bu - li šäy - da bū - läy,

a

Šu či - ray - lik čä - män ,im - dä gul - lär te - rä - män

Af - tab - ning til - lä nur - lä - ri - ni ë - mä - män!

II.*C*

Qul - lä - rim - dä säy - rä - di saz, til - dä

ūy - naq yäl - lä - lär,

282

I opened up, friends, like a flower
I would like to be the nightingale for this garden

Refrain:
I gather flowers in this beautiful garden;
I soak up the golden rays of the sun.

The lute sounded in my hands, and happy songs were on my lips.
The sun healed the wound in my heart. (Refrain).

My eyes shone, the bloody tears stopped flowing.
My fiery speech pierces the heart of my enemy (Refrain).

The three-part chain form is a national characteristic of Uzbek, as well as of Tajik, folk art: ABABA. The songs "Čärx" (Ex. 2) and "Čämändä gul" (Ex. 13) are examples of this form.

The Uzbeks clearly define various song forms in folk terminology. One-part and small two-part forms of simple recitative type are called *terma* and *čublama*. Small two-part forms with more developed melodies and refrains are called *košuk*.[5] A košuk with unison choral refrain, accompanied by playful or dance motions is called a *yalla*, or *lapar*, if it is performed as a dialogue. Finally, songs in large two-part form are called *äšulä*.

The musical content of simple Uzbek songs (terma, košuk and the like) is quite fixed. Their texts consist of complete individual thoughts in quatrains, freely following one another and often belonging thematically to different genres.[6] For the most part these texts are not fixed to specific melodies. As for songs of the ašula type, their musical content is more elaborated, individualized, and connected with texts on a specific subject, demanding unified melodic and emotional expression. Even here there are cases of various texts to the same melody, but these texts are entire multistrophic poems, and not individual quatrains with varying content, as in the terma and košuk forms. The ašula, a development from the two latter forms, is carried into the realm of Uzbek urban folk songs in musical style and text. The use of the term "terma" testifies to the ties between the songs of the Uzbeks and their Turkic neighbors, the Kazakhs and Kirghiz. The development of form in Uzbek folk songs prepares the way for the structures of art song, of which more below.

Uzbek Instrumental Music

Uzbek Musical Instruments.[7] As mentioned in the chapter on Tajik music, the instrumentarium of the Tajiks and Uzbeks is similar, and is quite varied. It includes earlier forms of all the basic types of instruments found in the symphony orchestra. Woodwinds are represented by the *nai* (transverse flute), *surnai* (oboe) and *košnai* (clarinet).[8] Brass instruments are represented by the *karnai* (a bass horn); percussion instruments consist of the *doira* (tambourine) and *nagara* (kettle-drum);[9] and strings include the *gičak* (fiddle), *dutār, tanbur,* and *rubāb* (plucked lutes) and the *čang* (dulcimer—a distant ancestor of the piano).[10] The Turkic element in the instrumentarium consists of the *qobuz* [horsehair—M. S.] fiddle, related to one of the main instruments of the Kazakhs (*kobiz*) and Kirghiz (*kiak*).

284

The dutar is spread among the Uzbeks both for solo play and as accompaniment for folk songs, often with the doira added.[11] The tanbur is an instrument of professional performers.

The development of this instrumentarium among the Uzbeks led to the formation of two ensembles, or orchestras, of local instruments: 1) the military orchestra, consisting of two surnais, two karnais, and naǧara, and 2) the chamber or concert ensemble, made up of the rest of the instruments listed above, used by themselves or for accompanying song.

Uzbek Instrumental Music.[12]   Instrumental music, like vocal music, is used by the Uzbeks for daily-life and social occasions, and also in military affairs. Let us note some cases of instrumental music as used in family life and public holidays. This consists mainly of dance tunes, called *raqs*,[13] and are usually played on the surnai, although some tunes are sung by unison chorus accompanied by rhythmic handclapping. Of the following two melodies, the first is played for a *tui*, or celebration on the birth of a child; the second, accompanied by handclapping, is a wedding dance song (Exs. 28, 29):

Ex. 28. Räqs. (Transc. A. Kozlovskii).   In march tempo.

Ex. 29. Räqs. (Transc. A. Kozlovskii).   Quickly.

285

An early transcription of Uzbek music from the 1880s is similar to Example 29. It is accompanied by the doira and the handclapping of spectators (Ex. 30).

Ex. 30. Räqs (Transc. A. Eichhorn).   Lively.

Here is an additional example of a more developed dance melody, played on the surnai with nağara accompaniment (Ex. 31):

Ex. 31. Räqs. (Transc. V. Uspenskii).   Quickly ♩=116.

Similar melodies are played as accompaniments for wrestling matches, tightrope walking, and other entertainments at public festivals. The following short melody is of this type, played by an ensemble of surnais, nağaras and karnais during balancing feats on a tightrope (*darbāza*) (Ex. 32):[14]

286

Ex. 32. Darbaz. (Transc. A. Kozlovskii).   Very lively

A tune for the horsemanship game *ulak* is slightly different, cast in a march-like rhythm (Ex. 33).

Ex. 33. Ulaq. (Transc. A. Kozlovskii).   Quickly.

287

The old Uzbek military marches are similar in style to the aforegoing holiday instrumental tunes. They are performed by an orchestra of *sarbāz* ("soldiers"), playing nais, surnais, karnais, and drums. These marches are called *sarbāzča* (soldiers' marches); one is given below (Ex. 34):

Ex. 34. Sărbazčă. (Transc. V. Uspenskii).   In march tempo.

As can be seen from all of the aforegoing examples, Uzbek holiday instrumental pieces have bright melodies, even rhythms, and concise structures connected to the forms of Uzbek folk songs.

Uzbek Epic Art

The Uzbek Epic. Compositions of epic art are called *daston* or *dastan* by the Uzbeks. They can be divided into two types: 1) dastans whose content is transmitted through straightforward recitation, and 2) dastans in which only the monologues and dialogues of the characters are sung, while the circumstances and descriptions of action are given in narrative style. Uzbek epic singers accompany their performances on the *dombra*, a two-stringed fretless lute.[15]

1) In the first type of dastan, verse lines are not usually grouped into strophes. Their musical setting consists of manifold repetitions of a single tune, corresponding to one poetic line, which is varied when repeated. Individual, textually complete excerpts of epic tales are concluded with a special cadence in a slower tempo.

The most popular Uzbek dastan of this type is the great cycle of heroic tales called *Körogli*, close to tales of the same name of other Central Asian and Caucasian peoples. The main hero of the tale, Körogli, appears as a brave warrior and defender of the national independence of his people. The Körogli tales preserve memories of the Uzbek people about their struggle with Arab invaders. We include below an excerpt from this dastan, dealing with Avaz, the closest associate of Köroğli.[16] The excerpt is given in the rendition of the famous Uzbek reciter Islam-šair (b. 1872). The addition of the word "šair" to the storyteller's name indicates that he is not only a singer who performs the traditional epic repertoire, but also a professional poet. The musical form of the excerpt is one line, with manifold repetition and melodic variation of the following basic tune (Ex. 35):

Ex. 35.
Voice.   Fairly quickly.

Here are three other variants of this tune (Ex. 36):

Ex. 36.

2) In Uzbek dastans of the second type, performed by storytellers in mixed prose-poetic form, the texts of the vocal episodes are usually in strophic form, and their musical expression is given in recitative or melodic style in both single strophe or more developed verse forms.

Dastans of this type belong thematically to epic-novelistic compositions approximating the literary form of the novel. Among these epics belong the following: *Earhad and Širin, Leili and Majnun, Taxir and Zuxra, Šahsenem and Ǧarib*, and others. Some of the subjects of these dastans appear among other peoples of the East. We have included an excerpt from the lyric-dramatic dastan *Taxir and Zuxra* in which Taxdir, searching for Zuxra, turns to one of the characters to ask where he should seek his sweetheart. This question has a recitative style (Ex. 37).

Ex. 37. From the tale "Taxir and Zuxrä" (Transc. F. Karomatov).   Fairly quickly.

Bek ūğ - li xä - bär   ber bi - zä,   Zux-rä qiz käy dä

dir,   qäy - dä?   Mäj - nun bū - lib   čiq - dim yū - lä,

Zux-rä   qiz   qäy - dä - dir,   qäy - dä?

*Bek ūğli xäbär ber bizä,   Kūzimni giryan äylägän,
Zuhrä qiz qäydädir, qäydä?   Bäğrimni biryan äylägän,
Mäjnun būlib čiqdim yūlä   Qarä bäğrim qan äylägän,
Zuhrä qiz qäydädir, qäydä?   Zuhrä qiz qäydädir, qäydä?

Xäbär alsäng väzir ūğli,   Taxir deyär kuyär jani,
Zuhrä qiz bağdädir, bağdä.   Bu šähärni äziz mehmani,
Päri sifät hur sūnali   Qirq känizlärni sultani
Zuhrä qiz bağdädir, bağdä.   Zuhrä qiz bağdädir, bağdä.

*stanzas alternate Taxir-Bek's son

Taxir: Tell me, bek's son
           Where is the girl Zukhra?
           Tell the traveler, who has become Majnun**
           Where is the girl Zukhra?

Bek's son: If you want to see her, cazir's son
           Then Zukhra is in the garden.
           She is like a fairy, with a houri's face
           The girl Zukhra is in the garden.

Taxir: She, for whom my eyes are full of tears
           She who kindled my heart,
           She, separated from whom I am lifeless
           Where is the girl Zukhra?

Bek's son: She calls her lover Tahir.
           He is a dear guest of this city.
           She is a sultana with a retinue of 40 girls;
           The girl Zukhra is in the garden.

*The bek's son does not suspect that Taxir himself stands before him (—V.B.)

**Majnun here = "mad," after the hero of the tale "Laili and Majnun."

The song of Šahsenem from the Khwarizm tale *Šahsenem and Ğarib* is an example of a more musically developed episode. Here, Šahsenem greets Ğarib, who has returned to her after long travelling. Recitative-like in its melodic outline, this song is cast in strophic form (Ex. 38).

Ex. 38. From the tale "Šahsenem and Ğarib " (Transc. Alimbaiev).

Tar.   Fairly quickly.

291

Kūlgä tušdi aq qärčigä baqišlim,
Xuš gäldingiz sävdägim säba gälibsiz.
Būl mänim janimä ütlär yaqišlim,
Xuš gäldingiz sävdägim säba gälibsiz.

Kūnglim suv ičmädi yarning xusnidin,
Härkim janä istär dūsti dūstindin,
Basgän qädämläring diydäm ustindän
Xuš gäldingiz dilim säba gälibsiz.

Näsibämiz čäkti äkäl qoyimä,
Qulaq salib ëšit būl färyadimä,
Jan päyandaz būlsin xaki payingä,
Xuš galdingiz dilim säba gälibsiz.

Šasänäm qiz äytär sändi dirdašim,
Firaqingdä aqär kūzimdä yašim,
Baš avvaldä yūğu qūšgän yūldašim,
Xuš gäldingiz dilim säba gälibsiz.

My bright falcon returned, my beloved,
Greetings, I rejoice at your arrival.
The fire of love is kindled in my heart.
Greetings, I rejoice at your arrival

I could not gaze enough at my beloved's beauty.
Everyone wishes his friend good health.
Every step of yours gladdens me.
Greetings, I rejoice at your arrival.

Fate separated us
Listen to my sighs, my pleading
Let my soul be a path for the dust of your feet
Greetings, I rejoice at your arrival.

Your close friend calls you Shahsenem.
My tears flow in pining for you.
My friend, you rewarded with joy from the start.
Greetings, I rejoice at your arrival.

Uzbek folk song began with the simple forms of terma and čublama, which spun off from epic recitation. Through its more complex styles, folk song greatly influenced the literary-musical genre of epic-novelistic dastans, which contrast strongly with their literary and musical beginnings in the epic.

THE EARLY PERIOD OF DEVELOPMENT OF UZBEK MUSIC (TO THE FIFTEENTH CENTURY)

. . . *Development of Uzbek Culture.* To this period belongs the activity of the famous medieval philosopher Al-Farabi (*ca.* 870-950), acclaimed as the second Aristotle, who was of Turkic origin from a place called Farab in the Bukhara area. Also at that time appeared the Turkic didactic poems "Kudatku bilig" ("Knowledge which Brings Happiness") written by Yusuf Balaguni in 1069-1070 (*see* Chapter 1) and the "Divan-i hikmet" ("Book of Wisdom") of Axme Yasavi who lived from 1103-1166 (*see* Chapter 2). At the time of the completion of the "Kudatku bilig," between 1072 and 1074, the Turkic linguist Mahmud al-Kašgari completed the *Dictionary of Turkic Dialects* ("Divan-i luğat-at Turk") in Arabic. Professional poetry also underwent significant development. Uzbek culture and that of neighboring peoples underwent a severe blow through the Mongul conquest of Central Asia in the thirteenth century (Čingiz Khan, 1206-1227), from which they only began to recover in the mid-fourteenth century.

292

Development of Uzbek Music Culture During This Period. The work of Mahmud al-Kašgari is of special importance in characterizing Uzbek musical art of the period before the fifteenth century. In it the author includes a series of excerpts of Turkic song texts in various meters and verse forms. These examples testify to the high level of development of poetic artistry of the Central Asian Turkic peoples, and relate more to the Uzbeks than to their Turkic neighbors. The book includes examples of not only five and seven syllable verse lines, but of the more complex types, such as lines of ten syllables (5+5), eleven syllables (6+5), twelve syllables (6+6), thirteen syllables (7+6), and the like.

In addition to examples of rhyme schemes typical of the folk quatrain (*aaba*), Mahmud al-Kašgari also includes the "crossed" rhyme (*abab*), single rhyme (*aaaa*), and single rhyme for the first three lines of a quatrain (*aaab*). All told, he registers all the types of rhyme schemes of folk and art prosody, which had already become well developed by the eleventh century.

The poems of Axme Yasavi were used by dervishes or calandars (itinerant Muslim monks) for religious hymns, performed in strophic form as solo songs with choral refrains. They derived from the cult singing of the ancient Magi, priests of the fire worshipping cult. They were also used for laments, and an example of this was given earlier as a professional mourner's song (Ex. 7).

The monumental work of al-Farabi has major significance for medieval musicology not only locally but, to a well known extent, even on a world scale. He wrote it in Arabic and titled it *Kitab al-musiqi al-kabir* ("The Great Treatise on Music"); there is a French translation of this work in R. d'Erlanger, *La Musique arabe* vol. I, Paris, 1930. It deals with questions of the origin of music, musical aesthetics, the theory of music, and the construction and acoustical properties of musical instruments. The appearance as early as the tenth century of such an outstandingly significant musicological work testifies to the great maturity of musico-theoretical thought at that time. Later, the military and political upheavals experienced by the Uzbeks (along with the rest of the Central Asian peoples), though causing great losses to musical culture, nevertheless did not stop its development, which bore fruit in the following period.

UZBEK MUSIC IN THE FIFTEENTH CENTURY

Development of Uzbek Music Culture in the Fifteenth Century.[17] The blossoming of Uzbek general and musical culture is tied to the rise of Samarqand (and later Herat) to the position of a major center of Central Asia in the later fourteenth and early fifteenth centuries. The activity of Mir Alisher Navai (1441-1501) belongs to this period. He was a remarkable poet and the founder of the Uzbek literary language,[18] and was also active as an official. Also active at this time was Zahir-ud-din Babur (1483-1530), poet and author of the famous *Babur-name* ("Memoirs of Babur"), who founded the Baburid, or Great Moghul Empire in India.

Navai, who patronized the arts and sciences, assembled the cream of Herati society. He was preeminent in musical theory and acted as a critic of musical art who was well acquainted with Herati musical life. He also wrote a number of musical compositions himself, as Babur tells us, saying that "in music he composed good things," and that he had "some good naqšes and pišravs." The poetic artistry of Navai displayed the beauty, richness, and strength of the Uzbek literary language. His work was widely used by Uzbek and Tajik composers for creating vocal compositions of the professional style. Babur possessed unusual poetic talent and, after Navai, played a major role in the development of Uzbek literature and poetry, and also influenced the development of Uzbek music.

Uzbek Art Music. While the work of Mahmud al-Kašgari can be used as evidence for the significant development of musical professionalism among the Uzbeks of the eleventh century, the historical and literary sources of the fourteenth and fifteenth centuries give a full idea of the great achievements of that period.

Complex forms of art song became widespread. These correspond in dimensions and structure to the multistrophic poetic texts they set, with well elaborated subjects. They have been described in the chapter on Tajik music culture under the term multistrophic forms. The *Šašmaqām* cycle, whose origin might be linked to Bukhara, became common musical-artistic property of both the Tajiks and Uzbeks. Parallel to the maqāms of this cycle, Uzbek professional singers created maqāms known as "Tashkent" or "Ferghana" maqāms, named for their areas of origin.[19] They differ from the Bukharan maqāms in 1) less strictness in style, 2) greater rhythmic freedom, 3) approximation of the melody to urban song, and 4) the introduction of "genre" sections, such as the *kaškarča* in lively Kashgar style (Kashgaris being close to Uzbeks in origin, area, and language). Usually the Tashkent or Ferghana maqāms consist of a small number of sections (up to five or six), and are concluded with an *ufār* or section in dance rhythm. The first section of the maqām "Gulyar-šahnāz," ("Gulyar") is a good example (Ex. 39).

Ex. 39. "Gulyar" (Transc. V. Uspenskii).
Tanbur.

Moderately.

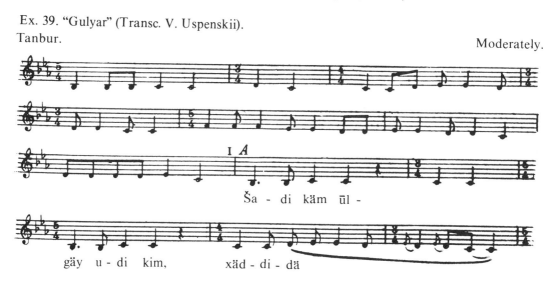

Ša - di käm ūl -

gäy u - di kim,   xäd - di - dä

bär - ja   ë - sä

B

Xar g̃ - tär   sa -

hib - lä ri   här fi - kri -

kim   be - ja   ë sä,

C

Da - g̃i häs - rät'

bir - lä yan - gäy   iš - kä kim

da - ra   ë - sä,

D

Gul - dän   äy,   ril - g̃u - si

ul   bul - bul - ki   be

pär - va   ë - sä,

E

Yul - lä - gäy   mäq - säd sä - ri

g̃a - ul - fä - ti   da - na   ë - sä.

II C

Yar ey!

Bäh - ri därd - gä uč - rä - gän - a -

šiq - qä äf - ğan - dän nä - sud

Pa - rä kŭng

li - gä yä - nä ča - ki gi - ri

bän - dän nä - sud,

Sev - gi - gä

xäm - däm bū - lib ūr - tän - gän

jan - dän nä - sud

Ul - ki - ši kim qäd - ri qil -

mäs väs - li ja -

nan - dän nä - sud

A - šiq ul kim här zä - man

296

kūz yaš - lä - ri   där - ya   ë - sä.

Vay - da - dey!

Bäs - dir ë   dil

ën - di be - hu - dä nä - va

häm   qil - mä - ğil,

Tub siz iš   qing bir - lä ya -

- ri   il - ti - ja   häm   qil - mä - gil

Väs - li yar

is - täb ri - ya   bir - lä du a

häm   qil - mä - gil

Be - xä - bär   sän se - vdi - gän

yuz - ni kä - ra

häm qil - mă - gil

E

Ya - ri as - ta - ni - dä

yat - gän kim ki - čin šäy - da ĕ - sä

Vay da - dey!

F (Rit.; coda)

Ya - ri - as - ta - ni - dä yat -

gän kim ki - čin šäy -

- da ĕ - sä Yar ey!

Happy is the wise one who knows the limits of the law.
He who understands the meaning of words will be rewarded.
He who is in love and passionately pines and suffers.
The nightingale, forgetting the rose, will miss her for ages.
The friend who is wise and devoted shows the true path.
If you love hopelessly, sighs are of no use.
If your heart has broken, tearing your clothes is of no use.
If your heart has cooled, then it is of no use.
If you have no word for your sweetheart, there is no use in meeting.
Tears flow ceaselessly when one loves truly.
Heart, be calm and don't sigh in vain.
If there's no reply to love, don't call out to the cruel one.
If you want happiness, don't tempt fate.
If there's no love in your heart, don't hide yourself away.
He who lives his life at his love's doorstep loves truly .

298

The lyric love text of this song consists of fifteen-syllable verse lines in *ramal* meter and *muxammas* (five-line) strophe form. The verse meter here determines the basic melodic contour; the strophic structure dictates the construction of each verse, or section, of the piece, and the number of strophes gives the total number of parts of the whole composition. Its scalar structure and tonal plan consist of a threefold presentation of Aeolian (A, B, C in Ex. 40) and Dorian (D, E) c-minor with a modulation to the subdominant scale, Aeolian f-minor (C) and to Mixolydian F-major (in D, Ex. 40).

Ex. 40.

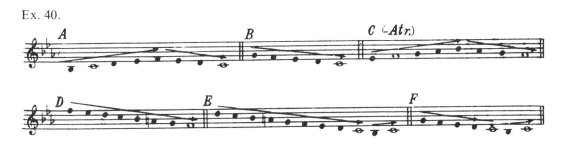

As can be seen from the following scheme, while each section has a complex internal structure, the overall pattern is a large two-part design with a repeat of the second section and a coda.

$$\overline{\underset{\text{I. } ABCDE}{A}} + \overline{\underset{\text{II. } CDCDE}{B}} + \overline{\underset{\text{III. } CDCDE}{B}} + \overline{\underset{\text{coda } F.}{a}}$$

The general style of art song in the Ferghana Valley is called *kättä äšulä* ("large songs"). These songs are cast in verse forms and set to lyric texts of professional poets; they are close to the usual äšulä genre, but have a special melodic-recitative style, free and supple declamation of the text, and introduction of exclamations in the high register on words of the refrain. The kättä äšulä are sung without instrumental accompaniment in an emotionally heightened manner. The singers hold a tray or dish in front of their mouths and manipulate it for the desired acoustic effect. Usually two or three singers perform kättä äšulä, alternating and competing with one another, while the last verse is sung in unison. Here is an example of the compositional style of the kättä äšulä (Ex. 41):[20]

Ex. 41. "Kättä Äšulä" (Transc. V. Uspenskii).   Moderately, freely.

Me - ni mähv äy - lä - gän ul dil - bä rim - ning čäš - mi

šah la - si. Kūn - gil mul - ki - ni ta - raj äy - lä - gän

iš - qing - ni yäǧ ma - si. *Dad!*

ū - lim - din zär - rä väh - mim yuk vä - le

qūr - qu - vim än din kūp, Qä - čan ūl - gäy mä -

nu ket - käy ba - šim - din yar - ning säv - da - si.

Musico-theoretical Works. Musico-theoretical works appeared in connection with the development of musical art in the period under discussion. Abdul Qadir (d. 1435), from Maraga in southern Azerbaijan, was the great theoretician of this time. He lived the second half of his life in Samarqand and Herat, and was a great authority. Among his few preserved works is a valuable and unique treatise which handles the question of musical form in great detail. The following forms are mentioned, in use today among the Uzbeks and Tajiks: *tarana, pišrav, sowt, tarje, naqš, muxammas*, among others.

UZBEK MUSIC FROM THE SIXTEENTH TO THE EARLY TWENTIETH CENTURIES

Uzbek Music from the Sixteenth to the Nineteenth Centuries. Central Asia was put into a position of feudal fragmentation through the conquest of the region at the outset of the sixteenth century by Uzbek nomads, who established feudal states such as the Emirate of Bukhara and the Khanates of Kokand and Khiva . . . . The gravity of the feudal yoke called forth a struggle by the Uzbek workers with the oppressors, which was reflected in songs of social protest and of the fight for liberation against the power of the khans. The progressive Uzbek intelligentsia took part in this struggle, sending forth such representatives in the seventeenth and eighteenth centuries as the poets Turdi (d. *ca.* 1701) and Mašrab (1657-1711), to whose works composers wrote songs which became quite popular.

Turdi took part in the popular uprising against the Bukharan emir Subhanqulikhan in 1690. Calling on the Uzbek tribes to unite, Turdi severely and angrily denounced the khans and emirs. . . . Mašrab led a wandering life as a "madman"-dervish, and was famous as a fearless defamer of the feudal rulers, mullahs, and *išans* ["holy men"—M. S.]. He was executed for his free thinking through the intrigues of the orthodox, fanatic Muslim elite.

The following are the major theoretical works of the period, all linked to Bukhara: *Risāle-i Šašmaqām* ("Treatise on the Šašmaqām") by the sixteenth-century musicologist Kaukabi (d. 1576) and the *Risāle-i musiqi* of Dervish-ali, written in the first half of the seventeenth century. They were both discussed in Chapter 4. In addition to theoretical works, so-called *baiaz* were produced. These were anthologies of song texts used by outstanding art singers. The baiaz approximate Kaukabi's "Treatise on the Šašmaqām" in basic style and are major musico-historical materials.

During the period under discussion, the folk song continued to survive, lightening work, accompanying life, and affirming the belief in the eventual triumph of social justice. Art music in its traditional forms played a great role in the life of the Uzbek intelligentsia. The achievements of art music were used by the emirs and khans in court life, but there they were limited to those styles that corresponded to the class interests and whims of the feudal rulers, who pretended to the title of patrons of the arts and sciences.

UZBEK MUSIC AFTER THE ANNEXATION TO RUSSIA
(THE LATE NINETEENTH AND EARLY TWENTIETH CENTURIES)

. . . The creation of the major administrative center at Tashkent on Uzbek territory played an enormous role in the development of the culture of the Central Asian peoples. This was also aided by the organization of scientific and research work by representatives of the Russian intelligentsia in the areas of Central Asian history and ethnography, including geographic discoveries, geologic explorations, and the like.

Uzbek Music Culture of this Period. The musical life of Uzbekistan during this period was based on the solid, age-old Uzbek musical life discussed above. There is a great quantity of literary evidence concerning the love of the Uzbeks for music and its great dissemination in both daily life and at folk festivals. *Nowruz*, or New Year's, was especially richly celebrated in the larger cities of Uzbekistan by *sail*s, or popular festivals,[21] lasting several days . . . .

During the sail, carnival processions were arranged in the evenings, with music and illumination of streets along the parade route. In one of the descriptions of such a torch-lit carnival held in the suburbs of Bukhara, it is said that boats took part "with baldachins covered with red calico and hung with lanterns with reflecting mirrors." It seemed as if boys sat in these boats, but actually the boats were "fixed to the waists" of the boys who carried them. After the "floating" dancing boats came "an elephant and a gigantic fantastic fish"; next came "two enormous snakes made of muslin stretched on metal hoops; each hoop had a candle, so that the snake was illuminated, like a lantern. A stick ran from each ring, held by a man. The snakes seemed to be swimming in the air." In the center of the parade they carried figures "of giants three times life-size with papier-maché heads." These figures represented Rustam and other heroes of the ancient epics, whose actions are described in the *Shahname*, and they could move their hands and head. The parade concluded with "a cavalcade of wooden horses" fastened to the waists of *masxarabāz*, or comedians, who portrayed horsemen with horses in their hands and shields on their backs. The whole procession moved to the continual sounding of wind instruments and tambourines, and unison singing. In this picture of the carnival parade one, of course, sees the preservation of the most ancient forms of local folk holidays.

Compromising on political grounds with local traditions, the representatives of czarist officialdom did not hinder the Uzbek population from organizing their national holidays in the large administrative centers such as Tashkent, Samarqand, and other cities. But they demanded Uzbek participation in official holidays organized on so-called czar's days, *i. e.*, birthdays of members of the royal family. For the most part, Russian military orchestras played in city parks and Uzbek wind ensembles in special, removed places to introduce a bit of exotic color into the holiday.

The Uzbek song tradition was enriched in this period by new content, connected with the new conditions of life of the people. The possibility emerged for Uzbeks to become acquainted with Russian folk songs and with Western European music, mostly due to the Russian military orchestra, which played in public places. Songs arose to the texts of Uzbek poets who struggled against the fossilized forms of the old way of life toward the development of Uzbek culture and the propagation of progressive ideas evoked by acquaintance with enlightened Russian democratic thought. These poets were Muqimi (1851-1903) and Furqat (1858-1909). Muqimi is one of the most popular Uzbek poets, to whose texts many Uzbek songs are set in the ašula genre. Outstanding in his lyrical gift he was also a satirist . . . . As an example of a song to his lyric text, let us take "Färganäčä" ("Ferghana Melody"), with a text cast in the poetic form of the *murabba* ("quatrain") with an original rhythm, $3/8+3/4$, and a supple, flowing melody (Ex. 42).

Ul kun janan yuzni taban äyläding,
Äbr ičindä ayni pinhan aylading
Qamätingni särvi būstan äyläding,
Qumrilärni zari nalan äyläding.

E, zalimi bedadigär sitämgär,
Qilmäs takäygäčä färyadim äsär,
Bemaringdän almäy ketib bir xäbär,
Qilmäs išni heč bir insan äyläding.

Yūk ūzingdek heč bir jälladi qatil,
Täšläb čiqib nazik bellärgä qakil,
Baqmäy ūtib ašnalärgä täğafil,
Beganägä lutfi-ihsan äyläding.

Määšimdur hijranidän zähru ğäm,
Artiqčädir baz ustigä bu äläm,
Räqiblärdän nä iš qurdim šul aqšam,
Väsling härämigä mehman äyläding.

Ruxsaringdin qät-qät lalä dağ ičrä,
Käpki šäyda aram äyläb tağ ičrä,
Jilvä bilän tävusläring bağ ičrä,
Räftaringgä mähvi häyran äyläding.

Išqing bilän išim ahu-fiğanlär,
Xäsrätingdä rängim būldi sämanlär,
Müqimiygä berib ähdu päymanlär
Axir va'dälärni yalğan äyläding.

The large beautiful eyes of the enchantress destroyed me.
The fire of love burned the treasure of my heart.
Death is not so fearful;
Only the loss of cares for my beloved is fearful.

When my beloved uncovered her face
The moon hid her face in shame.
When she walked in the garden, supple as a cypress,
The turtle-doves sighed in anguish.

O unfair, cruel offender,
How long will you remain deaf to my moans?
Leaving, you did not inquire about my illness.
You acted as if no one else would have.
There is no other executioner as cruel as you.
With braids hanging down to your waist.
You walked past me, not looking at your friend,
And you were kind and friendly with a stranger.

My food is bitter poison from longing.
The pain of this is great.
How much I suffered from my rivals that night,
When you allowed them into the closeness forbidden to me.
Seeing your cheeks, the tulips were wounded,
And the partridges hid themselves in the mountains, embarassed.
You captivated the peacocks in the garden
With your graceful carriage.

I sigh and moan from love for you.
I have become yellow as straw from pining.
You gave Muqimi so many promises
And always cruelly deceived him.

While in the preceding song Muqimi does not go beyond the bounds of lyric images and feelings, in the next ğazal, "Šunčälär!" ("Enough"), he reaches a peak of pathos in heated protest against trifling with the poet's feelings and against servility before wealth, reflected in the agitated syncopated melody which sets the text of the ğazal (Ex. 43).

Ex. 43. "Šunčälär!" (*Uzbekskie narodnye pesni*, vol II, p. 38).

Xäs - tä - yu mä' - yus ë - tib äb -
gar qil - maq šun - čä - lär

Zulm ilä qähru ğäzäb izhar qilmaq šunčälär,
Ašiqi bečarägä azar bermaq šunčälär.

Gul deban sevgän kišining kukrägigä niš urib,
Xastäyu mä'yus ëtib, äbgar qilmaq šunčälär.

Tūtiu širin suxän ä'yarlärning bäzmidä,
Bizgä kelgändä gäpirmäy, zar qilmaq šunčälär,

Sizgä kim äydi muhäbbät ählini qil ixtisab,
Qūrqitib ūz äybigä iqrar qilmaq šunčälär.

Kelšä aldingizgä bay surät yakāsi tugmälik
Izzät ilä šad minnätdar qilmaq šunčälär.

Gärči kelšä ëski tūn bizdek duogūyi fäkir
Kämbägälning ëskisidän ar qilmaq šunčälär.

Xär bälayi jäbr kelsä yanmägäy xärgiz Muqim,
Asiq ählini uruban xar qilmaq šunčälär!

Enough of spite, anger and suffering,
Enough of insulting the poor lover.

Enough of piercing the lover's heart, which cherishes you like a flower.
Enough of bringing him to despair and suffering and making him ill.

At parties you are a sweet-tongued parrot for others,
Enough of not speaking to me and insulting me!

Who told you that you could judge a lover?
Enough of frightening them, forcing them to confess guilt.

When a rich man with buttons on his collar comes to you,
Enough of showing him joy and tenderness.

When a poor admirer like me comes in an old cloak,
Enough of shaming him for his modest clothing.

As much as you insult him, Muqimi will not leave you.
Enough of degrading and beating the one who loves you.

The same text of Muqimi is also performed to a different melody, called "Ändijan sämasi" ("Andijan Melody"), which seems unified by a single emotional outcry in its impulsive style. This is facilitated by the introduction of a tune for the first line of text which is sung an octave higher at its repetition (Ex. 44).

Ex. 44. "Ändijan sämasi" (*Uzbekskie narodnye pesni*, vol. I, p. 78).   Fairly quickly. (♩ = 100)

In the Soviet period this poem of Muqimi is performed in a new version, containing an impassioned protest against the oppression of Uzbek women.[22]

Furqat was a contemporary and friend of Muqimi and, like him, was a subtle lyric poet. He heatedly denounced ignorance and apathy and fervently fought for the Uzbek people's acquisition of progressive Russian culture . . . . The work of both poets, well received in Uzbek music, prepared the way for the first revolutionary Uzbek poet, Hamza Hakimzade Niazi, of whom more below.

The Study of Uzbek Music. The beginning of the study of Uzbek music dates to the 1870s and is linked to the name of August Eichhorn, a well qualified violinist and member of the Bol'shoi Theater Orchestra in Moscow, who came to Tashkent as a military conductor. He was also a composer of pieces in popular genres. Eichhorn undertook extensive work in transcribing the music of the Kazakhs, Uzbeks, and other Central Asian peoples and left behind a special monograph on Uzbek music, along with a considerable body of transcriptions.[23] Eichhorn was especially interested in the study of Central Asian musical instruments, and made two collections of these instruments. The first collection appeared at the Polytechnic Exposition in Moscow in 1872, from which it was sent to the International Exposition in Vienna. The second collection was displayed in St. Petersburg in 1885 and is now located in the Glinka Central Museum of Music Culture in Moscow.[24]

Eichhorn showed great keenness in posing theoretical, artistic, and historical problems connected to the study of the music of the Uzbeks and other Central Asian peoples. His transcription of an Uzbek dance melody was given above (Ex. 30). We can add several more of his transcriptions. One of them is the Bukharan triumphal military march "Särbazčä" ("Soldiers' March," Ex. 45).

Ex. 45. "Särbazčä" (Transc. A. Eichhorn).   In march tempo.

Another is the earliest transcription of the Uzbek song "Läyzangul" ("Trembling Flower"), which has many variants, testifying to the firmness of Uzbek song tradition (Ex. 46).

Ex. 46. "Läyzangul" (Transc. A. Eichorn).   Fairly quickly (♩ =116).

Qa - šing qa - rä   būl gun - čä - e   läy - zan - gul,

Kū - zing qa - rä   būl - sä - či - e,   läy - zan - gul.

Instead of your eyebrows being black,*
It would be better if your eyes were black

*No English pun intented.

A third melody is for surnai, and is marked by assymetrical structure and great internal unity (Ex. 47).

Ex. 47. Melody for surnai. (Transc. A. Eichorn).   Lively.

One must also note Eichhorn's transcription of three variants of a popular Uzbek melody which is performed in Bukhara, as well as other Uzbek cities, both for lyric songs and military marches. It is also widespread not only in the Near

East and Central Asia, but also in the Caucasus. There it became known to Glinka, who used it for the "Persian Chorus" of his opera *Ruslan and Liudmilla* (Ex. 48).

Ex. 48. Popular Uzbek melody. (Transc. A. Eichorn).   In march tempo.

tambourine and drum.

In march tempo

It is interesting to note that in folk tradition this melody was also called the march of Iskahdar-khan, (Alexander the Great).

Eichhorn was the first harmonizer of Uzbek melodies.[25] His arrangement of the Uzbek song "Miskin" ("The Poor One") is an example of his style (Ex. 49).

Ex. 49. "Miskin" (Transc. A. Eichorn).   Moderately.

The first three published Uzbek melodies were printed by I. Dobrovol'skii in his *Asiatic Musical Journal* (1816-1818). The first Uzbek melody performed on a large stage in concert arrangement was the song "Karaibersam kurinmaidi," with the following text:

I aim my glances in vain at the road;
I have no saddle; only my whip is left for me.

There is no saddle, and where the saddle-band
   should be I only have my whip;
I don't miss the saddle, but my beloved, who went far away.

The song was first published in 1889 by R. A. Pfennig in the journal *Etnograficheskoe obozreniie* and was later arranged for voice and orchestra by N. S. Klenovskii and was included in his 1893 ethnographic concert in Moscow and published the following year in *Sbornik narodnykh pesen (etnograficheskii kontsert) russkikh i drugikh narodnostei* ("Anthology of Folk Songs [Ethnographic Concert] of Russians and Other Nationalities"), which went through five editions. The song "Karaibersam kurinmaidi" is yet another variant of the melody which served as a basis for Glinka's "Persian Chorus." Klenovskii handled it in the oriental style used by composers of the Russian school for the melodies of Caucasian peoples, *i. e.*, with the use of augmented seconds, which does not at all correspond to the character of Uzbek music.

311

F. V. Leisek, who lived in Tashkent as a military conductor, also put out transcriptions of Uzbek melodies. He used the materials of these transcriptions for composing an *Asiatic Potpourri* of Uzbek, Kazakh, Tatar, and Bashkir songs for brass band. This potpourri was performed many times at the Turkestan Exposition of Tashkent in 1890. Not noted for artistic worthiness, Leisek's potpourri nevertheless played a great role in bringing together the music cultures of the Central Asian peoples, inasmuch as the stage on which it was performed (as reported in the newspaper *Turkestanskie vedomosti*) was always surrounded by a crowd of Russians, Uzbeks, and Tatars.

V. S. Uspenskii (1879-1949) played the main role in the transcription of Uzbek folk and professional music and the study of musical folklore in the first two decades after the Great October Socialist Revolution. In 1924 he published the first transcriptions of the Bukharan Šašmaqām. We are indebted to him for the discovery of "Khwarizm notation."[26] He also transcribed a series of Tashkent maqāms, Uzbek folk songs, and other monuments of folk musical art. Uspenskii was a highly qualified musician, trained at the St. Petersburg Conservatory. He played a significant role in the history of the development of Uzbek Soviet music culture as a composer, ethnographer, and music educator.

The Musical Life of Tashkent. As the major administrative center of Central Asia, Tashkent had a large body of military and official intelligentsia among its Russian inhabitants. They developed music life from the earliest years of the annexation of Uzbekistan to Russia. They organized amateur concerts, mostly for charitable purposes, with local performers. They also put on productions of popular operas and operettas, and had small chamber ensembles. All of this activity led to the creation of the Tashkent Musical Society in 1884, which numbered five hundred members in the 1890s. Among them were over eighty singers (soloists and choir members). An officers' symphony orchestra was organized under the aegis of the society.

After the inauguration of the trans-Caspian Railway in 1888 (first brought to Samarqand and then ten years later to Tashkent), communication with Central Russia was made easier. As a result, tours of individual artists and of whole opera and operetta troupes began in Tashkent and other cities of Central Asia.

The choir of Agreneva-Slavianskii came to Tashkent in 1889. In 1891 the French operetta troupe of Lassalle completed its Central Asian tour with a trip to Bukhara. The Tiflis opera toured in Tashkent in 1894 and 1898. In 1895 and 1899 the Ukrainian musical-dramatic troupe put on performances. Among individual artists who visited Tashkent, noteworthy were the fourteen-year-old pianist Kostia Dumchev (1895) and "the king of flutists," the Czech Adolf Tershak, who travelled to all the principal countries of the world, from North and South America to Australia, China, and Japan. He was awarded a golden star by the emir of Bukhara for his performance there. In 1902 the famous singer Alma Foster came to Tashkent, and in 1903 the pianist Iadvig Zaleskii. In the early twentieth century Tashkent became one of the major musical cities of the Russian Empire.

Creative musical activity also flourished. In the 1870s and 1880s Eichhorn put out a number of his dance and salon pieces on Central Asian themes: the "Tashkent" polka, the waltz "In the Broad Steppes of Turkestan," the piece "A Moonlit Night at the Ruins of Samarqand," among others. Leisek was exceptionally prolific in composing military marches for all occasions. The most significant occurrence in Tashkent's musical activity was the work of G. I. Gizler. A doctor by profession, he was a student of V. N. Paskhalov (1841-1885), the author of popular romances of his day. Among Gizler's Tashkent compositions were the 1905 cantata "Song of the Prophetic Oleg" and the 1906 operetta *Berthold Schwarz*, the comic subject of which was associated with the inventor of gunpowder. Gizler also wrote an opera, *Psyche*, and a number of romances and other compositions.

Among the major musical and social figures of Tashkent were F. V. Leisek and V. M. Mikhalek, a cellist, who was formerly the conductor of the Imperial Theater in St. Petersburg. Mikhalek displayed broad talents in the 1890s as an organizer, conductor, and music educator.

The development of concert life in Tashkent had a great influence on the progressive Uzbek intelligentsia, which became acquainted with Russian music. Their excitement is reflected in Furqat's poem "The Grand Piano:"

Then I heard some
Different music, friends!

I was at a Russian concert last night—
There's art and mastery!

I confess I lost control
And wept tears of excitement.

As if I did not comprehend my own soul
As I did that of the composer at that moment.

The poet describes his excitement at coming into contact with the new and bright world of musical art, and also dreams of the possibility of Uzbeks composing such artistically significant and effective music:

Even if it takes twenty or thirty years
For our grandsons to master the secret of this music,
Furqat will consider himself comforted hundredfold.

The dreams of Furqat became reality in the Soviet period.

Uzbek Song in the Prerevolutionary Years. . . . Two songs of those years can be introduced as examples. The first is "Ärsilläri-näxšilläri" which appeared in 1914-1915 and was sung in Jarkent during the mobilization of Uzbek youth into bands for railway construction along the Chinese border. The content of this song involves the use of Russian words such as *vagon* ["railway car"—M. S.] and *rabochii* ["worker"—M. S.], which speaks for the importance of the work ties between Russian workers and the Uzbek proletariat and peasants. In addition, the march-like rhythm, evenness of melody, and laconicism of individual phrases brings to mind the influence of the style of Russian revolutionary songs (Ex. 50).

Ex. 50. "Äršilläri-naxšilläri" (Transc. V. Uspenskii).   Moderately. (♩ = 96)

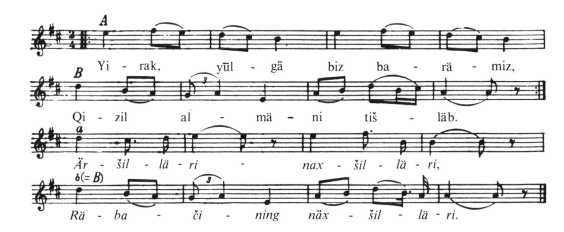

We are going far away
Biting a red apple
If we are healthy, we'll return.
Working on the railway.

The second songs "Märdikarlär vaqiäsi" ("Song of the Mardikars") tells of the 1916 uprising of the Uzbeks who were forceably directed (with the aid of cannons) toward defense work, and who swore to dethrone the oppressor of the peoples of czarist Russia, Nicholas II . . . . The song is marked by an active, strict melody and march-like rhythm (Ex. 51).

314

Ex. 51. "Märdikarlär vaqiäsi" (*Uzbekskie narodyne pesni*, vol. I, p. 57).   Fairly quickly.

Payizingni jildirgän
Ūtxanäsi minän dūngälägi,
Diviniskkä ketišdi
Märd yigitning bir būlägi.

Diviniskkä ketmäs ëdi
Märd yigitning bir būlägi,
Diviniskkä ketkizgän
Nikaläyning zämbärägi.

Ūttiztädän ryäd qilib
Nikaläyning bäräkidä turǧizdi,
Bäräkidä uč kun säqläb
Qarnimizni ačgä qaldirdi.

Alib čiqib ūttiztädän
Qizil uygä qämädi,
Rat-rat saldätni qūyib,
Mehnätkäšlärni surgizdi.

The pistons and furnace
Set the train into motion
Some of the brave youths
Went to Dvinsk.

Some of the brave youths
Wouldn't have gone to Dvinsk
They were sent to Dvinsk
By Nikolai's cannons

Lined up thirty in a row
They drove us into Nikolai's barracks.
They kept us hungry in the barracks
For three days.

Calling us up in thirties
They put us in red houses (=boxcars).
Leaving companies of their soldiers
They sent us off as workers.

315

Paezdni häm yurgizdi, Kämpirlärni "vay baläy" deb, Yulimizgä urgizdi.	They sent off our train Waking old women bar our way With wails of "o my son."
"Diviniskkä yūl būlsin, Qäräğäyzaring kul būlsin! Yigitlärni qiynägän Nikaläyning yuq būlsin!"	"Your road is to Dvinsk May your forests burn! May Nikolai rot, Who oppresses youths!"
Utxanäsini qičqirtirib, Istänsägä yurgizdi, Kūk teräkkä etmäsdän, Saz dutärimni sindirdi.	The train, hooting, Left the station. We didn't get as far as our own poplars When my resonant dutar broke.
Ūttiz sutkä yūl yurdik, Sïzränni bäräkigä tuširdi Kūkrägimni yağläb qūyib, Tūrt ёllik ninäsin kirgizdi.	We rode thirty days, And got to syzrana. They stuck a sharp needle Into my wounded chest (= inoculated).
Qardä qäräğäy kesgänmän, Heč haqimdän kečmaymän, Alib ūtib Ädäskä, Imarätigä qärätdi, Tizzämizdän qan surib, Ūz faydäsigä yärätdi.	In winter we felled tall pines; We will never forgive that. They transferred us to Odessa, Drove us out for construction. They drained the blood from our knees; We made a building for their benefit.
Ūng qūlingdä bir qässab, Čūčqäni suyädi behisab, Bizni tūqqiz ay išlätdi, Nikaläy degän qan jällob.	To the right, a butcher Slaughters countless pigs.* The blood-sucker named Nikolai Sent us to work for nine months.
Istäntsägä čiqqändä Här paizddän qalmäymän, Bizni išlätgän Nikaläyni Täxtidän ağdärmay qūymäymän!	When I get to the station I won't miss any train. Nikolai made us work; I won't miss dethroning him!

*This would have been particularly repulsive
to the Uzbeks, who are Muslims.

Hamza Hakimzade Niazi (1889-1929). The progressive enlightening, and later revolutionary activity of Hamza Hakimzade Niazi was immediately linked to the struggle for social justice and liberation in Uzbekistan. He was a true son of the working people and an untiring fighter for his rights, as well as being the founder of Uzbek national music culture.[27]

Hamza was born in 1889 in Kokand to a family of a *tabib*, or Uzbek doctor. The father wanted his son to receive religious training, and sent him in 1905 to a medrese in Kokand. The work at the medrese did not satisfy Hamza, and he spent much of his time reading and studying the classics of Uzbek literature and the poetry of the progressive poets of that time, such as Muqimi and Furqat, as well as works of Uzbek folk art. The events of the revolution of 1905-1907 had an especially great effect on Hamza's world view. While still at the medrese Hamza began to write poems, following the denunciatory line of Muqimi and Furqat's works. Hamza's progressive leanings led to a profound conflict with his father, which forced him to leave home and move to Namangan . . . .

Hoping to carry his forward looking ideas to the broad working masses in the most impressive way, Hamza, for the first time in Uzbek history [in 1915—M. S.], turned to the creation of dramatic works, although there were no realistic possibilities of putting them on due to the lack of an Uzbek theater. His dramas *Bai ila xezmatči* ("The Bai and the Pauper") and others began to be produced by artists in his front for agitation called "The Itinerant Drama Troupe" . . . .

In his pedagogical work, Hamza placed enormous stress on the study of the Uzbek folk song. Thus, beginning in 1915, he put out a number of song anthologies, calling the first of them *National Poems for National Songs*. In it he provided his poems with special arrangements of Uzbek melodies, suiting the style and character of the texts to the music. Considering Uzbek songs as the blossoms of folk art, he named his remaining seven anthologies for various flowers. On the dust jacket of his last anthology, Hamza remarks that its content consists of songs "about the burdensome situation of his collaborators."

Hamza put about forty poems in his first seven anthologies, set primarily to Uzbek tunes and also to Kashgar and Tatar melodies, which testifies to the breadth of his artistic and cultural-political views. Starting with the second anthology, Hamza indicates the name of the song tune to which the verses should be sung, gives the text of the first verse (along with all of the words of the refrain added in performance), and also indicates phonograph recordings, if any.

Hamza was a master of Uzbek instruments (dutar and tanbur). In 1928, N. N. Mironov transcribed a series of [Hamza's—M. S.] Uzbek melodies without words. The latest work toward establishing Hamza's heritage was the anthology of his songs published in 1949 in Tashkent, called *Kuškilar*. Here is one of the songs from that book, the Uzbek folk song "Atinbibijan," in the form of a lapar dialogue (Ex. 52):

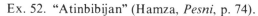

Ex. 52. "Atinbibijan" (Hamza, *Pesni*, p. 74).　　　　　　　　　Very Moderately.

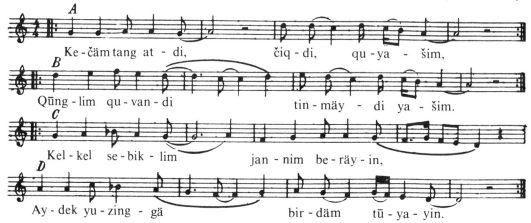

*Kečäm tang atdi, čiqdi kuyašim,　　　　Boy:　Dawn comes, the sun rises
Kūnglim quvandi, tinmäydi yašim.　　　　　　My soul rejoices, I cannot hold back tears.
Kel-kel seviklim, janim beräyin,　　　　　　　Come beloved, my soul is yours,
Aydek yuzinggä birdäm tuyäyin.　　　　　　　If only to see your face for a moment!

Sälam äläykūm, Atinbibijan,　　　　　　Girl:　Greetings, my beloved!
Ūynäb keläyin, ertä kelibmän.　　　　　　　　I came early, and can walk with you.
Čiqdi ësimdän, nan algänim yūq,　　　　　　　I forgot to bring along breakfast,
Här väqt sūrärmän keč qalgänim yūq.　　　　　　Fearing to be late.

Ërtä etirgän tängrimgä qulluq,　　　　　Boy:　I am in rapture at meeting you
Ketmä seviklim, janim täsädduq.　　　　　　　Early in the morning.
Kel-kel seviklim, janim beräyin,　　　　　　　Don't leave, dear,
Baǧlärdä sengä gullär teräyin.　　　　　　　I will gather roses for you from the garden.

*verses alternate boy-girl-boy.

In making his anthologies, Hamza departed from the old practice of the baiaz songbooks, but in this followed more serious goals: the study of folk song. Thus, he was actually the first Uzbek collector of folk songs. In the eighth anthology, published in 1919, revolutionary songs are included with melodies composed by the author himself, which have become extremely popular among the Uzbeks . . . . Among them the most popular down to today are "Yäšä šura!" ("Hail to the Soviets!") and "Xoi isčilär!" ("O, Workers!"). With these he made a generous contribution to the development of Uzbek song, enriching it in emotional, melodic, and idea content (Exs. 53, 54).

Ex. 53. "Yäšä šura! (X. Hamza, *Pesni*, p. 11, Transc. E. Romanovskaia).   Moderato.

Buz - mä kūng - ling,   baq bu Šū - ra
Ber - di man - gu   in - ti
- bah.   Tam - či har qa   -   nin - ga al
- ding   Il - mu - ur - fan   ërk - kä jah.
Yä - šä Šū - ra!   Yä - šä Šū - ra!
Sen yä - šäy - dir   -   gän zä
- man.   Iš - či ūğ - li   šuh - rä - ting -
din.   Bal - qi - sin rū   -   yn jä - han.

for ending.

Yä - šä Šū - ra!   Yä - šä Šū - ra!   A!

Buzmä kūngling, baq bu Šura   Don't give up; look, the Soviets
Berdi mangu intibah.   Have awakened you.
Tamči här qaninggä alding   For every drop of blood you shed
Ilmu-urfan, ërkkä jah.   You receive freedom, enlightenment and knowledge.

319

Yäšä Šūra! Yäšä Šūra!	Hail to the Soviets!
Sen yäšäydirgän zäman.	This is your epoch,
Isči ūgli šuhrätingdin	May your glory, worker's son,
Balqisin rūyn jahan.	Be carried around the whole world.
Čar hukumät väqtidägi	When you remember that you were
Qulligingni ūyläsäng,	A slave under the czar,
Šadliging mängu tugänmäs,	Your joy will be boundless,
Qänčä ūynäb, kuyläsäng.	Your happiness endless.
Išlä, išlav väqti keldi,	Labor, the time for work has come;
Yatmä ğafil bändälär!	This is no time to be careless.
Bitsin ëndi ëski turmuš,	Let the old life rot,
Ul qulaq u jändrlär.	With its kulaks and gendarmerii.
Ëski turmuš bağlärin qūy!	Let only black crows
Qärğä-zağlär qišläsin.	Winter in the gardens of the old order,
Yängi turmuš bağläridä.	And in the gardens of the new life
Yaš kungillär yäšnäsin!	Let young hearts rejoice.
Yäšä Šūrä! Yäšä Šūrä!	Hail to the Soviets!

Ex. 54. "Hay isčilär!" (Hamza, *Pesni*, p. 19. Transc. A. Kozlovskii). Andante.

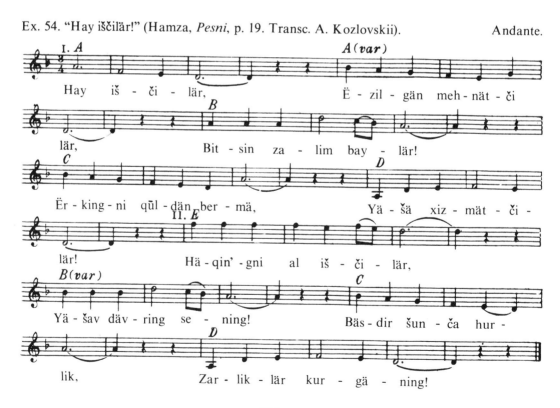

Hay iščilär, Ëzilgän mehnätčilär, Bitsin zalim boylär!. Ërkingni qūldän bermä, Yäsä xizmätčilär!	Oh workers, Oppressed workers, Away with the bais, exploiters. Don't give up your freedom Hail to the workers!
Xähingni al iščilär, Yäšav dävring sening! Bäsdir šunčä xūrlik, Zarliklär kūrgäning!	Seize your rights, workers; Your time has come. Enough of former suffering And oppression.
Bay būlsin xizmätčilär, Ëmäsmu bir insan! Iščining negä umri Baylär učun qurban?! Yäsä xizmätčilär!	Let the workers prosper. Are they not people? Why should the life of the poor Depend on the rich?
Tokäylär biz yurämiz, Qūlu ayak bağli?! Bir pärčä qatgän nangä Yuräq bägir dağli?!	How long will we Walk constrained? Like with a tortured soul For a piece of stale bread?!
Bir sūzgä bašimizdä Yuz qamči! Iščilär! Yarilib tinmäsdän Qarä qan tamčilär. Yäsä xismatčilär!	For one word a hundred lashes Fell on our heads! Workers! From wounds Flowed black blood.
Bitsin zalim baylär! Ëšan, mingbašilär! Yäšäsin ëndi mängu, Qarä mehnätčilär.	Away with the bais, oppressors: Ishans and mingbashis (=officers) Hail forever To the workers.
Qurallän mehnätčilär! Būlsin dunyä sening, Bäs ëndi qullik kūrib Ärslär kelgäning! Yäsä xizmatčilär!	Arm yourselves, workers! Let the world be yours. Enough of suffering Age-long slavery.

Having begun as a democrat-enlightener, Hamza Hakimzade Niazi grew into an outstanding revolutionary poet, playwright, composer, and agitator-propagandist, giving all his strength to the consolidation of Soviet power in Uzbekistan, the power of the workers. In 1920 he entered the ranks of the Communist Party, and in 1926 was chosen as a deputy to the Second Kurultai (Congress of Soviets) of Workers' Deputies of the Ferghana Valley. In 1929, coming to the village of Šahimardan (now Hamzaabad) to clean out the counter-revolutionaries (kulaks and sheiks), he was treacherously murdered by enemies of the Uzbek' people. In all fairness he must be considered the founder of Uzbek national musical style, born during the flames of revolution. . . .

Notes to Chapter V

1. For a variant of "Uzgäncä," *see* Romanovskaia (1957: 106).

2. This represents a particularly valuable contribution to the sample of Uzbek folk songs given, since the traditional puppet theater, now vanished, has been only scantily described; the transcription of Example 20 was made by Uspenskii in the 1920s (presumably in a manuscript available to Beliaev).

3. *See* Chapter 3, note 22.

4. *Gulsara* was one of the first operas composed on the basis of Uzbek folk tunes. Gliere, a Russian composer best known in the West for his "Russian Sailor's Dance," was aided by Sadykov, an Uzbek.

5. It would be interesting to know if this košuk is related to the Kirghiz lament genre of the same name.

6. *I. e.*, genres in Beliaev's sense of theme (love, work and so forth).

7. For the most thorough presentation of Uzbek instruments and instrumental music, *see* Karomatov (1972). A survey of instruments used by the Uzbeks of Afghanistan can be found in Slobin (1969b).

8. A paired single reed aerophone. The sibizgi, a small one-pipe single reed aerophone should also be mentioned, as should the diversity of end- and side-blown flutes under the single term "nai."

9. Other "percussion" instruments include: *qošuq* (spoon castanets), qaivaq (stone castanets) and *safail* (two short metal rods with a circling metal jingle). Again, *see* Karomatov (1972).

10. Also the *sato,* a type of bowed tanbur, should be included.

11. An interesting feature of Uzbek music culture is the frequency with which women play the dutar. Romanovskaia (1957: 66) collected a large number of women's songs for the dutar from the Ferghana Valley in 1931 (now housed in the archives of the Institute for Research in the Arts of the Uzbek Academy of Sciences). In other areas of Central Asia, women rarely played lutes or fiddles, being mostly restricted to tambourines and/or jew's-harps (*see above* for Kazakh modern exceptions).

12. Unfortunately, Beliaev does not take up the full range of instrumental music; notably lacking are the repertoires of the dombra and dutar. For the former, *see* Karomatov (1962). For dutar music, surprisingly, there seems to be no significant source at all, (save for a short section in Karomatov, 1972) even for transcriptions of pieces. This is especially regrettable in that the dutar is a major lute-type, and its polyphonic style is an interesting variant of Central Asian multipart instrumental music. In addition, the dutar repertoire spans the areas of classical music, a sort of "light classical" style, and purely folk music, and is the only instrument to do so (with the possible exception of the tambourine).

13. *Raqs* is Persian for "dance."

14. Oboe and drum accompaniments are well known across the Near East and North Africa as accompaniment to sport events.

15. For transcriptions of dombra music used in epic recitation, *see* Karomatov (1962). The Uzbek dumbra (or dümbüra) is a close relative of the Tajik *dumbrak*, and is known among Uzbeks and Tajiks of Afghanistan in slightly different shape as *dambura*.

16. In most versions of the epic, Avaz is the adopted son of Köroğli.

17. For the most complete history of Uzbek music, *see* Veksler (1965).

18. The modern (*i. e.*, Soviet) literary Uzbek language, based on the Tashkent dialect is, like Navai's Čağatai, heavily Iranized.

19. To indicate the great variety among local maqām traditions, which also vary from performer to performer, and for the sake of completeness, a comparative table of various Uzbek and Tajik maqāms is given below, taken from available transcriptions. Only the first three maqāms (*Buzruk, Rāst, and Navā*) are given, as these are the only ones for which all seven variant transcriptions were available as of mid-1972.

The sample is rather lopsided, in that there has only been one thorough publication of Tajik maqāms, that edited by Beliaev (1950-1958). The version labelled "Bukhara A" is given in Akbarov (1958), and it is not clear what the source is. "Bukhara B" is Rajabi's transcription (Akbarov, 1959). The edition led by Karomatov is in the process of publication. "Khwarizm A," like the following Khwarizm variants, is cited in Akbarov, 1958; it represents those sections of the maqāms which were put into Khwarizm tanbur tablature in the late nineteenth century "Khwarizm B" is the work of a celebrated Khwarizm musician, Matiusup Xarratov, and was published under the title *Ocherki istorii khorezmskoi muzyki* without musical notation in Moscow in 1923 (Akbarov, 1958: XXXIX). "Khwarizm C" is the transcription of M. Iusupov contained in Akbarov (1958).

The listing gives us insight into the formational process of the maqāms. Some titles of movements are clearly local, such as "tarāna-i khwarizm," while others (a considerable number) bear the name of a particular artist who added his personal stamp to a given maqām through stylistic individuality, e. g., "Sakil-i Niazjan xoja." Still other names indicate periodic additions to established movements: "Muxammas jadid," or "New Muxammas." A similar process of development marked the growth of the Persian *avāz* cycles, and indicate the fact that while model suites may be generally fixed in order and number of movements, as long as the tradition remains alive, there is always room for addition and modification. It seems unlikely that new movements will be added to maqāms in the Soviet period, as they have become solidly established as "classics of Uzbek national musical art." Similar crystallization can be seen in many Asian traditions, e. g., the Japanese Gagaku repertoire, whereas others (notably, the gamelan traditions of Java and Bali) continue to undergo lively change. For a comparative table of Uzbek and Tajik maqāms, *see* Appendix to Chapter 5.

20. In kättä äšulä singing, male singers reach an extraordinary degree of vocal tension. The highest pitched sections are left to especially gifted soloists.

21. *Nowruz* celebrations called *sails* were also noted in Chapter 4 as typical of Tajik culture. Here we have just one small example of the intermingling of traditions and observances that characterize the Uzbek-Tajik area, especially in the Bukhara region, from which the following description stems.

22. It is rather rare to find a poem by a well known poet altered so significantly for Soviet performance.

23. As noted in Chapter 2, Beliaev completed an excellent edition of Eichhorn's unpublished works (translated from German) on Kazakh and "Sart" (Uzbek-Tajik urban) music, including the musical examples given here (Exs. 45-49) and many more; *see* Beliaev (1963).

24. A number of the Eichhorn instruments are readily visible in display cases at the museum; to see others, special permission must be obtained. Some are "temporarily" housed in Leningrad.

25. The next several pages, describing prerevolutionary work on Uzbek music and the music life of Tashkent under czarist rule, are of particular historical interest in that they provide data on pre-Soviet musical acculturation in Central Asia. Many activities and policies strongly pressed in the Soviet period are outgrowths of patterns established in the preceding fifty-year czarist rule (1867-1917).

26. *See* Chapter 4, note 62.

27. Hamza is the major hero-martyr of Soviet Uzbek music.

Beliaev (Tajik)	Bukhara A	Bukhara B	Karomatov
		MAQĀM-I BUZRUK Instrumental Section	
Tasnif	Tasnif	Tasnif	Tasnif
Tarje	Tarji	Tarji	Tarji
Gardun		Gardun	Gärdun
Muxammas	Muxammas	Muxammas	Muxammas
Muxammas-i Nasrullah	Muxammas-i Nasrullah	Muxammas-i Nasrullah	Muxammas-i Nasrullah
Saqil-i Islimi	Saqil Islimi	Saqil Islimi	Saqil Islimi
Saqil-i Sultan	Saqil Sultan	Saqil Sultan	Saqil-i Sultan
		Vocal Section	
		First Group of Šu'ba	
Saraxbar-i	Saraxbar	Saraxbar	Saraxbar
Tarana 1-6	Tarana 1-5	Tarana 1-6	Tarana 1-6
Talqin-i uzzal	Talqin uzzal	Uzzal talqini	Talqin-i uzzal
Tarana 1,2	Tarana		Tarana
Nasrullai	Nasrullai	Nasrullai	Nasrullai
Tarana 1-4	Tarana 1-4	Tarana 1-3	Tarana 1-3
Nasri uzzal	Nasri uzzal	Uzzol nasr	Nasri uzzal
Supariš-i av- valin	Siporiš		
Ufar-i uzzal	Ufar	Ufari	Ufar-i uzzal
Suporiš-i axarin		Suporiš	

UZBEK AND TAJIK MAQĀMS (FROM TRANSCRIPTIONS)

Khwarizm A	Khwarizm B	Khwarizm C
Maqām buzruk	Maqām buzruk	Maqām buzruk
Pešrav 1,2,3	Pešrav 1,2,3	Pešrav
Muxammas	Muxammas	Muxammas
	Sausul	
Saqil Islimxani	Saqil Islimxani	Saqil Islimxani
Saqil Niazjan Xoja	Saqil Niazjan Xoja	Saqil Niazjan Xoja
Saqil Sultan	Saqil Sultan	Saqil Sultan
		Ufār
Maqām buzruk	Maqām buzruk	Maqām buzruk
Tarana 1-4	Tarana 1-4	Tarana 1-3
Talqin	Talqin	Talqin
Nasrullai	Nasr-i Nasrullahi	Nasrullai
Nasr-i Ajam	Nasr-i Ajam	
Suvari	Suvari	Suvari
Naqši	Naqši	
Muqadima-i nasr-i Uzzal	Muqadima-i nasr-i Uzzal	
Nasri		
Nasri uzzal	Nasri uzzal	
Ufar	Ufar	Ufar

Beliaev	Bukhara A	Bukhara B	Karomatov
			Second Group of Šu'ba
			1. Sowt-i sarvinaz
Sowt-i sarvinaz			
Talqinča-i sowt-i sarvinaz			
Kasqarča-i sowt-i sarvinas		(Same)	(Same)
Saqiname-i sowt-i sarvinaz			
Ufar-i sowt-i sarvinaz			
			2. Muǧulča-i Buzruk
Muǧulča-i buzruk			
Talqinča-i mugulča-i buzruk			
Kaškarča-i mugulča-i buzruk		(Same)	(Same)
Saqiname-i muǧulča-i buzruk			
Ufar-i muǧulča-i buzruk			
			3. Iraq
			(Beliaev-Iraq-i Buxara)
Iraq-i Buxara		Iraq	Iraq
Talqinča-i Iraq-i buxara		Talqinčasi	Talqinča-i Iraq
Čapandoz-i Iraq-i buxara		Čhapandozi	Čapandozi Iraq
Ufar-i Iraq-i buxara		Ufarisi	Ufar-i Iraq
			4. Bebokča (Beliaev only)
			5. Sinaxuruš (Beliaev only)
			6. Rak
Rak			Rak
Mustahzad-i rak			
			Talqinča-i rak
Kaškarča-i rak			Kaškarča-i rak
Saqiname-i rak			Saqiname-i rak
Ufar-i rak			Ufar-i rak
Supariši- rak			

Khwarizm A   Khwarizim B   Khwarizim C

Beliaev	Bukhara A	Bukhara B	Karomatov

MAQĀM-I RAST

Instrumental Section

Beliaev	Bukhara A	Bukhara B	Karomatov
Tasnif-i rast	Tasnif	Tasnif	Tasnif-i rast
Gardun-i rast	Gardun	Gardun	Gardun-i rast
Muxammas-i rast	Muxammas	Muxammas	Muxammas-i rast
Muxammas-i ušaq	Muxammas ušaq	Ušaq muxammasi	Muxammasi ušaq
Muxammas-i panjgah	Muxammas panjgah	Panjgah muxammasi	Muxammas-i panjgah
Saqil-i vazbin	Saqil vasmin	Vazmin saqili	Saqil vasmin
Saqil-i rak-rak	Saqil rig-rig	Rak-rak saqil	Saqil-i rak-rak

Vocal Section

First Group of Šu'ba

Beliaev	Bukhara A	Bukhara B	Karomatov
Saraxbar-i rast	Saraxbar	Saraxbar	Saraxbar-i rast
Tarana 1-5	Tarana 1-3	Tarana 1-4	Tarana 1-4
		Suporiš	
Talqin-i ušaq	Talqin ušaq	Ušaq talqini	Talqin-i ušaq
Tarana	Tarana	Taronasi	Tarana
Nasr-i ušaq	Nasr-i ušaq	Ušaq nasr	Nasr-i ušaq
Tarana 1	Tarana	Tarana 1	Tarana 1
Tarana 2 (daramad-i saba)		Tarana 2	Tarana 2
Nowruz-i saba		Saba naurazi	Nauruz-i Saba
Talqinča-i saba Talqinča		Talqinčasi	Talqinča-i
Supariš-i avvalin Sipariš			Nauruzi Saba
Ufar-i ušaq	Ufar	Ušaq ufari	Ufar-i ušaq
Supariš-i axarin			

Khwarizm A	Khwarizm B	Khwarizm C
Maqām Rast	Maqām Rast	Maqām Rast
Tarji	Tarji	Tarji
Pešrav gardun	Pešrav gardun	Pešrav gardun
	Murabba-i kamil	
Muxammas	Muxammas jadid	Muxammas
Muxammas ušaq	Muxammas feruz	Muxammas
	Muxammas jadid feruz	
Muxammas panjgah	Muxammas	Muxammas ušaq
Panjgah	Murabba-i rast	
	Murabba-i rast mirza	
Saqil vazmin	Sakil rast	Saqil vazmin
Saqil	Saqil muxurkan	
	Ufar	Ufar

Maqām rast	Maqām rast	Maqām rast
Tarana	Tarana	Tarana
Suvori	Suvari	Suvari
Naqš	Naqš	Naqš
Talqin	Talqin	Talqin
Nasri ušaq	Nasri ušaq	
Nasr-i saba	Nasr-i saba	Saba
Ufar	Ufar	Ufar

Beliaev	Bukhara A	Bukhara B	Karamatov
			Second Group of Šu'ba
			1. Sowt-i ušaq
Sowt-i ušaq		Ušaq sowti	Sowt-i ušaq
Talqinča-i ušaq		Talqinča	Talqinča
		C	Čapandazi
Kašqarča-i Sowt-i ušaq		Kašqarčasi	Kašqarča
Saqiname-i sowt-i ušaq		Saqinomasi	Saqiname
Ufar-i sowt-i ušaq		Ufarisi	Ufari
			2. Sowt-i Saba
Sowt-i saba			
Talqinča-i sowt-i saba			
Kaskarča-i sowt-i saba		(Lacking)	(Same)
Saqiname-i sowt-i saba			
Ufar-i sowt-i saba			
			3. Sowt-ikalan*
			Sowt
			Talqinca
(Lacking)		(Same)	Kaškarča
			Saqiname
			Ufar

MAQĀM-I RAST

Instrumental Section

Beliaev	Bukhara A	Bukhara B	Karamatov
Tasnif nava	Tasnif	Tasnif	Tasnifi nava
Tarje nava	Tarji	Tarji	Tarje'i nava
Gardun nava	Gardun	Gardun	Nağmai orazi nava
Nağma oraz	Nağmai oraz	Oraz na'masi	Muxammasi nava
Muxammas nava	Muxammas nava	Muxammas	Muxammasi bayat
Muxammas bayat	Muxammas bayat	Bayat muxammasi	Muxammasi husaini
Muxammas husaini	Muxammas husaini	Husain muxammasi	Saqili nava
Saqil nava	Saqil	Saqil	

Khwarizm A	Khwarizm B	Khwarizm C

*Beyond Sowt-i kalān, Karomatov (1969:203) cites the following possible additions for the Uzbek Maqām-i rast: Ušaq-i samarqand (Ušaq-i Xoja Abdul Aziz) and Ušaq-i Kokand as variants for the Sowt-i ušaq section and an additional section called **Gulyar-šahnaz**, with the following sections: Gulyar, Šahnaz, Čapandazi gulyar, Ušaq, and Kašqarca-i Ušaq.

Maqām nava	Maqām nava	Maqām nava
Pešrav	Pešrav	Pešrav 1,2,3,4
Muxammas	Pešrav zanjiri	Pešrav zanjiri
Muxammas bayat	Muxammas nava	Katta muxammas
	Muxammas bayat	Muxammas bayat
Saqil	Saqil	Saqil
	Nim saqil	Nim saqil
	Ufar	Ufar

Beliaev	Bukhara A	Bukhara B	Karomatov

Vocal Section

First Group of Šu'ba

Beliaev	Bukhara A	Bukhara B	Karomatov
Saraxbor nava	Saraxbor	Saraxbor	Saraxbori nava
Tarona 1,2,3,4	Tarona 1,2,3	Tarona 1,2	Tarona 1,2
Talqin bayat	Talqin bayat	Bayat talqini	Talqini bayat
Tarona 1,2	Tarona	Tarona	Tarona
Nasr bayat	Nasr bayat	Bayat nasri	Nasri bayat
Tarona 1,2,3,4	Tarona 1,2	Tarona	Tarona 1,2
Oraz nava	Nasri oraz	Oraz	Orazi nava
Tarona 1,2,3,4	Tarona 1,2,3	Tarona 1,2,3	Tarona 1,2,3
Husaini	Nasr husaini	Husaini	Husaini nava
1st suporiš nava	Suporiš		
Ufar bayat	Ufar	Bayat ufari	Ufari bayat
Final suporiš			

Second Group of Su'ba

I. Sowt-i navā

Beliaev	Bukhara A	Bukhara B	Karomatov
Sowt nava		Sowt	Sowt
Talqinča-i sowt-i nava		Talqinča	Čapandoz
Kaškarča-i sowt-i nava		Kaškarča	Talqinča
Saqinoma-i sowt-i nava		Saqinoma	Kaškarča
Ufar-i sowt-i nava		Ufar	Ufar

II. Muǧulča-i nava

Beliaev	Bukhara A	Bukhara B	Karomatov
Muǧulča-i nava			
Talqinča-i muǧulča-i nava		(same)	(same)
Kaškarča-i muǧulča-i nava			
Sāqinoma-i muǧulča-i nava			
Ufār-i muǧulča-i nava			

III. Musta'zod-i nava

Beliaev	Bukhara A	Bukhara B	Karomatov
Musta'zod			
Talqinča'i musta'zod-i nava			
Kaškarča-i musta'zod-i nava		(same)	(same)
Saqinoma-i musta'zod-i nava			
Ufar-i musta'zod-i nava			

Khwarizm A	Khwarizm B	Khwarizm C
Maqām nava	Maqām nava	Maqām nava
Tarona; Suvori	Tarona; Suvori	Tarona; Suvori
Talqin	Talqin	Talqin
Taronai xorazmi	Taronai xorazmi	
Nasri bayat	Nasri bayat	
Nasri oraz	Nasri oraz	Oraz
Mukaddimai dugah husaini	Mukaddimai dugah husaini	
Nasri dugah husaini	Dugah husaini	
Talqin mustahzod	Talqin mustahzod	
Naqš	Naqš	Naqš
Suvorai dugah husaini	Suvorai dugah husaini	
Talsin dugah husaini	Talqin dugah husaini	
Ufar	Ufar 1,2	Ufar

Bibliography

Beliaev's Bibliography

Antologiia uzbekskoi poezii. [Anthology of Uzbek poetry.]. Moscow, 1950.

Beliaev, V. M. "Formy uzbekskoi muzyki." [The forms of Uzbek music.]. *Sovetskaia muzyka*, nos. 7-8, 1935.

——*Muzykal'nye instrumenty uzbekistana.* [The musical instruments of Uzbekistan.]. Moscow, 1933.

——*Rukovodstvo dlia obmera narodnykh muzykal'nykh instrumentov.* [Handbook for the measurement of folk musical instruments]. Moscow, 1931.

Pekker, Ia. "Pevets novoi zhizni (Khamza Khakim-zade Niiazi)." [Singer of a new life.]. *Sovetskaia Muzyka*, no. 11, 1949.

Uzbekskie narodnye pesni [(in Uzbek) Uzbek songs.]. vols. 1 and 2. Tashkent, 1929.

Vyzgo, T. *Uzbekskaia SSR.* [The Uzbek SSR.]. *Seriia Muzykal'naia kul'tura soiuznykh respublik* [The music culture of the Soviet Republics.]. Moscow, 1954.

The general bibliography on Uzbek music is too large and, for the most part, too inaccessible to warrant a full listing. A good representation of the literature is listed in Slobin (1967).

NOTES ON BIBLIOGRAPHY

Aside from the bibliography for Beliaev's output cited earlier (B. Krader, 1968 and Beliaev, 1971), the reader is directed to the following three sources which, taken together, are quite comprehensive:

1. Emsheimer, E. "Musikethnographische Bibliographie der nicht-slavische Völker in Russland." *Acta Musicologica* XV (1943): 34-63.
2. Slobin, M. Bibliography at end of entry "Zentralasien" in *Die Musik in Geschichte und Gegenwart*, vol. XIV Kassel: Bärenreiter.
3. Waterman, R. *et al.* "Bibliography of Asiatic Musics, Thirteenth Installment." *Notes of the Music Library Association* VIII (1950): 100-18.

For surveys of local music cultures in Western languages, the reader is restricted at present (1974) to the encyclopedia entry just cited (Slobin, 1967) and to the extensive article of Johanna Spector (1967). Spector's article is drawn from Soviet sources (primarily Beliaev's works) and contains a wealth of detailed information and excellent reproductions of old photographs. The data are restricted almost completely to the professional classical music of the urban Uzbek and Tajik milieu, with some reference to Turkmen music.*

Other useful collections of data can be found among the works of Ernst Emsheimer and in R. Lach's early, limited *Gesänge russischer Kriegsgefängene* (Akad. d. Wiss. in Wien, Phil.-hist kl., Sitzungsber. 183, 189, 211 and 218), based on data collected from World War I prisoners of war. For other, scattered studies, see the bibliographies listed above.

With interest in Central Asia currently on the increase, it is to be hoped that more research will be completed (and published) on this fascinating area of Asia.

---

* A brief survey by Slobin appears in *Encyclopedia Brittanica* under "Central Asian Peoples, Arts of (Music)." The forthcoming sixth edition of *Grove's Dictionary of Music and Musicians* contains an extensive entry under "Central Asian Peoples."

WORKS CITED IN NOTES

Akbarov, I. A.
   1958   *Khorezmskie makomy.* Vol. VI of *Uzbekskaia narodnaia muzyka.* Tashkent: Gos. izdat khudozh. lit.
   1959   *Bukharskie makomy.* Vol. V of *Uzbekskaia narodnaia muzyka.* Tashkent: Gos. izdat. khudozh. lit.

Aksenov, A.
   1964   *Tuvinskaia narodnaia muzyka.* Moscow: Muzyka.

Ambramzon, S. M.
   1963   *Kirgizy Narody srednei azii i kazakhstan.* Narody mira, vol. II. Moscow: Izd-vo ANSSSR, 154-320.

Aravin, P.
   1968   Review of Erzakovich, 1966. *Sovetskaia muzyka,* no. 12, 102-05.

Bachmann, W.
   1969   *The Origins of Bowing.* Leipzig: VEB.

Beliaev, V. M.
   1924   "Khoresmian Notation." *The Sackbut.*
   1933   *Muzykal'nye instrumenty uzbekistana.* Moscow: Gos. izdat.
   1935   "The Longitudinal Open Flutes of Central Asia." *Musical Quarterly,* 19: 84-89.
1950-1958   (ed.) *Šašmaqām*, vols. 1-4. Moscow: Gos. izdat.
   1960   (ed.) *Abdurrakhman Dzhami: "Traktat o muzyke."* Tashkent: Izd-vo ANU-zSSR.
   1963   *Muzykal'naia fol'kloristika v uzbekistane.* Tashkent: izd-vo ANUzSSR.
   1964   *Persidskye tesnify.* Moscow: Muzyka.
   1971   *O muzykal'nom fol'klore i drevnei pis'mennosti.* Moscow: Sovetskii kompozitor.

Braginskii, I. S.
  1956   *Ocherki iz istorii tajikskoi literatury.* Stalinabad: Tajikgosizdat.

Carrere d'Encausse, H.
  1967   Chapters 4-9 in *Central Asia: A Century of Russian Rule.* Edited by E.
          Allworth. New York: Columbia University Press.

Castagné, J.
  1930   "Magie et exorcisme chez les Kazak-Kirghizes et autres peuples turks orien-
          taux." *Revue des Etudes Islamiques*, 4: 53-151.

Cazden, N.
  1969   "A Revised Mode Classification for Traditional Anglo-American Song Tunes."
          Paper read at the 14th Annual Convention of the Society for Ethnomusi-
          cology, at the University of Michigan.

Centlivres, P. and M., and Slobin, M.
  1971   "A Muslim Shaman of Afghan Turkestan." *Ethnology* V (2): 160-73.

Chadwick, N. and Zhirmunsky, V.
  1969   *Oral Epics of Central Asia.* Cambridge: University Press.

Dansker, O.
  1965   *Muzykal'naia kul'tura tajikov karategina i darvaza. Iskusstvo tajikskogo
          naroda*, vol. 2, Dushanbe: Donish, 174-264.

Dernova, V.
  1967   (ed.). *Narodnaia muzyka v kazakhstane.* Alma-Ata: Kazakhstan.

Dupaigne, B.
  1968   "Aperçus sur quelques techniques afghanes." *Objets et Mondes*, VII (1):
          41-84.

Emsheimer, E.
  1941   "Ueber das Vorkommen und die Anwendungsart der Maultrommel in Si-
          birien und Zentralasien." *Ethnos* V, 109-21.
  1956   "Singing Contests in Central Asia." *Journal of the International Folk Music
          Council*, VIII, 26-

Erzakovich, B.
  1961   *Kenen Azerbaev.* Moscow: Sovetskii kompositor.
  1966   *Pesennaia kul'tura kazakhskogo naroda.* Alma-Ata: Nauka.
  1967   "Vrachevatel'naia pesnia bakhsy," In Dernova 1967, 99-108.

Ghirshmann, Ia.
  1960   *Pentatonika i ee razvitiia v tatarskoi muzyke.* Moscow: Sovetskii kompo-
          zitor.

Gippius, E.
  1964   Introduction to Aksenov, 1964.

Huth, A.
  1954   "East Turkestan." *Grove's Dictionary of Music and Musicians.* London:
          Macmillan.

337

Irons, W.
1969   "The Yomut Turkmen: A Study of Kinship in a Pastoral Society." PhD. Dissertation, University of Michigan.

Karomatov, F.
1962   *Uzbekskaia dombrovaia muzyka*. Tashkent: Gos. izdat. khudozh. lit.
1966   *Buzruk*. Vol. I of *Šašmaqām*. Tashkent: "Tashkent."
1968   *Rast*. Vol. II of *Šašmaqām*. Tashkent: "Tashkent."
1969   (with I. Rajabov). "Schaschmakom." *Beitrage zur Musikwissenschaft*, #2, 91-9.
1970   *Nava*. Vol. III of *Šašmaqām*, Tashkent: "Tashkent."
1972   *Uzbekskaia instrumental'naia muzyka (nasledie)*. Tashkent: Guliam.

Karryev, B. A.
1968   *Skazaniia o Ker-ogly*. Moscow: Nauka.

Kon, Iu.
1961   "K teorii narodnykh ladov." *Voprosy muzykal'noi kul'tury uzbekistana*. Edited by Karelova, Tashkent: Goz. izdat. khudozh. lit. 108-29.

Krader, B.
1968   "Viktor Mikhailovich Beliaev." *Ethnomusicology*, XII (3): 86-100.

Krader, L.
1966   *The Peoples of Central Asia*. 2nd ed. The Hague: Mouton.

Kulakovskii, L.
1962   *Pesnia: ee iazyk, struktura, sud'by*. Moscow: Sovetskii kompozitor.

Lebedinskii, L. N.
1965   *Bashkirskie narodnye pesni i naigryshi*. 2nd ed. Moscow: Muzyka.

Manas (anthology).
1961   *Kirgizskii geroicheskii epos Manas*. Moscow.

Marcel-Dubois, C.
1941   *Les Instruments de musique de l'Inde ancienne*. Paris: Presses universitaires de France.

Meredith-Owens, C.
1936   "Arud." *Encyclopedia of Islam*. Leiden: Brill.

Moser, H.
1885   *A travers l'Asie centrale*. Paris: Librarie Plon.

Nurjanov
1956   *Tadzhikskii narodnyi teatr*. Moscow: Izdatel'stvo ANSSSR.

Poppe, N.
1965   *Introduction to Altaic Linguistics*. Ural-altaische Bibliothek, vol. XIV. Wiesbaden: Otto Harrasowitz.

Rejepov, S.
1966   *Sakhi Jepbarov*, Moscow: Muzyka.

Romanovskaia, E. E.
1957   *Stat'i i doklady*. Tashkent: Gos. izdat. khudozh. lit.

Sachs, C.
1962   *The Wellsprings of Music*. New York: McGraw-Hill.

Sarybaiev, B.
1967   "Drevnii kazakhskii narodnyi instrument jetygan." In Dernova, 1967, 122-26.

Semenov, A. A.
1946   (ed.) *Sredneaziatskii traktat po muzyke Dervisha-ali (XVIII V.)*. Tashkent.

Slobin, M.
1967   "Zentralasien." *Die Musik in Geschichte und Gegenwart*, vol. XIV. Kessel, Bärenreiter.
1969a   *Kirgiz Instrumental Music*. New York: Asian Music Publications.
1969b   "Instrumental Music in Northern Afghanistan." PhD. dissertation, University of Michigan, UM 7014644.
1971   "Rhythmic Aspects of the Tajik Maqām." *Ethnomusicology*, XV (1), 100-04.
1974   *Music in the Culture of Northern Afghanistan*. Viking Fund Publications in Anthropology. Tucson: University of Arizona Press.

Smirnov, B.
1971   *Mongol'skaia narodnaia muzyka*. Moscow: Sovetskii kompozitor.

Spector, J.
1967   "Musical Tradition and Innovation." *Central Asia: A Century of Russian Rule*, Edited by E. Allworth, New York: Columbia University Press.

Szabolcsi, B.
1935   "Eastern Relations of Early Hungarian Folk Music." *Journal of the Royal Asiatic Society*, 483-89.

Tajikova, G.
1968   "K voprosu o sootnoshenii metriki stikhoslozheniia s metroritmikoi napeva v tajikskikh pesniakh." *Izvestiia ANTajSSR otdelenie obshchestvennykh nauk* 2, 84-94.

Thompson, S.
1955-1958   *Motif-Index of Folk Literature*. 6 vols., rev. ed., Bloomington: Indiana University Press.

Tkachenko, T.
1967   *Narodnyi tanets*. 2nd ed. Moscow: Iskusstvo.

Tleubaeva, A. E.
1967   "O pripevakh kazakhskikh narodnykh pesen." In Dernova, 1967, 171-84.

Tsuge, G.
1970   "Rhythmic Aspects of the Avaz in Persian Music." *Ethnomusicology*, XIV (2): 205-27.

Uspenskii, V. S. and Beliaev, V. M.
1928   *Turkmenskaia muzyka*. Moscow: Gos. izd-vo.

Veksler, S. M.
1965   *Ocherk istorii uzbekskoi muzykal'noi kul'tury*. Tashkent: Uchitel'.

Vertkov, V., *et al.*
1963   *Atlas muzykal'nykh instrumentov narodov SSR*. Moscow: Muzyka.

Vinogradov, V. S.
    1939   *Muzyka sovetskoi kirgizii.* Moscow: SNK Kirgizskoi SSR.
    1952   *Toktogul satylganov i kirgizskie akyny.* Moscow: Gos. izdat.
    1958   *Kirgizskaia narodnaia muzyka.* Frunze: Kirgizgosizdat.
    1961a   *Muzykal'noe nasledie toktogula.* Moscow: Gos. izdat.
    1961b   *Voprosy razvitiia natsional'nykh muzykal'nykh kul'ture v SSR.* Moscow: Sovetskii kompozitor.
    1968   *Muzyka sovetskogo vostoka.* Moscow: Sovetskii kompozitor.

Winner, T.
    1958   *The Oral Art and Literature of the Kazakhs of Russian Central Asia.* Durham: Duke University Press.

Wolcott, R.
    1970   "The Xomi of Mongolia." Paper read at the Fifteenth Annual Convention of the Society for Ethnomusicology, Seattle, Washington.

Zataevich, A. V.
    1925   *1000 pesen kirgizskogo (kazakhskogo) naroda.* Orenburg: Muzgiz.
    1931   *500 kazakhskikh pesen i kiu'iev.* Alma-Ata: Muzgiz.
    1934   *250 kirgizskikh p'es i napevov.* Moscow: Gos. izdat.
    1963   *1000 pesen kazakhskogo naroda.* 2d ed. Edited by V. Dernova, Moscow: Gos. izdat.

Zhanuzakov, Z.
    1964   *Kazakhskaia narodnaia instrumental'naia muzyka.* Alma-Ata: Nauka.